On the Wrong Side

On the Wrong Side

My Life in the KGB

Stanislav Levchenko

PERGAMON-BRASSEY'S
International Defense Publishers, Inc.

Washington   New York   London   Oxford   Moscow
Beijing   Frankfurt   São Paulo   Sydney   Tokyo   Toronto

U.S.A. (Editorial)	Pergamon-Brassey's International Defense Publishers, 8000 Westpark Drive, Fourth Floor, McLean, Virginia 22102, U.S.A.
(Orders)	Kampmann & Co., Inc., New York, New York, U.S.A.
U.K. (Editorial)	Brassey's Defence Publishers, 24 Gray's Inn Road, London WC1X 8HR
(Orders)	Brassey's Defence Publishers, Headington Hill Hall, Oxford OX3 0BW, England
PEOPLE'S REPUBLIC OF CHINA	Pergamon Press, Room 4037, Qianmen Hotel, Beijing, People's Republic of China
FEDERAL REPUBLIC OF GERMANY	Pergamon Press, Hammerweg 6, D-6242 Kronberg, Federal Republic of Germany
BRAZIL	Pergamon Editora, Rua Eça de Queiros, 346, CEP 04011, Paraiso, São Paulo, Brazil
AUSTRALIA	Pergamon-Brassey's Defence Publishers, P.O. Box 544, Potts Point, N.S.W. 2011, Australia
JAPAN	Pergamon Press, 8th Floor, Matsuoka Central Building, 1-7-1 Nishishinjuku, Shinjuku-ku, Tokyo 160, Japan
CANADA	Pergamon Press Canada, Suite No. 271, 253 College Street, Toronto, Ontario, Canada M5T 1R5

Copyright © 1988 Pergamon-Brassey's International Defense Publishers, Inc.

First printing 1988, Second printing 1988, Third printing 1988

Library of Congress Cataloging-in-Publication Data

Levchenko, Stan.
    On the wrong side.

    1. Levchenko, Stan.   2. Soviet Union. Komitet gosudarstvennoi bezopasnosti—Officials and employees—Biography.   3. Spies—Soviet Union—Biography.   4. Defectors—Soviet Union—Biography.   5. Espionage, Russian—History—20th century.
I. Title.
UB271.R92L435   1987   327.1'2'0924 [B]   87-7154
ISBN 0-08-034478-X

British Library Cataloguing in Publication Data

Levchenko, Stanislav
    On the wrong side: my life in the KGB.   1. Union of Soviet Socialist Republics. *Komitet gosundarstvennoĭ bezopasnostĭ*——Biography
I. Title
327.1'2'0924   HV8224
ISBN 0-08-034478-X

Printed in the United States of America

To M. and K.
*Without whose inspiration
this book probably
would never have
been written*

CONTENTS

PREFACE

I address this book to the people of the free world who experience a freedom that is not shared by hundreds of millions of people. I do not address this book to the professionals in the intelligence communities of these free countries; the memories included in this volume are often too personal for that. But I think those intelligence professionals will still find points to ponder in these pages. I hope to reach you who have always been free and cannot conceive of life where one's every move is dictated or monitored. You absorb the spirit of freedom with your mother's milk. I will give you a glimpse of "the other side" so that you may understand how much you are blessed.

I also speak to the occasional Soviet reader who, despite Soviet censorship, will somehow read this book. Let me address you directly: Give thought to the problems of the Soviet Union that I describe and make your own assessment of the system, which is imposed upon you by the leadership of the Communist Party of the Soviet Union. Perhaps then you will understand that man described by your government as "the traitorous Levchenko."

I feel a deep love for and a profound commitment to my adopted country, the United States of America. I have found a new home here. More important, for the first time in my life, I feel that I am free to express my own political views and able to be true to my own ideals. I have become a part of a nation that welcomes people of free spirit, those who have been deprived of even the most elemental human rights in other countries. I work very hard to contribute to the protection of my new country and the free world, and it is my earnest hope that this book will help you recognize the threat posed by the Soviet leaders and their most dangerous tool—the KGB.

The first book about my life was published in Japan in 1984, and it was received with a healthy interest and extensive coverage in the Japanese media. I still get many interesting—sometimes touching—letters from Japanese readers, who provide me with valuable suggestions regarding any new editions of the book. I am most grateful to my Japanese correspondents.

That first book was addressed to the Japanese people specifically. Although this book also examines a bit of the data and information revealed in the first one, the purpose of this one is, as the title shows, to present my personal memories. I am opening my life and my soul to you, and the experience has been wrenching.

I do not mention the real names of some of the Japanese agents whom I handled in Tokyo for the KGB because I did not want to bring unnecessary sensationalism into this account. The governments of the United States and Japan have knowledge of all of my activities in Japan as a Soviet intelligence officer; they also are aware of all of the KGB agents whom I knew in Japan. As I understand it, most of the Japanese citizens who were recruited by the KGB have been thoroughly investigated by the authorities of that country.

I do not mention in my book the real names of some of my personal friends in the Soviet Union. To do so would have immediately made them more vulnerable to persecution by Soviet authorities and the Soviet security police. Names do not matter much. What is more important is to make you aware of the extent of KGB activities and to inform you of the methods and operations employed by the KGB.

Any success in this work is attributable to the encouragement, moral support, and professional guidance of Dr. Franklin D. Margiotta, president of Pergamon-Brassey's, and of my editor and colleague, Mrs. Jewell Alexander. This book would not have been possible without that charming lady. She and her husband Alex have become my close personal friends, and I think of them as my family. Finally I must thank Lisa McCormack who helped with the final polish of my words.

I have opened my heart to you in this book. I have tried to share my views, my emotions, my concern, and my personal life. Now that I have done so, this book has become a needed catharsis. I feel better now, more tranquil, serene, and spiritually fortified. "Honest confession is good for the soul," they say, and in making my confession to you, I have learned that it is true.

Stanislav Levchenko

KILL DEVIL HILLS, NORTH CAROLINA

I feel as old as the ocean itself . . . as though I've felt and experienced everything there is, and I am tired. I've walked for hours along the shore of the Atlantic, mesmerized by the powerful waves. Last night, in an inn by the sea, I listened to my tapes of classical Japanese music. The voices of the ancient instruments blended with the sound of the surf, and I remembered my beloved Japan. Today, on the wet sand, it's as though the sounds of the shamisen and fue have merged with the rhythms of the crashing sea. I am calm now, but I'm still tired. I'm so alone.

This morning, the white sands led me on, past a pier jutting out to the restless waves, past a woman whose glistening body was sprawled on a blanket in the sun. Further on, I circled around a clutch of children with voices as shrill as the cries of the gulls, and I was a child again . . . a lonely little boy on a Moscow street.

Memories . . . the dreams and the nightmares flood in, washing away the peace, and I live it all again. In my mind I cry again at the crushing pain, feel again the shattering loneliness, see again a hospital crib. . . . The death of my father . . . Anastasia . . . the beatings.

Japan! The joy of living there. My KGB masters, my enemies . . . and, oh God, the guilt. The danger . . . the decision, the act, the escape. . . . The loss of my wife and son. Soviets in pursuit . . . the danger.

How did the street boy from Moscow become the man who traveled? Japan . . . Egypt. . . . How did Major Stanislav Levchenko of the KGB become the free man who lives and works in the United States?

1

It Hurts:
The Early Years

KILL DEVIL HILLS, NORTH CAROLINA

The children on the beach break into my thoughts. One little boy is crying, and the other children are running after him, screaming.

"Don't cry, Billy! It was just a tiny jellyfish. Don't cry!"

"But it hurts!"

My memories take over. Why are the children screaming? My stomach is on fire. Everything is spinning . . . whirling, whirling away into the dark. . . . It hurts!

MOSCOW, 1941–1964

World War II and I made our entrance together. I couldn't have picked a worse time. One month and six days after Germany attacked the Soviet Union, I was born in Moscow, the capital city. Today, I live and work in the United States of America in one of its largest cities. I was born a Soviet citizen. I'm now an American. The purpose of this book is to trace one man's journey from there to here.

I have been told that those early months of World War II were confusion wrapped in chaos. Moscow was strained to the bursting point as refugees from the western front swarmed into the city, only to be evacuated to some other town farther east. Confused! Chaotic! It's almost as though those early days of my infancy set the pattern of my life. I guess it was fitting for war and me to come in together.

I always lived in Moscow. My father was a military officer stationed in the capital city during those days of World War II, so my mother and I lived there also. I don't remember much of it, though. In fact, I barely remember my mother, who died giving birth to my stillborn brother when I was three years old. Within hours after my mother was buried, my father received orders to report to the western front, and I was left behind in Moscow with some relatives. There was nothing else Father could do with me.

I don't remember who those people were or how we were related. The time I lived with them is just a blurred picture of noise, faceless adults, and countless children. I don't have any idea exactly how many families shared that one apartment—six or seven, I should think—using one kitchen and one bathroom. I became a street urchin, always playing outside the apartment, soaking up every word the older boys said, and innocently getting into all kinds of mischief.

My first clear memory of that wretched period is when I was four years old. As usual, I was with a crowd of children in the courtyard when a delivery truck drove in—a massive Studebaker van, sent to the Soviet Union through the American aid program. We had never been that close to an American vehicle before, and in seconds there were children swarming all over and around it. I clearly remember climbing up on the running board and having to reach far up to catch hold of the edge of the open window.

5

"I dare you to ride it," someone whispered.

"You're crazy!" someone else hissed back.

The driver couldn't see me as he started to drive out, but I was there, hanging on for dear life. I still remember the thrill of it as the truck gained speed. I was so proud. There I was, taking the dare when the bigger boys were afraid to risk it.

I don't suppose I'll ever know exactly what happened. I don't know if the driver hit a bump or whether the van swerved a little bit. Whatever it was, it jarred me loose from my hold on the window, and I fell. The big front wheel ran right over me as the driver backed up. Strangely, I didn't feel any pain at all. In fact, I got up and started to walk. Everyone in the yard was staring at me in horror. I can still hear the gasps and a few screams. Then time began to move in the slowest of slow motion. I had taken no more than three steps when the pain started. I reached a bench and sat down.

"It hurts . . . ," I began to say as I felt myself falling into a black pit and whirling around as I lost consciousness.

Father told me months later that for the first few days the doctors were not sure I would live. It was the skill of a young and talented woman that saved me. Doctor Anastasia, a pediatric surgeon on the hospital staff, simply wouldn't give up. It was several weeks before I opened my eyes and was conscious enough to really see her. She leaned over my crib and smiled at me when she said, "Hello, Stas. Are you going to wake up for a little while now?"

I was in the hospital for six long lonely months. Father would come to visit, but he could never stay long. Always he would have to leave too soon to go back to the front. Sometimes Anastasia would stay with me for a few extra minutes, but most of the time I was alone, completely bedridden. I had totally forgotten how to walk, and it took me weeks to learn to use my legs again. Baby though I was, I still remember the wrenching loneliness, the grim monotony of the hospital walls, and the bars around my crib.

I was five by the time I was released from the hospital, and there had been many changes. The war ended in 1945, and my father was once again stationed in Moscow. He had also been dating Anastasia since before my release. She was an attractive woman, very tall and brunette, and divorced with a daughter named Kira, who was a little older than I. It must have been difficult for Anastasia to work at the hospital and bring up her child all alone. On looking back and trying to remember those years between age five and eight, I realize that there was much that I probably missed or misread. But of one thing I am sure: Anastasia adored my father. Certainly I was not surprised when they married. I was then about six years old.

They hadn't been married very long when Father was assigned to a post in Yugoslavia as a military adviser, and we four—Father, Anastasia, Kira, and I—moved to Belgrade, where our new home was a comfortable house surrounded by fruit trees and flowers. It was quite a change from our one small room with communal kitchen and bath. Later, I realized how hard it must have been on Father and Anastasia to begin their marriage in one room occupied by four people. At a time when a couple most needs privacy, there they were, crowded into one intolerable room. It is certainly no wonder that we all loved our little house in Belgrade.

I liked living in Yugoslavia. Whenever Father managed to take a vacation, we traveled. I was fascinated by the forests, the mountains, the quaint little sea resorts, and the cheerful people. I was intrigued by everything that was different from life at home—the language, the clothes, even the music on the radio. Then one day in 1948 Father came home, his face ashen.

"What's wrong?" my stepmother asked at once.

"We have to go home," he answered. "Back to Moscow. Start packing."

"Why? What in the world has happened?"

"I'll explain later," Father replied curtly.

I never found out what the crisis was all about, but some two months after our return to Moscow, Yugoslavia's President Tito abruptly severed relations with the Soviet Union and expelled all of the Soviet military and civilian advisers. The Soviet Union sent special planes to Belgrade and evacuated all Soviets within forty-eight hours.

Back in Moscow, Father was given new housing, a relatively large room in a big apartment in a house that had been built before the October Revolution. Eight other families lived with us in that apartment, sharing a communal bathroom and kitchen. I might have been too young to notice accurately what life was like in such an overcrowded fishbowl when I had been there before, but I was now old enough to decide that I didn't like it. We had lived in our own house for almost two years, and all of us had developed a taste for privacy. Our return to one single room was nothing short of culture shock.

Father would shout at us when any of us complained: "These are privileged quarters! Very few people live as well as this!"

He was right, of course. We were fortunate in the place that we'd been given. The rooms were very large, and the apartments had been adapted so that each one was now laid out like a miniature hotel, with a wide central hall and numbered rooms on either side of it. Several rooms had been combined into a large kitchen with separate cupboards and individual stoves for each family. This was a privilege indeed. But some terrible quarrels erupted in that kitchen. If one cook got a little too nosy about what a neighbor was cooking, or if someone tasted food from another's pot without permission, all hell would break loose!

Our room was large enough that the beds could be screened off from one another, and a tiny sitting area and dining table could be accommodated. We used furniture that Father had kept after my mother's death and some that had been provided by Anastasia; all of it was heavy and dark. They had sold everything they didn't want to keep before we went to Yugoslavia, and with the money they had been able to buy a few things in Belgrade—rugs, some pretty ornaments, even one or two paintings.

The fact is that people can get used to anything, and this kind of communal living was a necessity. The western part of the Soviet Union was nearly destroyed in World War II, and displaced persons had to be housed some way. New construction could not keep up with the needs of survivors, let alone the normal population growth. Indeed, the Soviet Union has never really caught up, and housing is still a critical problem, especially in the large cities.

The real drawbacks to living in a communal apartment were the one bathroom, the communal telephone, and the lack of privacy. There were over thirty people in ours, yet it was palatial compared to most. But in the mornings! Bedlam! A long line would form with people waiting their turn for the toilet. They would mutter and gripe, "Well! I guess he has to read the whole paper before he can do his job!" or "For goodness sake! Don't they have a mirror in their room?"

Fights and quarrels would break out, and the noise from nine rooms would surround us. We knew everything about everyone else— who beat their wives, who beat their children, who made love and when, who were super-clean, who were the slobs. Yet with all of the infighting, a strange kind of camaraderie emerged in our group, almost a familial feeling. We might fight among ourselves, but woe to anyone from the outside who started a fight with one of us.

Because there was only that one toilet for over thirty people, most families kept and depended on chamber pots. Or, if they were lucky enough to own one from earlier times, commode chairs. The job of emptying the pots, washing them out, and putting them out to air in a special little cubicle in the courtyard usually fell to the oldest daughter. It was a task no one liked, and Kira, Anastasia's daughter, was no exception. She managed to pass the job on to me more times than I like to remember.

One Sunday afternoon Father took me for a walk around the neighborhood. I was nine years old, fiercely proud of my father, and it, was wonderful to stroll along beside him, savoring the feeling of having him all to myself. He broke the silence suddenly.

"Son, I have to warn you," he said with a voice that told me he was very serious, even troubled. "You must never mention to anyone that I have been to Yugoslavia. I need your promise that you won't ever tell any of your friends or anyone else that you have lived there."

I was dumbfounded. I was also upset because I had been proud to be able to boast to my friends that *my* father, as a high-ranking military officer, had been honored with a foreign assignment.

"Why, Father? Why?" I was close to tears, and he knew it.

"You are too young to understand," he said gently. "Perhaps some day I can explain. Meanwhile, I need your promise not to say a word. Do you understand?"

I said I did. But I didn't.

"Stanislav Aleksandrovich," he continued (and I knew that he was in earnest: he was using my whole name), "there is something else. Those two books you brought back from Yugoslavia—put them in the most out-of-the-way corner of our bookshelf."

Those books had been a present to me from one of Father's friends, a major in the Yugoslav army. I was too young at the time to have learned that someone could be in favor one moment and out the next. As I matured, that incident came back to me over and over, each time laden with more significance.

Father managed to get me into School Number One of Moscow's Sokolniky District in 1949. About half of the subjects were taught in English. The teachers were among the best in Moscow. Father was very proud of me. He used to say that if I studied hard and was well organized, I could become a foreign service officer and travel abroad. It didn't take me long to realize that most of the pupils in the school were the sons of privileged men in the Communist party and the government. This was an elite school; the students dressed very well as opposed to those at my old school, where we were all shabby and some of my classmates looked underfed.

For all of my father's pride, I was not an outstanding student. I seriously studied those subjects that interested me; others I ignored as much as I could. I excelled in Russian language and literature. I was good in English, English-language literature, and English history. I would spend hours reading poems by Longfellow, novels by Somerset Maugham, and, later on, short stories by Edgar Allen Poe. I was, however, mediocre in mathematics, physics, and chemistry.

While I was in that special school a schism developed between my stepmother and me. Our relationship deteriorated to near-crisis levels. I found it hard to talk to her, let alone confide in her. I felt increasingly uncomfortable and apprehensive in her presence, and her behavior toward me became unpredictable and ambivalent. We were all still living in the same room, so I began to stay away from the house as much as possible, playing in the yard or visiting public libraries.

My stepmother was by nature a nervous, high-strung perfectionist. It bothered her enormously that I had the opportunity to go to Moscow's most prestigious school, yet I was wasting the chance, as she viewed it. My father was not worried. He knew that boys are often late bloomers and that when I was just a little older I would outgrow the phase. But I think that Anastasia saw it as a waste of money. Besides, she also felt that she owned me. After all, it was she who had saved my life. In any case, she demanded that I become the top student in my class. Each time I made a two or three instead of the perfect five, she would fly into a rage that always ended in my being beaten, often very severely. She knew that if my father ever found out about those beatings he would be furious. So, after each of them, she threatened that if I said a word to Father I would be treated even worse. I believed her.

Father was always very busy, and during the week there was little time for us to be together. But on Sundays, his one day off, he spent as much time with me as he could. He liked to collect books, and he took me to bookstores that offered works by famous Russian writers and Russian translations of European classics. Repeatedly he stressed that I could become a truly well-educated person only if I were an avid reader, that reading would enhance my knowledge of life. My father was a thinking man, an honest man, an honorable man, and one who never stopped learning. I never heard him utter a criticism of the party or any official. He was a military scientist; toward the end of his life he chaired the chemistry department of a military institute. He loved Mother Russia and her history, but he did bend the law a little by keeping a few proscribed books by pre-Revolution writers. He often warned me not to mention those books. "It is sometimes necessary to hide the truth," he said, "but you must never hide the truth from yourself."

Sometimes in my sleep I still hear my father's voice saying those words. They have become the guiding rule of my life. Indeed, I doubt that I could have made the critical decisions I have made without such guidance. I will always remember my father as a big man—earnest, hardworking, sensitive, and somehow remote.

It is strange what memories stand clearly from the past. They are not always the most important personal events. For instance, I can remember with perfect clarity March 6, 1953. I was twelve years old. I remember still the feeling of unreality, of disorientation, when Radio Moscow announced that the leader of the Soviet people, Josef Vissarionovich Stalin, had died. The entire student body congregated in an unnatural silence. Everybody—teachers and students alike—looked stunned and subdued. The school superintendent, a World War II veteran who had lost an eye in combat, made a lengthy speech about what a tragedy Stalin's death was for the Soviet Union and its people. Sometime during the speech, he started to cry. Tears poured from his good eye while his glass eye stayed completely dry. Some of the students giggled. Classes were canceled, and I went home, walking past the Sklifasovskiy Hospital, which had the largest emergency ward in Moscow.

Late that afternoon some neighbors told us that hundreds of people were brought to the hospital by vehicles of all kinds—ambulances, military trucks, anything that could move. Most of the injured had been hurt by the stampeding crowds gathering to see Stalin's body on display. Many were already dead before they even reached the hospital. There is no doubt that there was much confusion in Moscow. Troops had to disperse the grief-stricken mobs because people sincerely mourned Stalin's death. It was as though the entire nation were suddenly left rudderless.

Grief soon turned to dismay. For example, my father was issued a summons directing him to witness the trial of one of Stalin's closest friends. Convened only a few short months after Stalin's death, this military tribunal met in secret to try KGB Security Chief Lavrenti Beria on charges of "crimes against the Russian people." These crimes included mass murders and bizarre tortures. Undoubtedly, he was guilty. At least, the tribunal found him guilty and sentenced him to death. But the trial also uncovered the disturbing fact that Beria had acted at the direct orders and the behest of Stalin himself. "Uncle Joe," as the West called Stalin, was once and for all revealed to be as ruthlessly Machiavellian as any of history's other dictators. The crimes were Stalin's; Beria became the scapegoat. Every day of that trial my father would come home in a state of shock, brooding at the table for long periods without speaking. Then he would burst out, "I cannot believe it! I cannot believe," suddenly lowering his voice to a whisper, "that those as highly placed as Beria could commit such atrocities against their own people."

One night as I listened to him, wide-eyed with shock, I thought for the first time in my life something I have thought many times since: "The real Russia that Father loves and this 'new' Soviet Union are not the same thing at all. Russia is Mother Russia, and the Soviet Union is . . . ?" I felt a chill of foreboding.

Later that year, Father got sick. After he'd visited the doctor, he came home in the middle of the day, something he never did. In a rare display of affection, he put his arm around me, and he looked at me. I had the strange feeling that he was memorizing my face.

"Stas," he said softly. Clearing his throat, he continued, "Stas, I have cancer. I'm dying, I think."

I was stunned. "How do you know? Did the doctors say so?"

"Nobody has said so. Maybe they're afraid to," he said. "But I do have cancer."

Suddenly he began to cry. It was terrible. Then, overcoming his tears, he went on. "I won't be here to see you grow up, son. Promise me that you will grow up to be a decent man, Stas, and always remember that you are a gentleman. Always act with honor."

Father was hospitalized soon after that conversation. They performed surgery, but the cancer had spread to his vital organs. He was dying slowly, suffering terribly. Shortly before his death he was promoted to the rank of major general of the Soviet army, but I'm not sure he realized it. During his last days he was in a coma most of the time. He died six months after he was admitted to the hospital. I was devastated by the loss of my father, and I began to see myself as an orphan. I had never been able to reconcile with my stepmother, and I was not close to my stepsister. I had no one to ask for counsel and guidance. I was alone. I was as sad and alone as any child could be.

My stepmother had long ago revealed a deep-rooted, unhealthy jealousy of my dead mother, Lydia. She burned all photographs of my mother, and she insisted upon formally adopting me shortly after she married my father. At the time I had been happy about the adoption because I had so much wanted a real mother of my own. As time went by, however, I had come to view her actions as just one more proof of her determination to "own" me. One thing that Anastasia's action did for me was to remove from the records the fact that my real mother was Jewish (a help, no doubt, to my future career). What I regret is the loss of the pictures because my mother's face has grown so misty with time. Sometimes, when I'm on the edge of sleep, I almost think I can see her—my little mother. I guess we never stop missing the woman who gave us life.

When I was fourteen, I ran away from home several times as a protest against my stepmother's waspish temper and harshness. I would simply leave for a couple of days. With only a few kopeks in my pocket, I would buy some salted herring and a little bread and sleep on some construction site. When I came home, she would always promise to be kinder to me. She never was.

My final fight with my stepmother came when I was seventeen years old. I don't remember the cause of the furor. In fact, I had concluded much earlier that she never needed an excuse to set her off. Anything would suffice—a towel not hung up, crumbs on the floor, a cup of spilled tea—and she would explode. I knew her pattern well. First she would scream and yell, working herself into a towering rage, and next she would seize a broom, a stick, anything. Then came the beatings, often severe enough to leave marks on my body. At age seventeen, however, I was near a man's height and size, and I decided to stand my ground.

"If you hit me again," I told her, "I will turn you in to the police. I'll report you to the school. I'm not going to take these beatings any more."

She merely laughed at me. "Go ahead! Nobody will believe you. You—a troublemaker, always running away. Who will take your word against mine? I'm a respected doctor who works in a big hospital every day. Nobody will believe you!"

As she started toward me, I did not give way to her. Instead, I doubled up my fists and advanced toward her. "I will take no more beatings," I said. "This time I will fight back. This time it is you who will be hurt."

All at once the rage drained out of her. Her face turned white. She turned abruptly and walked away. I felt a moment of great elation—then an unaccountable surge of guilt. I remember reading somewhere that the young can never triumph over their elders without feeling inside that they are guilty of a breach of nature. It's true. I knew that I was right to stand my ground, but I felt awful for doing so. Besides, it solved nothing in our relationship. Instead, we treated each other with cold formality and a constant wariness. By the time I was eighteen, I was out of her reach, and the estrangement was complete.

Since I was ten years old, I had endured my stepmother's beatings because I had felt guilty. Once I remember running outside so that no one would see me cry and thinking that I must be a terrible boy or I wouldn't deserve these punishments. Now, as a grown man, I have read and studied child psychology, and I see the situation more clearly. Abused children always think they are the cause of their own abuse. I was an abused child, and it still hurts me. Deep in my heart, it hurts.

Despite the antipathy of my stepmother, my schooling went on, and I studied as usual, relishing the social sciences and disdaining the natural sciences. My history teacher was particularly stimulating. He was about fifty-five years old, with the face and bearing often seen in nineteenth-century paintings. He looked like an intellectual of old Russia. He spoke Russian eloquently and created for us a vivid picture of our culture. In teaching modern history, he was unorthodox: instead of glorifying the role of the Communist party in winning World War II, for example, he stressed the sacrifices and heroism of plain people.

I'll never forget my first glimpse of a real-life hero. What a disappointment! I was fourteen or so when we were all called to an assembly to hear a "Great Hero" of the revolution, Marshal Budyonniy. We were kept after school hours; none of us was very keen on wasting our time listening to a doddering old Bolshevik. The "Great Hero" arrived in a government limousine just in time to see us trying to escape the assembly and our teachers herding us back. Old he was; doddering he wasn't. The infuriated seventy-year-old rushed into the auditorium and cursed us and the teachers, all in obscenities I had never heard before.

The old boy never did pull himself together. His speech was rambling and illiterate, a collection of anecdotes, none very interesting. As we were leaving that day, one of my friends sidled up to me and whispered, "Do you suppose all 'Great Heroes' are like that old man?" I was asking myself the same thing.

When I graduated from high school in the summer of 1958, I thought the world would come to an end if I weren't accepted to the Moscow Institute of International Relations so I could become a diplomat. I wasn't accepted because I had not earned the grade marks for admission. So I applied to the Institute of Oriental Languages at Moscow University, somehow knowing from the moment my application went in that I would be accepted. I passed the entrance exam with high marks and began my studies in the fall of '58. My career as an expert on Japan began with that single step. From the very beginning I enjoyed everything I learned. In high school I had gotten my hands on a few books by Japanese authors. I can't remember the names of all of them now, but I do remember the surprise I felt at the work of Akutagawa Ryunosuke. After the first few lines of *Rashomon* I knew that the author was a genius and that he wrote about the same kinds of people as those in Russia. His work reminded me of the writings of Ivan Turgenev. Here was a writer from another land speaking to the very heart of Russia.

My college education planted the seeds for much that I became later on. If I hadn't had the advantage of learning to speak Japanese under the tutelage of the two professors I had, I couldn't possibly have become as fluent as I am. I owe much to four teachers: Mrs. Ivanenko and Katayama, professors of the Japanese language; Irina Lyvova, professor of Japanese literature; and Professor Galperin, the noted historian. All educated Soviets know about these people, and claiming to have been taught by one of them is like saying "I was taught by Albert Einstein" or "I learned literature as a student of William Faulkner." Ironically, three of these four wonderful teachers bear deep emotional and psychological scars from wounds inflicted on them by the Soviet system. That in itself is a commentary, I think.

The two Japanese language professors were brilliant, naturally talented teachers. Mrs. Ivanenko was a dragon-like woman who had acquired a military bearing from her years of working as an interpreter in a Japanese prisoner-of-war camp. Katayama had come to Moscow with her father, a prominent Communist who fled Japan in the 1930s. He died a few years afterward, and his ashes were interred in the Kremlin Wall in the same row with other Communist leaders, a high tribute for one who was foreign-born. When I first knew her, Mrs. Katayama was already fifty years old. Much of the time she seemed sad and subdued, sometimes nervous and emotional. She had trouble speaking Russian, and it was difficult for her to adjust to the realities of

Soviet socialism, though she was a Communist by ideology. She had a hard life, I think, because Soviets are afraid to befriend foreigners.

My professor of Japanese literature was Irina Lyvova, a Russian and one of the best specialists on Japanese literature in the Soviet Union, perhaps in the world. As a young woman she had been thrown into a Stalinist prison where she stayed, under false accusation, for ten years. She was an unbelievable instructor. She would pick up a book written in Japanese and read it and translate it in one operation. She personally guided me through the research for my thesis, and I remember her with gratitude.

Professor Galperin was the leading expert on Japanese history in the Soviet Union, and I was very lucky to be able to study under him. Intelligent and soft-spoken, he really knew how to captivate his students.

I was in college during the height of the "de-Stalinization" period, though we still didn't have much freedom of discussion, particularly about contemporary events. Even there, in the college, the KGB kept its sharp eyes on us. There were even people enrolled in the college who were secret informers. One of my classmates, turned in by one such informant, was arrested and later sentenced to eight years in prison for "Zionist propaganda," though it's hard to say what kind of propaganda a twenty-one-year-old student could have spread. A few students were summoned for conferences with the KGB officers on campus for criticizing Khrushchev's approach to handling cultural problems. They weren't arrested, but the KGB tried to—and probably did—recruit some as informants. It was fairly easy to spot the collaborators, and I avoided them as much as possible.

One of those collaborators was Vyacheslav Pirogov. He was two years older than I, but I was at his graduation party where he got drunk, as usual. He staggered around, acting like a full-fledged KGB officer and ordering people into a private room to discuss the possibility of their working for the KGB. Some of the guests were mad as hell at first, but somebody passed the word to play along and have a little fun with this drunken oaf. Every person there lined up and humbly allowed Pirogov to interrogate them, one by one. It was all in fun, and no one reported him to the officials of the Institute—a sign of true decency, I've always thought. Many years later, when I first reported to the embassy in Tokyo for my tour of duty, there was good old Pirogov, a real KGB man by then.

I was in college before I discovered girls. Ah, but when I did! I'll admit that those newfound wonders interfered with my school work quite a bit. After classes, my friends and I used to go to the Café Moskva on Mokhovaya Square, where we would spend hours just talking, talking, talking. We had just been introduced to the world of ideas, and it was heady stuff indeed. Naturally, many romances were born during those hours when students crowded the café. It seems to me that I fell in and out of love at least twice a week. A group would form at a table, I'd start talking to a girl—maybe one I'd known for years—and all at once I'd discover that she was beautiful. Instant romance. I went with one girl for nearly a year. She was almost seven feet tall; I'm only five-eleven. She was sweet, intelligent, and feminine, but nothing could come of it, even though she was good fun. Oh, we knew that people stared at us and that we looked a bit odd together. Sometimes after a few glasses of wine we would dance under the arch of the entrance to the old building of Moscow University, just for the fun of watching people gape at us in astonishment. But, as I say, nothing could come of it. I couldn't ever find a place to stand so that I could kiss her. We stayed good friends; she was a guest at my first wedding, and she cried and cried. "Stas, my dear," she kept saying, "your Yelena is so beautiful! Your wedding is so beautiful!"

I met my beautiful Yelena in 1959 when I was eighteen. She was a student in the Philology Department of Moscow University. All at once, instead of just going with a girl, I was courting a girl. One is much more difficult than the other. If a young Muscovite is just going with a girl, it is permissible to meet where the crowd goes and to be part of the group. Courtship is more serious. The couple wants to be alone, but they usually have no money. Even if they did, there are few places where they can go—an occasional movie or a meal in an inexpensive restaurant, and that's about it. Otherwise, there are only public parks—very cold in the winter—or public buildings, such as the museums, palaces, or art galleries. Yelena was easy to talk with, and soon we were spending all of our free time together. By early 1960, when we were both too young to know that companionship and love are not the same thing, it seemed like the most natural thing in the world to get married. Yelena's mother and grandfather were agreeable, so we married as most young Soviets do—in a registry office. Yelena wore a lovely white gown and veil. The wedding party, our relatives, and our friends all trooped down to the registry where we stood in line to get the necessary form filled out in a cubicle manned by a sour-faced ogre of a woman. There were wedding parties ahead of us and behind us. As one marriage was finished, another would begin. When our turn came, we were ushered into another room, which looked a bit like a reception hall. As a wheezy phonograph whined Mendelssohn's "Wedding March," we took our vows before a magistrate, and in three minutes, we were married. Yelena's family hosted a party at their home that went on into the wee hours of the morning.

We both earned only our stipends. I could not even afford to rent a room in an apartment. So we lived with Yelena's mother and grandfather in her grandparents' old log house in the suburb of Kuntsevo. It was the first time that I really experienced what life in a family could be like when there was no friction and when everyone worked together. For the first time I had a father-figure to emulate and revere. My own father, dear as he was to me, had died when I was in my early teens, and our relationship was that of adult to child. Yelena's grandfather and I developed a man–to–man closeness that I treasured.

A veritable font of history, Grandfather did more to teach me about the October Revolution than all of the history books I ever read. He had lived through it. A Bolshevik when he was a law student in the early 1900s, he had not only taken part in the Revolution but had also served as defense lawyer for many Bolsheviks in the months preceding it. He had been quite successful, too. Many were saved from jail in tsarist times due to his efforts.

After the revolution, Grandfather studied to become a biologist and gradually gained recognition for his work in genetics. He wrote fiery articles against one of Stalin's favorites, Professor Lysenko. Because he stuck to his guns, as it were, he was imprisoned in the 1930s and confined to the infamous Lyubyanka Prison. The information I gained from knowing that wonderful man has been invaluable to me. From him I got a true picture of the early Stalin era, rather than the history, complete with Soviet bias, that is taught in Soviet schools.

One other important lesson that I learned from Grandfather concerned the so-called collectivization of the Soviet farmlands. "Millions of skillful, talented farmers were branded 'kulaks' [parasites] and imprisoned or driven into exile," he recalled. "Many hundreds of thousands died of starvation because there was no one to work the land."

I am convinced that because of this action alone the base of Soviet agriculture was irreversibly damaged. Certainly, the Soviet Union today cannot produce enough food to feed its own people. The land is there; the know-how and incentives are not.

From my discussions with Grandfather, which sometimes lasted into the early morning, I began to suspect that the late secretary general of the Communist party, Mr. Khrushchev, had lied to our people during the de-Stalinization period. Khrushchev had claimed that Stalin and a very small clique of defective individuals were responsible for *all* of the atrocities of the 1930s, 1940s, and early 1950s. A small group couldn't have done the things they had done without the active support and participation of all who were part of the Stalin regime. Grandfather also said that by the late 1930s, when he was imprisoned, he understood well that the Soviet socialist government did not work *for* the people, but against them. He was the first Soviet citizen I had ever met who dared to say that the Soviet system would fall if it were open and truthful rather than secretive. He suggested that it survived through lies, half-truths, and the tyranny of fear.

When I look back on my marriage to Yelena, I see us first as students and then as a married couple. Our interests were not similar— she loved the structure of language, libraries, and semantics; I loved all things Japanese—yet we were good companions when we laid our own interests and studies aside. She was quiet, adaptable, even-tempered, and sweet, but somehow the love between us never deepened. It didn't lessen, but it didn't grow, either.

In the spring of 1960 the Ministry of Fisheries sent a letter to the Institute of Oriental Languages, offering summer jobs to students of the Japanese language. They needed interpreters for the Soviet state fisheries inspectors who patrolled the Sea of Japan. The state inspectors monitored the Soviet-Japanese Fishing Agreement, searching any Japanese fishing boats found in restricted areas. The pay for this summer work was 200 rubles a month for a period of three months. My student stipend was much lower, and for me 200 rubles was unheard-of wealth. I leaped at the chance to go to the Far East. Besides, the chance to see the sea again was an enticement I could not ignore. I signed on, and leaving my wife in Moscow with her family, flew to Khabarovsk, changed planes for Yuzhno-Sakhalinsk, and then took a train to Korsakov. Once there I boarded a civil inspection ship. I was just nineteen years old, and this was my first real job.

I was so seasick those first few days I thought I'd die. I couldn't eat anything; even the smell of food would send me to the rail. But I recovered quickly and began to enjoy the sea. It was fascinating. I could remember visiting the resort areas around the Black Sea when I was a child, but the Pacific was entirely different, changing colors, sometimes several times a day, from light blue to almost black, depending on the weather. Some days we would be swallowed by fog so thick that it was almost like traveling through milk. Other times, we would get caught in violent storms in which huge, menacing, and beautiful waves convulsed the boat from bow to stern.

One such storm almost killed me. The ship I was on was an old solid-iron military vessel that had been reassigned to serve as a civilian inspection ship. There were few amenities aboard; in fact, the only rail on the deck was a rope running through eye rods that, in turn, were fastened every yard or so into a two-inch-high iron facing that girded the deck. Just getting to the toilet (actually only a hole in the aft deck) could be a major challenge, especially if the seas were rough.

One night the old ship was wallowing through the pitch and roll of a major storm. The deck was awash from breaking waves and blowing spume. The noise from the sea and the high wind was deafening, and it was certainly no time to visit that toilet up there on the dangerous deck. But I woke up knowing I *had* to go. Holding on for dear life, I groped my way from the cabin to the deck above. I had just reached the open deck when a wave hit. The ship rolled, water washed across the deck, and I slid across the deck and over the side. There I hung with my fingertips gripping the sharp edges of the two-inch iron facing of the deck. If I had dropped, no one would have known it until the next day. Even if anyone had seen it happen, they could never have found me in the dark and the storm.

By some miracle of chance, one of the ship's officers just happened to come along. He spied me down there, barely clinging to that facing, and said matter-of-factly, "Stanislav, what are you doing down there?"

"Trying to find the toilet!" I shouted.

"It's not down there."

He reached out a huge hand, grasped my wrist, and with one quick heave, hauled me aboard. "Come with me, Stas," he said, grinning broadly, "I'll show you where the toilet is."

I think I learned about sailors in that instant. Certainly they are a different type of people from those I had always known. They are hard-working, good-hearted, good-natured, cheerful men always ready for a good laugh, a bawdy joke, or a rough-and-tumble adventure. Their tough profession may have made some of them into ruffians, but I found most of them to be diamonds in the rough. The sailors I knew lived daily with the dangers of the Pacific Ocean and always behaved with courage and valor. They braved any danger to help a comrade in trouble.

I enjoyed being a part of this crowd. I am glad, however, that I did not adopt some of their customs. Though most of my new friends drank excessively, only a few were alcoholics. They enjoyed drinking some very exotic types of liquor—from hair lotion to cough syrup—anything, as long as it had alcohol in it. Keeping bottled liquor on board the ship was strictly forbidden, and the sale of liquor was prohibited in most of the tiny ports the inspector ships visited. Soviet authorities were afraid of bloody, drunken brawls between the crews of the fishing boats crowded in each of the Kurile Islands' ports. There were no decent cafés, movie theaters, or hotels in that area. Indeed, I believe there are none now. Shore leave was just a chance to get rid of "sea legs."

One of the Kuriles is the tiny, rock-bound island of Shikotan, sparsely populated most of the year and buffeted by bad weather for all of the year. Its only importance rests in three fish-processing plants kept in operation almost around the clock during the summer months to serve the Soviet fishing fleet. Fish are caught in great numbers in these waters, and having the processing plants within close reach is a great advantage.

Covered in fog most of the time, this tiny spit of land jutting into the sea has been dubbed "the end of the world" by sailors who dock at the wooden pier of its shallow port. Still, to the woman-hungry sailors, Shikotan is a paradise. The reason? The processing plants are operated by women who are brought from the mainland each summer. On Shikotan, the ratio is seven women to every man.

The regulation prohibiting alcohol on that one particular island was an especially wise one. It does not take much imagination to see how much blood would flow if sailors, inspired by the presence of so many women, were free to drink to the point of bellicosity. Only champagne was ever allowed, and that only on national holidays.

About once a month a ship with a minuscule bar visited Shikotan. But since it was too big a vessel to enter the rocky harbor, it anchored some distance away and off-loaded goods for the island by barge. One of the funniest sights I ever witnessed was the night every man on that island swarmed out to the ship in little boats and canoes, on rafts and logs, on or in anything that would float. It was like watching pirates attacking a ship, and the "attackers" did not leave until every drop of alcohol was gone.

Shikotan's sole representative of authority was a one-horse policeman. His horse, the only one on the entire island, was well taken care of. He and the horse were constant companions. If anything had ever happened to one, the other would probably have died of loneliness. I became acquainted with this "man of authority" during our brief stops. Once, while the constable was visiting our ship, he and I were alone for a few minutes.

"Stas," he said, "You know this goddamned island. Fog! Rocks! No alcohol! Now, you are going from here to Sakhalin and then back to here. That's one month. Please, Stas, do me a favor. Bring me a couple of bottles of alcohol. Do me this favor, okay?"

He was not just asking me to bring him some liquor. He wanted pure, unadulterated grain alcohol. The request, of course, was against the rules. But the poor man pleaded so hard that I finally agreed to do it.

Returning a month later, we docked late in a fog thick as cream. It was dark before I set foot onto the wooden pier, knowing I would meet the policeman out there. I have experienced few things as eerie. The fog swirled around me, rising to shroud the already dim lights into a preternatural glow. Rats as big as house cats ran along the pier and, once or twice, over my feet. At last I heard the clip-clop of hooves on the wooden pier. When the figure loomed up out of the fog, it was terrifying. Something was on the horse's back, all right, but it did not seem to have a head. All the stories I had ever read about headless specters raced through my mind as I stood frozen. Then came the sound: "Stanislav?" It was the policeman's voice.

"Here," I answered.

"Horse, turn."

At last I could see what was on the horse's back—the policeman lying across the saddle on his stomach, head dangling toward me, feet dangling on the other side. "Do you remember the merchandise we discussed?" he said, using his most official voice, though his position destroyed the intended effect.

"Yes, sir."

"Did you bring it?"

"Yes, sir."

"Give it here! I'm desperate!"

I gave him the bottles of grain alcohol, one in each of his hands, and as he and the horse were turning away, I ran after them.

"Wait!" I said. "Why are you riding the horse like that?"

"Because I have blisters all over my goddamned ass!"

They disappeared into the fog.

The poor man did indeed have blisters on his posterior that, in turn, had been infected by his constant horseback riding. The cause of the blisters was a vitamin A deficiency: there were very few fresh fruits and vegetables on Shikotan. I can only hope that the alcohol I gave him brought him oblivion from pain and at least one good night's sleep.

The manners of my sailor friends were crude, of course, but there was a simplicity about them that was delightful. For instance, aboard Russian ships, the cook is usually a woman, and some of these lady cooks are very "kind" to their male companions. Our cook, the only woman among some two dozen men, slept with practically every member of the crew with the possible exception of the captain. To avoid confusion in assignations with her, the sailors kept a calendar with only one name written on each day's space. Amazingly, there were never any fights among these numerous Romeos.

Most evenings the sailors would gather in a large room to watch old movies. Other nights they would organize competitions to determine which man had the biggest penis. Each time, arguments erupted. Each time, the lady cook would be called in to act as judge. Armed as she was with expert knowledge, her verdict was always instantly accepted by everybody, and all of the contestants would go away happy, even though the winners differed from competition to competition.

Our ship cruised near the Southern Kurile Islands—Kunashiri, Iturup, and Shikotan. On several occasions, late at night, I had to embark on tiny Japanese fishing boats in the open sea with the state fishery inspector. The Japanese fishermen struck me as extremely brave. Who but people of great courage would dare to go more than 200 miles away from home port on small boats? The living quarters of the Japanese fishermen on board their boats were miserable, with the captain sleeping by the boat's controls. When we found evidence that these tiny boats had violated the fishery agreement, the state fishery inspector would often not fill in the papers because "these guys are really poor, and obviously they are not catching fish to get rich."

During this trip, I chanced to see the coast of Hokkaido: distant mountains rising from the sea, mountains covered with emerald green forests. I fervently hoped the day would come when I would actually be able to visit Japan, not just see it from afar. So close and yet so distant, just beyond reach, like a familiar dream.

Back in Moscow, I worked for six weeks as an interpreter at the first Japanese commercial exhibition in Sokolniki Park in Moscow. Although it was a part-time job, the personnel department of the Soviet Chamber of Commerce thoroughly screened the student applicants. When I took my application to the personnel officer, he read it through and then produced from his pocket a card identifying himself as a KGB major. I even remember his name—Kholopov. He told me that my part-time job was fraught with responsibility because several of the Japanese engineers or businessmen working for the exhibition were actually spies. He demanded that I report personally to him anything that I might notice that was the least bit unusual.

I was assigned as an interpreter for a Japanese company that produced steel cables, and I got to know quite a few Japanese engineers and businessmen. I was sure that none of them was a spy. I think Major Kholopov was using this pretext to collect information through the interpreters on the Japanese workers themselves, possibly for targeting them later on, either in Moscow or Japan. I often talked with my Japanese superiors at the exhibition, asking them about Tokyo, Osaka, and other Japanese cities. They gladly answered all my questions. My Japanese was by now fluent, and I communicated easily with them. It was exciting to talk at length to Japanese in Japanese.

The exhibition itself astonished me. The industrial exhibits showed the genius of the Japanese engineers and workers, and many of the products were superior to similar Soviet products. During many nights items on exhibit were stolen, especially cigarette lighters and other consumer goods. The KGB people said it was provocation by Japanese spies, but I knew that things had been stolen by some workers at the exhibitions, probably in some cases even by the KGB officers themselves.

In the summer of 1964, when I was twenty-three, I graduated from the Institute of Oriental Languages at Moscow University. In the Soviet Union, in exchange for free education, the government chooses one's place of future employment. I was told that I would work for the All-Union Research Institute of Oceanography and Maritime Fisheries as a junior researcher. I was bitterly disappointed. I didn't know what kind of future I'd have or whether I'd ever get to go to Japan. Why had I been trained as an expert on Japan if I was going to have to spend the rest of my life in fisheries?

Graduation from university marked the end of my formative years. The lonely little boy from the Moscow streets was now grown up. All of the pieces of my life had done their work, shaping and molding me. All of the influences had conjoined: the bits and pieces of my memories, the sadness, the loneliness, the lessons. All had determined what I would become. An expert on Japan. A KGB officer and spy. An American.

2

Undertow:
Being Pulled In

OUTER BANKS, NORTH CAROLINA

The waves were getting higher as the tide came in. The ground seemed to shake as the huge breakers crashed against the jetty. A Coast Guard Jeep went by, stopping a few hundred yards down the beach to raise the danger flags. Undertow!

"Get too close to that," I thought, "and you're pulled in!"

MOSCOW AND JAPAN, 1964–1967

$\mathbf{M}$y personal life underwent as many changes during the mid-1960s as my professional life had. In early 1964, when I was just settling in at the Institute of Oceanography and Fisheries, Yelena and I separated. Our life together in Yelena's home had been free of strife, even blandly content. We never quarreled and rarely disagreed. In our mutual affection, we were more like brother and sister, still living in our family home, than like husband and wife. Our love for each other had never grown, and each of us had matured enough to realize that our relationship lacked something essential to a genuinely happy marriage.

There was no reason to hurry about getting a divorce, so neither of us rushed into starting divorce proceedings. For a brief time life was placid and humdrum. Then one day a friend of mine said to me, "Hey, Stas, come to my party on Saturday. There's someone I want you to meet." I almost didn't go. At the last moment, I went along to the café where Nikolai's guests were gathering. I was one of the last to arrive, and my friend was genuinely glad to see me.

"Come over here," he said, motioning me toward a group of five or six people in an animated conversation; then, touching a dark-haired girl on the shoulder: "Natalia, I want you to meet Stanislav."

She turned toward me. She was the most beautiful woman I had ever seen in my life—tall, with a sensual figure, dark shining hair, brown velvet eyes, and the most kissable mouth in the world. Before that first night was over, I knew that I was madly in love. I have no idea what I said to her. She used to tease me about that later.

"I thought that you had a stutter," she said. "I wondered how anyone as good-looking as you could've been born with a stutter."

"Why? What did I sound like?"

"I don't know, darling. Something like B-B-B-B-," and she would give her adorable little chuckle.

I learned that Natalia was an architecture student, that her father was a senior Forestry Department officer in the Academy of Sciences, that she had one younger sister, and that her mother was a real intellectual. Both parents had impeccable credentials with the Communist Party of the Soviet Union (CPSU). Natalia lived with her parents in a tiny two-bedroom apartment, proof positive of her family's high position because her parents *owned* that apartment.

I took Natalia home that night and made certain that I would see her the next day. The morning found me as wide-eyed and sleepless as I have ever been in my life. As soon as offices were open for business I started divorce proceedings. When I met her later that day, the first thing I said was, "I love you!" The second thing was, "Will you marry me?" I thought my heart would jump out of my chest when she said, "I love you and YES!"

By the end of the week we both knew we couldn't possibly wait for that wretched divorce before sleeping together, and my darling Natasha figured out how we could manage it. She occupied one of the bedrooms in her family's apartment while her parents and sister slept in the other.

"Stas," she said, "you wait in the hallway until everyone is in bed asleep, and I'll smuggle you in."

She took her sister into her confidence, and that dear girl, after making sure their parents were asleep, guarded the way for us. Natalia let me into her room every night for over a month, and except for her sister, no one ever knew. In all the years I knew her, the sister never said a word to anyone. And that was a *big* secret.

If Natalia's father had ever found me in bed with her, he would have killed me. There's absolutely no doubt about that. Even now I shiver to think of the chances we took. Nevertheless, I'd do the same thing over any time. One lesson I did learn from those enchanted nights is that it is possible to make love *very* quietly! As soon as my divorce was final, in late 1964, Natalia and I were married. We lived with her parents in their apartment, occupying the same room where we had first made love.

Our baby son was born a year later, and the future seemed to hold all of the joy in the world. I was so proud of my lovely wife that it was unthinkable that anything could go wrong. Our son, Aleksandr, chubby and blond, brought us great delight. Natalia used to croon to him, "Where did you come from, little blond boy? Your daddy's hair is auburn, and your mother's hair is black." I'm not sure I ever told her that my hair was blond until I was seven.

For the first seven years of our marriage, we continued living in Natalia's family home, although her parents were not there all the time. When Natalia's sister married, the parents often visited her. In addition, her father's job allowed him to travel to places where her mother could also go. When Natalia's father died unexpectedly in 1971, her mother went to live with her sister, and we were given the apartment as more or less our own.

For almost two years I worked for the Institute of Oceanography and Fisheries, where I researched Japanese fishing off Soviet coasts and translated Japanese and English writings about fisheries. This was a safe little haven of "work, don't think, go home, go back to work." Then, on a slow day in 1966, my boss came by with a message that began the process of drawing me into the KGB.

"The Central Committee [of the Communist party] just called," he said, looking troubled. "You are to call them back. Right away! Ask for someone named Romanov."

I knew why he looked somewhat concerned. I was, too. Calls from the Central Committee were a rarity at the Institute, but when they did come, it usually meant trouble for somebody.

"Oh, no! What do they want with me?"

"I don't know, but you'd best call back. NOW!"

I didn't exactly run to a phone, but I didn't waste any time, either. I was put right through to Mr. Romanov's office. He told me that he wanted to see me as soon as possible. "You have been recommended by the university for a job we want you to undertake in the International Department, so it's essential that I see you at once," he said.

Recommended? For what? I knew very little about the International Department. The Soviet press rarely mentioned that department during the mid-Sixties. The following morning I went along to the Bureau of Passes, where I was given an official pass that would get me into the International Department of the Central Committee. I found the towering building in which the International Department's offices are located and showed my pass to an armed sentry. I was awe-struck as I took the elevator to the fifth floor. The building was so quiet it was eerie.

The office I was looking for wasn't easy to find. Tucked away along a rear hallway, the door was marked with only one word: ROMANOV. Romanov greeted me cordially enough, but I still found him to be terse and enigmatic. He allowed a small silence to build up after I was seated—a move that, predictably, put me on the defensive.

"Levchenko," he finally began, "a man with your education and knowledge shouldn't be rotting in a second-rate outfit like the Oceanography and Fisheries Institute."

I didn't speak. During the past two years with the Institute I'd been loaned to the International Department to work as an interpreter from time to time, but no one in the important offices upstairs had ever talked to me at all. I didn't know what to make of this. I figured the best thing to do was be quiet and wait.

"I think I can promise you a chance at a more rewarding career."

Another small silence.

"We want you to become a secretary/interpreter for the Moscow correspondent of *Akahata.*"

I already knew that *Akahata* was the official newspaper of the Japanese Communist Party. I still kept quiet.

"Ostensibly, your job will be to act as an aide for the *Akahata* correspondent, helping with translations, some filing, and so on. Actually, your job won't be that simple."

I probably looked startled. I certainly felt startled.

"In fact," continued Romanov, a little smile on his face, "you must report to the Japanese sector of the International Department on every step the correspondent makes in his contacts with both foreigners and Soviet citizens alike. You will also make the same reports to me personally."

By that time I was surprised as well as startled. I knew, as does every educated Soviet citizen, that one of the responsibilities of the International Department was to maintain good relations with all the Communist parties in the noncommunist world. But this man was telling me that the Central Committee systematically spied upon these foreign parties. I was shocked. There seemed to be absolutely no logic to treating friends with so much distrust. My somewhat naive and idealistic approach to the world would be challenged a thousand more times as my horizons were expanded. I would eventually be caught in the undertow and participate in another primary responsibility of the International Department—the planning and running of influence operations abroad.

Before my interview was finished, I had learned even more. Romanov indicated that there were many things I would learn about the mechanics of these operations. I was told that most of the foreign correspondents of Communist newspapers from abroad were paid by the Soviets, not by their own countries or newspapers. The source of the money for these salaries and the "cover" for the entire operation was the Soviet Red Cross.

"We use the Red Cross," Romanov said, "because no one must

know that you are assigned to the International Department. So far as anyone else is concerned, you will be working for the Red Cross."

I learned in later years just how devious this cover actually is. The Alliance of the Russian Red Cross and the Red Crescent Society of the USSR—the full title of the Soviet Red Cross—is a member of the International Red Cross. It unfailingly pays its dues and gives lip service to its endorsement of the seven guiding principles of the Red Cross. These principles require: (1) service to humanity, (2) by volunteers, (3) services are to be given universally, (4) in unity with other nations who are Red Cross members, (5) with neutrality, and (6) with impartiality. The seventh and most important guiding principle demands that these services to humanity be given with total "independence from governments, from government actions, and from governmental or political purposes." The Soviets use their relief organization and its funds, contributed by ordinary Soviet citizens to help people in trouble, to support foreign newspaper correspondents. Then, adding insult to injury, they go back to the same pot for money to hire others to spy on them.

Mr. Romanov told me to think over the offer. I did. When I went back for the second meeting, things got a little heated.

I refused his offer. He was furious.

"Do you understand," he demanded, "that the only way for you to have any kind of career is with party organizations? If you don't take advantage of this chance, you'll probably spend the rest of your life pushing paper at the Oceanography and Fisheries Institute."

I assured him that I meant no offense. I explained that I planned to apply for a postgraduate position at the Research Institute of Oriental Studies. This branch of the Soviet Academy of Sciences accepts a limited number of carefully selected students who can earn graduate degrees through their work but whose primary task is advanced research on various aspects of Far Eastern politics, economics, and sociology.

"I'm determined that my career, my life's work, will be in the field of research," I concluded.

"You will stand a better chance of being accepted after a successful period of work at the Japanese desk of the International Department. I sincerely hope that you change your mind," he said ominously. "If you don't, your future could be badly damaged. The International

Department is powerful, you know, and an unsatisfactory reference from us would bar you forever from what you want to do."

Obviously, Romanov wasn't placated. His threat wasn't even subtle. I gave in, at least partially. For a little over three months I reported to the office of the Japanese desk daily, doing translations from *Akahata* and other Japanese newspapers and putting them into the various files the department maintained on Japan. In spite of Romanov's thinly veiled threats, I still refused to work for the *Akahata* correspondent. During much of this period the chief of the Japanese desk, Ivan Kovalenko, was out of the country. When he came back, he called me in almost at once.

"Have you changed your mind about the job with the *Akahata* correspondent?" he asked.

Risky though it was, I said no.

He gave me a nasty look. "OK, if you want to be a fool, it's your funeral. Go to the Institute of Oriental Studies."

Not long after that uncomfortable interview, the notice came through that I'd passed my entrance exams for the Institute of Oriental Studies. When I reported for the orientation, I was told my adviser would be Igor Latyshev, a doctor of sciences in his early forties. Considered one of the rising stars as an expert on Japan, he had graduated from the Moscow Institute of Oriental Studies in the 1950s and had spent several years as a *Pravda* correspondent in Tokyo. Since that time he had worked, directly or indirectly, for the International Department.

In our first meeting Dr. Latyshev told me that if I wanted to succeed in a career as a Soviet expert on Japan, the subject of my study should be both contemporary and political. After long consideration I decided to study the history of the post–World War II Japanese peace movement. To my surprise Dr. Latyshev seemed doubtful, but he finally agreed.

"If you want to do a serious study on that subject," he warned, "you will have to write your thesis for in-house use only."

I wondered why, but he gave no real explanation. He just smiled cryptically and said, "You'll find out."

I found out all right. Indeed there were reasons why a study on that subject had to remain an in-house document only. In 1963–1964, the Japanese peace movement had split into two major groups: Gensuikin, supported by the Japanese Socialist Party (JSP), and Gebsuikyo, led by the Japanese Communist Party (JCP). During these years the

JCP had chosen an independent course from Moscow's. In addition, a JCP splinter group, the Voice of Japan, had emerged under the leadership of the veteran Japanese communist, Yoshio Shiga.

It didn't take me much time to unravel this trichotomy in the Japanese peace movement, but when I began to write my thesis I couldn't discover exactly what the position of the International Department was. From what I could determine, the position was confused and ill-defined. They wanted to support Gensuikin (JSP) because it was relatively sympathetic to the Soviet Union. On the other hand, though nominally aligned with communism, Gebsuikyo had declared its independence from the USSR and was frequently critical of Soviet policy. Both organizations, however, criticized the American presence in Japan.

The paradox, then, was this: although the Japanese Communist Party had chosen an independent line, neither the International Department nor the Soviet Union could afford to lose one of the largest and most active Communist parties in the world. The International Department had no recourse but to try, consistently and unsuccessfully, to reach a compromise with the JCP.

My adviser, Dr. Latyshev, had warned me that my postgraduate work would not be easy. "Your thesis can be successful only if you can give viable recommendations to the International Department on ways to cope with the situation. They are aware of the complexities in dealing with the Japanese peace movement. I just hope they don't expect you to find solutions when they haven't been able to do it for themselves."

That was a possibility, and we both knew it.

"Don't forget, either," he added, "that your thesis will only be approved as an in-house document if the International Department—in the person of Kovalenko, the chief of the Japanese sector—likes it." I know now that educational institutions in the West operate very differently.

I had chosen a formidable task indeed. In order to get a better feel for the realities of the Japanese peace movement, I worked part-time as a consultant for the Soviet Peace Committee.

The committee and the Afro-Asian Solidarity Committee have their offices on Kropotkinskaya Street in a beautiful 200-year-old mansion that once belonged to a Russian nobleman. It is also used as the headquarters for a major "ploy in deception" by the Soviet leaders, a deception they use against very sincere and dedicated partisans for peace in the free world countries. It's in these groups and others like them that the Soviet Union finds fertile ground for recruiting agents of influence. These agents are not necessarily ideological socialists or communists, but in their zeal to rid the world of nuclear weapons or to achieve world peace, they can frequently be manipulated into supporting exactly what the Soviet Union wants them to support: dividing and weakening the West, though not through peace or by eliminating nuclear weapons.

I worked for the Soviet Peace Committee during the Vietnam War years. My job was primarily concerned with propagandizing against that war. If I had to give a job description of my work for the "peace" committee, it would read:

> Applicant must be able to design and implement propaganda programs, to plan protest demonstrations, and to draft orders to Soviet fronts in other countries. Applicant must direct all efforts toward convincing America that there is a worldwide rejection of the U.S. presence in Vietnam and that there is no other way to restore peace than for the United States to withdraw from Southeast Asia.

At the end of a long day, I'd join a crowd that often gathered in the cellars of the old mansion, where a photographer for the Soviet Peace Committee kept his darkroom. A resourceful fellow, the photographer had devised an inexpensive and ingenious way to entertain frequently and well. He would tie a piece of string to a piece of stale bread and put it on the top step near the open outside door leading to the cellar. Pigeons and an occasional dove would come to investigate, and my friend would carefully lure them down to the cellar. There he'd wring their necks, remove their feathers, and dress them. When he had caught enough to make a meal, he would send out a little memo: "Time to watch the birdie!" This was our cue that after work there would be a banquet of tasty little birds, grilled over a charcoal fire, and lots of vodka, served in the photographer's cellar hideaway.

Those were real parties: food, music, laughter, and enough rowdiness to last a lifetime. After we had eaten our fill and were relaxed, couples would pair off and disappear into the empty cells of the old dungeons.

During this part of 1966, I was lucky in making friends with several people who were active in the Japanese peace movement. Among them was Professor Ichiro Moritaki, who chaired the organization for the survivors of Hiroshima. From him I learned firsthand something about the sincerity of the Japanese people who were working for world peace. I learned that Japan, after its defeat in World War II, had undergone a remarkable and dramatic psychological revolution that affected the whole nation. As a result, virtually the entire nation was dedicated to democratic ideals and to the search for a peaceful world.

Part of my job with the Soviet Peace Committee was to travel with the Japanese delegations visiting the Soviet Union. The committee, with the help of the local Communist party organizations, orchestrated these visits so that the visitors saw only the most appealing sights. They traveled to Potemkin-like villages—the best collective farms and the best state farms—places that were atypical of real Soviet agriculture, which has been staggering under incalculable burdens for more than sixty years.

After writing about two-thirds of my thesis, I abandoned it in disgust. Dr. Latyshev had been right about the difficulty of the task. It was impossible to tell enough lies to make my thesis acceptable to the International Department while still including enough truth to make it useful. Given the sensitivities of the doctrinaire Soviet system, there simply was no way to make meaningful recommendations about the situation in Japan. This ensured that I would not be awarded the degree I so desired, but the government already had plans for me.

Once again, by some miracle, I landed on my feet. As it turned out, the officers in the International Department, including Kovalenko himself, thought that I was a fairly respectable specialist on the Japanese peace movement. They also respected my fluency in Japanese. One winter day my adviser at the Institute told me that the International Department planned to send me to Japan as an interpreter for a delegation of the Moscow Council of Trade Unions.

I was so excited I couldn't stand still. At last I would have the chance to see with my very own eyes the country I had studied for so many years! Getting there wasn't easy. I had to submit countless papers on my personal history for review by the Central Committee and the KGB, only to wait another six weeks or more before being summoned to the exit visas department. I was interviewed for two hours. The interviewer had a spacious office, an impressive mahogany desk, and comfortable chairs. There was a voluminous file on his desk, and I was startled when I read the title: "Dossier on Stanislav Aleksandrovich Levchenko." It must have been 250 pages thick with KGB reports on my loyalty and behavior. Obviously, their agents and ever-present informants had been very busy.

At the end of the session, the interviewing officer gave me a long, pontifical lecture on the way a Soviet citizen should behave abroad. He warned me about the tricks of American imperialists who, he said, were chasing Soviet citizens all over the world, trying to recruit them or compromise them. I should stay away from bars and avoid walking the streets of Tokyo by myself. He warned in dire tones that the Japanese intelligence services would try to collect information on me and would never miss a chance to recruit me.

I also had to visit the International Department, where I had an equally long conversation with Kovalenko, my old "friend," the chief of the Japanese desk. I wouldn't have been human if I hadn't thought of the day some years before when this same man had barked, "It's your funeral. Go to the Institute of Oriental Studies." I also knew that I was damned lucky. I could've fallen off that high wire I was walking any time along the way.

"Now, Stanislav," he began, surprising me with his informality, "your mission is to serve as an interpreter for the delegation. You will also meet with members of the Japanese peace movement, primarily the Gensuikin people, and extract from them current intelligence on their future plans and positions on political platforms."

I had expected these instructions, but I was unprepared for what followed. Kovalenko was brutally frank about the chairman of the Moscow Council of Trade Unions. I got the impression that by his informality Kovalenko was subtly admitting me into the "inner sanctum" of the Japanese desk, if not into the whole of the International Department.

"Pay absolutely no attention to that fool chairman," Kovalenko spat out. "And he is a fool. Do what he says only during negotiations with the representatives of the Japanese trade unions; the rest of the time ignore him. Your job is to work for the International Department."

In April 1967, the delegation from the Moscow Council of Trade Unions flew from Moscow to Khabarovsk, where we boarded a train to the port of Nakhodka. From there we sailed on the *Dzerzhinsky,* a passenger ship bound for Yokohama. The first thing I saw of Japan was its harbor; enormous supertankers and cargo vessels and mammoth white-painted oil reservoirs and factory chimneys dominated the view that I had from the ship's deck. After so long a wait, I was at last entering Japan. And I was nervous.

Our delegation was driven to the Takanawa Prince Hotel in Tokyo, and I was all eyes. I stared in fascination at the beautiful modern buildings that stood side by side with old, traditional houses. I almost felt that there was something unreal about the first Buddhist temples and Shinto shrines I saw, and the lush Japanese gardens were complete marvels. I was struck by the neatness: in the people's dress, in the streets, in the shops. But Tokyo is bewilderingly overpopulated, and the rush hour crowd made me dizzy. How can so many people be crammed together in one place? I wondered. Yet everywhere I looked, there were self-confident, relaxed, smiling faces, not at all like the sour and anxious expressions on the faces of Muscovites during rush hours. The traffic astounded me. I'd never seen so many cars moving so fast on such narrow streets in my life, yet somehow everything functioned efficiently.

Of all the things I wanted to try firsthand, Japanase food topped the list. I remember how squeamish I'd felt the first time I learned that they eat raw fish. But, determined to taste it, I went to a small sushi and sashimi restaurant. Delicious! Delicate! Delightful! I've since become a connoisseur of all kinds of Japanese food, but nothing will ever match the wonder of that first time.

I had to steal two or three hours a day to meet with representatives from Gensuikin and Gebsuikyo to gather the information I'd been charged with getting about the various factions of the peace movement. The feud between the two parties was deepening, with representatives constantly running back and forth to Moscow to curry favor. One of my jobs in Tokyo was to try to sort out which group should receive Moscow's support on which issues.

A number of the members of Mr. Moritaki's organization for the survivors of Hiroshima came all the way from Hiroshima to meet me in Tokyo. We shared an enjoyable evening at a good restaurant, discussing their organization and its relationship with other peace groups. It was business, really, but I felt that they actually had come just to see me personally.

We were in Japan for only ten days. Even so, I was reluctant to leave.It took me three full days to write my report for Kovalenko, so much had I learned. I took it to him personally.

"Well done," he said. "We think your trip to Japan was very

successful and are considering including you as a consultant in the delegation of the Komsomol that's going to Japan in July."

I was happy, of course. Members of the Komsomol are always well received in other parts of the world. The Komsomol is the Soviet youth organization, and the representatives that can go abroad are the brightest and most personable that can be located. I'd been so busy during my short ten days in Tokyo that I'd not done much sightseeing at all. Even so, a corner of my heart already belonged to Japan. Another visit there seemed like a godsend.

So, in early July 1967, I joined a select group of Komsomol leaders and functionaries to take part in the Japanese youth festival on the shores of Lake Yamanaka. Delegation members were the secretaries of the district and regional Komsomol committees, minor functionaries, and carefully chosen workers; as additional "window dressing" there were a few athletes, singers, dancers, and other celebrities.

One of these celebrities was Vladimir Komarov, one of the brightest of the Soviet cosmonauts. We ran into a powerful storm a day or two out on our voyage, and almost everyone aboard got seasick. The cosmonaut, who had gone through years of training and had traveled in space, had some words of advice.

"Keep moving," he said. "Run. Do calisthenics. Exercise. Be active."

But after Komarov saw one of the passengers throw up, he too succumbed.

"I was tricked," he said when he began to recover. "No one ever told me that seasickness was contagious."

Sadly, on his next mission to space Komarov was killed. His Soyuz spacecraft malfunctioned, placing him in an incorrect orbit. Ground Control would have been able to bring him down safely, but a parachute that should have opened to slow his reentry failed. Knowing that he would die on impact, Komarov nevertheless calmly talked all the way down, supplying valuable data to those on the ground. He is still remembered as a hero, still honored for his courage. I'm glad I met him because he was a good human being.

Unexpectedly, the Japanese placed us in the Olympic Village dormitories, where, oddly enough, the entire compound was surrounded by barbed wire. The gates were locked from 11 P.M. until 8 A.M. The Soviets liked these arrangements because it made it easier for the KGB counterintelligence officers posing as members of the youth group to watch the real members of the delegation. For most of us the confinement was frustrating.

I finally decided to do something about it. One day when a group of us were talking about life in Japan, I mentioned the huge fish market in Tsukiji.

"It's the largest in the world, you know," I said knowledgeably.

"If you know so much about it, why don't you arrange to show it to us?" one of them asked.

I'd never seen it, but I wasn't going to admit it.

I knew that to see the real action, one had to arrive at Tsukiji no later than 5:30 A.M. I got in touch with the delegation's chauffeur, a nineteen-year-old son of a Russian emigré named Morozov who spoke both Japanese and Russian, and arranged for him to park outside the compound a little before 5:00 A.M. We slipped out of our rooms, climbed over the fence, and got into his car. Actually, it was Morozov who was the guide at the fish market, but everybody was so interested that they didn't notice.

Picture a roofed area encompassing thousands of square meters and a catch weighing thousands of tons, ranging from tiny herring to leviathan tuna. Everything within that area is surgically clean, perfectly organized, and bustling. Never missing a beat, within half an hour the market personnel transport the night's catch from the boats to booths, where it is sold to individuals or auctioned to businesses. This is Tsukiji market, and not one of us in the party who visited it that morning regretted for a moment the risks we had taken to get there.

A day or two later we went to Lake Yamanaka, one of the most beautiful places on earth, for a series of symposia with a few hundred Japanese youth. There was a marked difference between Soviet and Japanese delegates. All of the Soviets, myself included, had been instructed by the International Department on how to use such opportunities for making propaganda statements and political speeches. Our speeches were aimed at glorifying the policies of the Soviet government and the Communist party, while at the same time trying to convince those young Japanese that all Soviets supported these policies. We condemned the U.S. presence in Japan and denounced the American military.

The earnest young Japanese delegates, on the other hand, were pouring their hearts out to us. They shared their everyday problems, their personal difficulties, confidences on their professions and universities, and their hopes and dreams. Most of all, they were trying to find ways to achieve peace.

Meanwhile, I met with representatives of Gebsuikyo, Gensuikin, and the Japan–Soviet Friendship Society to get information for the International Department. Back in Moscow, my reports were commended.

Someone asked me recently, "Stan, people who know you are aware almost at once that you are a nonconformist, even a rebel at heart. How did you survive all those years?"

I have pondered that at length, and of course there is no single or simple answer. It is true that I was always introspective, that I questioned everything and often reached personal conclusions that were contrary to accepted policy or procedure. But, more important, I was young and ambitious, yearning for a successful career. Also, at that time I sincerely believed that what I was doing was right and necessary for the good of my country. Believing that, I worked hard to master the skills of my trade, which was to woo and seduce foreigners into accepting the Soviet view. As the years passed, I became more sophisticated and more mature, more capable and more effective. I will never forget the elation I felt when an argument I'd originated came back to me out of the mouth of an enthusiastic Japanese supporter. I took pride in knowing I was good at my job.

Then came the "bait." The International Department announced that the time had come for me to move from the Soviet Peace Committee to the Soviet Afro–Asian Solidarity Committee. What looked like a promotion was actually a lateral move in the International Department of the CPSU. I was being pulled closer to the undertow of events that would eventually draw me into the KGB.

3

The Right Bait

OUTER BANKS, NORTH CAROLINA

Several fishermen approached my strip of beach, stepping carefully through the white dunes and tall sea oats. At a point where the ocean current broke across the shallows, they began baiting their hooks.

"What's running?" I asked.

"Blues," a fair young man replied with a flash of white smile. "Those guys really put up a fight."

"Yeah," his friend spoke up, "but you gotta hook 'em first."

"Oh, hell," the smiling young man rejoined, "you can hook anything with the right bait."

MOSCOW AND JAPAN, 1967–1973

When I transferred from the Soviet Peace Committee to the Soviet Afro-Asian Solidarity Committee (SAASC), both organizations were actively involved in a gigantic active measures campaign to force the United States to abandon Indochina, thereby allowing it to fall to Communist control. Active measures is a term used to identify operations designed to influence actions in other countries, to shape their political stances or decisions, and to lead their people to opinions that best serve Soviet aims. Active measures are not to be confused with conventional espionage or counterintelligence. Instead, active measures involve a large part of the Communist party, KGB, and the state structure and are an integral part of, and a supplement to, traditional diplomacy as practiced by the Soviet Union.

At that time I was totally committed to the cause of getting the United States out of Indochina. I could only see superpower America with its superior weaponry attacking defenseless Vietnamese peasants. I was unreservedly dedicated to the objectives that both committees appeared to endorse: peace and nuclear disarmament.

My dedication didn't blind me to the hypocrisies practiced by both the Soviet Peace Committee and the Soviet Afro-Asian Solidarity Committee. Both were financed largely by contributions solicited from the public, and it soon became obvious to me that the Soviet Red Cross wasn't the only organization being exploited. The Russian Orthodox church was forced to make large donations for the "cause of peace." Well-known public figures, from athletes to entertainers, were coerced into soliciting contributions from the public. The very poorest people gave things they couldn't afford to give away—their few pieces of family jewelry or money that should have been spent on food.

When I joined the Soviet Afro-Asian Solidarity Committee, it was engaged in manipulating the Afro-Asian People's Solidarity Organization (AAPSO), headquartered in Cairo, into mirroring Soviet policy. AAPSO, created in the 1950s after the Bandung Conference, was not under Soviet control in the beginning. In those early years the president of Egypt, Gamal Abdel Nasser, played an important role in it and proved to be a moderating influence. Since the late 1950s and early 1960s, the International Department has gained control. Under it, the

Afro-Asian People's Solidarity Organization has become one of its most militant fronts, providing moral, financial, and material support to so-called national liberation movements, such as those in Angola, Namibia, and Vietnam, thus extending Moscow's influence in the Third World. By the mid-1960s, AAPSO was totally under Soviet control and had become the front for providing training facilities to Palestine Liberation Organization (PLO) guerrilla fighters and to the People's Movement for the Liberation of Angola (MPLA) guerrillas before their takeover of Angola. The Soviet army and the KGB helped furnish the military training.

Three or four active-duty KGB officers were assigned to the staff of the Afro-Asian Committee specifically to recruit agents from among the leaders of these national liberation movements. The chief of the student section was a Mr. Smirnov, a KGB lieutenant colonel, whose main job was to decide which students would make good agents and then to recruit them. That particular activity was considered strategically important because, when these students returned home, some would rise to successful careers, perhaps even becoming members of their own governments.

My job put me in charge of operations affecting Japan, India, and other Asian countries. I took an active part in meetings and discussions with all the delegations from these nations' Afro-Asian Solidarity Committees and often accompanied them during their travels in the Soviet Union. A major part of my job was to write detailed reports about every foreigner I met, analyzing their backgrounds, political views, and personal vulnerabilities. All reports were submitted to the International Department and copies sent to pertinent departments of the KGB's First Chief Directorate, which directs foreign intelligence operations.

Afro-Asian Solidarity Committee conferences with foreign groups are completely stage-managed by the Soviets, who get copies of every speech days ahead of time. If there is anything in these speeches they don't like, their agents of influence and contacts within those committees or countries try to remove those parts that displease them. If that fails, they arrange for rebuttals to be given by members of organizations under tighter Soviet control.

One of the most interesting things that happened to me during those early days in the Afro-Asian Solidarity Committee concerned Yasir Arafat of the Palestine Liberation Organization. This was before the PLO had an official mission in Moscow, though negotiations were under way. Arafat visited Moscow regularly for talks held under the auspices of the Soviet Afro-Asian Solidarity Committee, but the Soviets present at those talks were ranking officials of the International Department, the KGB and GRU (Chief Intelligence Directorate of the Soviet General Staff), and the Soviet Ministry of Foreign Affairs.

I was present at two of the meetings between Arafat and the International Department. The thing I remember most was Arafat's obsession with his personal security. His Palestinian bodyguards were armed to the teeth. The PLO commander in chief who visited Moscow with Arafat carried a huge revolver on his belt. Arafat was an ordinary-looking, middle-aged man who smiled constantly. At the same time, his eyes were everywhere, never still, always searching. The paradox between the smiling middle-aged man and his cold, suspicious eyes certainly made it easier to accept him as the head of one of the most active terrorist groups in the world.

In these discussions with Arafat, the major focus was upon Soviet and PLO positions on issues in the Middle East. Interestingly, the Soviet representatives tried, without success, to have the PLO tone down its rhetoric, which was hostile to the existence of Israel as a state. Arafat did not support this position, and it was clear that the Soviet Union and the PLO had similar, but different, motives in the region.

The Soviet Afro-Asian Solidarity Committee also organized and managed the Vietnam Support Committee (VSP), designed to work against the war in Vietnam. One of its most important jobs was handling the American soldiers who deserted while on leave in Japan. Before being flown to their final destination in Stockholm, each group of deserters spent three to four weeks in Moscow or some other city in the USSR so the Soviet propaganda machine could use them to generate anti-American publicity.

I accompanied many of these deserters on their travels, but only after becoming a KGB officer myself did I learn that the smuggling of these deserters into the Soviet Union was entirely a KGB operation. In the late 1960s and early 1970s some Japanese (often intellectuals and university students) were active members of an organization called BEHEIREN; its name is an artificial anagram composed of the beginning letters of a Japanese phrase meaning "Peace to Vietnam Committee." The KGB recruited a BEHEIREN secretary, working through him to get in touch with American deserters. The Japanese organization was made to order for this purpose because one of the first actions it had undertaken had been to help GIs desert and hide in Japan. The

KGB arranged to meet Japanese fishing boats in Soviet waters in the Northern Territories where the GIs were received by Soviet Border Guard ships.

Some of the GIs I met were just scared young boys who wanted to get out of the war. Others were legitimate pacifists who, because of religious or moral beliefs, didn't believe in war or killing. A few opposed the Vietnam War because it was undeclared. And then there were the disreputable characters who would have deserted under any circumstances.

I had one experience with a group of six of these GIs that deserves special mention. As soon as this group reached Moscow, they requested political asylum in the Soviet Union.

"We gonna settle down in Moscow," they kept repeating.

Now, that was not part of the plan. The International Department and the KGB weren't averse to using these GIs as propaganda tools, but they certainly didn't want to keep them as permanent residents. So I was called in by A. Dzasokhov, the secretary-general of the Solidarity Committee.

"We can't keep them here, Levchenko," he declared. "Let Sweden cope with them. Now, Levchenko, you meet with them and talk them out of trying to stay here. I don't care how you do it, but talk them out of it. Use any conceivable argument you need to use. Do what must be done. You can even be critical of us Soviets if you have to. Understand?"

"Yes, sir!" I answered. I left the room smiling. I knew I was going to have some fun with this assignment, and I did. When I met with those GIs the next morning, I lowered my voice as though I didn't want anyone to hear me except them.

"Now, listen closely," I said, "because I could get shot for telling you what I'm going to say right now. But you need to know the truth about things here." Then I proceeded to tongue-lash the Soviet Union and life in the USSR so severely that the GIs unanimously decided not to seek asylum in Moscow.

For two or three years the BEHEIREN-KGB pipeline worked well. Then something happened. Usually, the GIs would arrive in Moscow where they would be met by several officers from the Solidarity Committee, and after a briefing, one of us would escort them to Moscow's Hotel Sputnik, where they were quartered. They had their meals together, again escorted to and from the restaurant by one of us.

One evening a young marine got out of his room before the

evening's escort arrived, made his way to the only restaurant he had been to in Moscow, bought a bottle of vodka, and proceeded to get drunk. By apparent coincidence, two American women who worked at the U.S. embassy happened to be dining at the same restaurant.

"I'm buying the drinks," the marine announced in English. "Anybody want to drink with an American marine?" As Soviets are very slow to make friends with foreigners, none of the local citizens accepted his offer; the American women, however, joined him at once.

"How great to hear an American voice," one of them gushed. The other asked, "How did an American marine wind up in Moscow?"

Before the rest of the GIs had arrived at the restaurant, the marine had told them the whole story of his desertion, and the women had convinced him that he wanted to go back home to the States. Weeping as a drunk man often does, he begged them to help him get back. The ladies, who just happened to have a car parked conveniently close to the door, were able to get him out of the restaurant, into their car, and to the embassy. As the car passed them, the Soviet guards near the embassy gates could see someone lying down on the floor.

The stream of American deserters dried up after that.

"It was bound to happen sometime," everyone said. "It was just bad luck, a coincidence" was the official opinion of the incident.

I have never been able to accept that opinion. As a professional intelligence officer, I see far too many coincidences in the episode. First, the marine ended up at just the right restaurant, and no one saw him en route there or in the hotel after he'd left his room. Second, the two women just happened to be in a restaurant not usually frequented by Americans. Third, while the marine had ordered a bottle of vodka, not enough of it had been consumed to make a healthy young man drunk. Finally, he had attempted to hide as the car entered the American embassy gates.

In my professional judgment, the incident with the marine was a well-executed intelligence maneuver. I strongly suspect that it was engineered by U.S. Naval Intelligence, and I believe there is some evidence to support my view. Later I learned that the marine testified before Congress when he returned to America. I believe that the workings of the pipeline were traced from Vietnam through Japan to Moscow, then exposed by that daring young marine. The significance of stopping the stream of deserters through Japan can't be overlooked.

In one of the last groups that came through the pipeline there was a handsome young black GI whom the others in the group called

Romeo. Every time he was asked why he had deserted, he would fling his head back, go into a little strut, and say, "I'm a lover, not a fighter."

As we soon found out, he was telling the truth. By the time we got him billeted into the hotel, he had already lined up rendezvous with four or five women. He flirted with every woman we met. He took a lot of ribbing from his friends because of his flashy clothes and his cologne, a powerful scent of which he seemed to have brought along at least a quart. One of the other soldiers remarked that you could tell when Romeo joined a crowd because you could smell him before you saw him.

An escort officer from the Solidarity Committee was intrigued by Romeo's success with women. He leaned over at dinner one evening and asked Romeo, "Is it true you haven't slept without a woman companion in your bed since you've been here?"

"That's true, babe. Hell, six days ain't long."

"Come on, Romeo, you can tell me. What's the secret of your success with women?"

Replied Romeo in a perfect stage whisper: "They likes . . . ,"— he paused for dramatic effect—"They likes to *smell* me!"

My job was not limited to such simple tasks as escorting deserters from Vietnam. The main mission of the Afro-Asian Solidarity Committee was to wage anti-American campaigns (called anti-imperialist campaigns), many of which I planned in writing. By that time I was a skilled propagandist and knew the tricks. Normally, my monographs were sent to the International Department. If they were accepted, they were sent on to the Politburo, which would then approve them as the official program of the Soviet Union. One of my approved papers outlined ways to instigate anti-Vietnam War campaigns in Asia, Africa, Europe, and Latin America. The leadership of the Soviet Afro-Asian Solidarity Committee and that of the International Department were so close that it was not unusual for me to see the personal signatures of the late President Brezhnev or party ideologist Suslov on secret committee directives.

I went back to Japan several times between 1966 and 1970 as an interpreter, a member of one or another of the committees, or as a member of a trade union delegation. If they needed me in Japan, my title would be changed to fit the occasion. During one of these visits I went to Hiroshima to attend a commemoration of the anniversary of the atomic bombing.

I had just finished a particularly cynical and hypocritical assignment and was feeling its effects. The commemoration in Hiroshima was one of the most touching and impressive I've ever experienced, and the contrast between my kind of work and the sincerity of those people was not lost on me. The ceremony was dignified, the participants were prayerful and meditative, deeply concerned that the world and its children should never again experience war. I now see that moment as a milestone in my own ideological journey to the free world.

The next step in my journey toward espionage was a detour rather than a straight progression. It seemed that every time I was going to change directions, the first clue would be a phone call. This time was no different. I got another interesting phone call in 1966, summoning me to a military conscription center.

The colonel who interviewed me introduced himself as a member of the GRU (the Chief Intelligence Directorate of the Soviet military). After a few civilities he rose from his chair and surprised me by saying, "Let's go for a walk. We can't talk here."

Outside in the park-like grounds, he told me that in the event of a sudden war, plans were already in place. "Agents will be parachuted into strategic locations throughout the Western world," he said. "You could be dropped near Liverpool because you can speak English. Besides, you know about the country itself." The only important fact that I could recall on the spur of the moment was that Liverpool was a major British port.

"We want you to volunteer to train for such a wartime mission," he added, "and I'm not going to lie to you. If you were ever called upon to execute the mission, you probably wouldn't survive for more than a few days. But the information you could gather would be invaluable."

"If I did survive, how would I get out?" I asked.

After a long pause he answered, "Well, once you were there, we'd tell you."

We looked at each other and both of us burst into laughter.

For six weeks during the summer of 1966, I was trained by the military. I learned to recognize nuclear storage sites, was given a crash course in agent radio use, and was trained in cryptography. The following summer, my six weeks of training included learning to parachute from a tower, survival by living off the land and foraging for food, and the use of small arms.

I enjoyed those summers. The GRU officers I met were totally dedicated to national defense and approached their jobs with single-minded devotion. The work was straightforward, physically and mentally satisfying, and I felt honored to be a part of the GRU. I learned that the GRU in general felt nothing but contempt for the KGB, but they also knew full well that in any contest between them, the KGB would win. However, the mission of the GRU was specific enough to divorce them for the most part from the party-line hypocrisies that characterize the KGB. In short, the GRU provided a cleaner life.

I was scheduled to undergo a third summer of training in 1968 when I was summoned again before a GRU officer who reluctantly told me that my contact with GRU was being terminated. I was to begin cooperating with the Second Chief Directorate (SCD) of the KGB. I was so furious that I saw red!

The Second Chief Directorate is one of the major directorates of the KGB. Responsible for all counterintelligence operations in the Soviet Union, it is accountable for both the investigative and the punitive functions. Americans are always a little shocked at what is clearly a conflict of interest in these two functions, but then Americans have grown up with a system of checks and balances and take it for granted that those who investigate a person's behavior ought not to be the same ones to mete out punishment. The SCD has countless informers who provide a constant flow of information on almost every Soviet citizen, as well as on foreign tourists, diplomats, newsmen, and businessmen. Paid informers penetrate dissident organizations, entrap people into expressing their honest opinions and then report on them. The SCD monitors the activities of all foreigners with the cooperation of other organs of the KGB. Of all the assignments in the world, this was the one I wanted least. I dreaded the idea that I would be used against Japanese visitors to the Soviet Union.

In my fury at this news I treated the GRU officer to a protracted and fluent display of Russian profanity. He sat there listening impassively until I ended with a particularly obscene Russian epithet.

"Yobannye tyuremsshiki!" I concluded.

He sighed softly and said, "We know. We don't like it either, but, dammit all, you still have to go!"

Although I cooperated with the KGB, I basically remained on the same treadmill. By this time I knew it well: escort visitors through the Soviet Union, showing off the model farms, factories, schools, hospitals, and children's nurseries that were specially maintained to show to visitors; stay on my toes and conceal anything that could mar the carefully staged shows; hide the truth at all costs; report at length about any foreigners; devise and implement methods of seducing foreigners to the Soviet view. I broke this routine with trips to Japan nearly every year, still on business for the Afro-Asian Solidarity Committee.

Each time I went to Japan, my perceptions of that prosperous and harmonious country provoked the same questions about the Soviet system. I would see a burgeoning economy, streets crowded with automobiles, ample food supplies, and stores packed with consumer goods—all in a nation that had absolutely no governmental regimentation.

Increasingly, I found that merely doing my job was very stressful. Each day I hated what I was doing just a little bit more. The idealism of my early youth had gradually disappeared, worn away by the abrasive realities of my work. Finally I came to face what the Spanish call the "moment of truth," the time when one recognizes the real loss of innocence. I had to admit the immorality of what I was doing. There is no spiritual emptiness to equal such a moment, and few can live in a spiritual desert forever. Certainly I could not. So the journey from interpreter to spy sent me at last in search of solace, and the Eastern Orthodox church is incredibly and beautifully satisfying in that regard.

While it is not illegal to belong to a church in the Soviet Union, the country is officially a godless state. But the fact that it's not illegal to practice a religion does not in any way protect the religious practitioner from persecution.

I had been given no religious training, of course. So at first, my examination of the church was merely as an observer, one who watched from the outside. I was surprised to realize one day that, in terms of commitment to what ancient peoples called "the unknown God," I had become an insider. That was the beginning of a conversion that took years to complete.

One aspect of my job that had given me much pleasure had been showing visitors the cultural centers of Russia: the palaces, museums, and cathedrals. In the beginning I saw only the physical beauty of these places. But gradually, so gradually that I can't even remember when it began, I started to experience something deeper. Sitting quietly while visitors were led through a church by one of the priests, I'd watch the faces of those who had come in to pray. Sometimes their faces would be drawn and anguished, sometimes worried and scared. What always astounded me was that, once they had knelt in prayer, their faces would clear, their brows would smooth out. By the time they'd get up to leave, they looked serene, even happy. It was a phenomenon I never tired of watching.

Little by little I came to appreciate the pageantry, the beauty of the music and art, and the splendor of the icons. Little by little I began to hear what the priests were saying. Little by little I began to believe in the God who gave solace to people who asked for help. But I didn't know what to do about it. I didn't dare go to the priests and request catechism classes, because I was in a line of work that would arouse their suspicions and because I could never be sure that I could trust whomever I spoke to. So I became a secret Christian.

I had always frequented the Moscow libraries, but now I started a deliberate search for everything I could find about the Eastern Orthodox church and the modern religious arguments affecting the twentieth century. I read accounts of the ninth-century schism with the Roman Catholic church, everything I could find by or about John of Damascus, the works of Augustine and Thomas Aquinas, and everything I could about the church's rituals. In thus educating myself, I had to exercise caution. I read in the reading rooms under assumed names, rarely checked out books, and when I did, took care that their titles were innocuous.

What hurt most about my secret conversion was that I didn't know any prayers. I had no idea at all how to pray. I believed deeply in this wonderful, helpful God, and I didn't know how to contact Him. I finally began thinking little business letters to Him, addressing Him "Dear Sir" and apologizing for not knowing how to do it right. But I could feel that someone was reading my mail, and I was comforted.

My faith was sometimes all that kept me sane, but I never told my wife about it. I never told anyone at all, and though the sacraments are required of members of the Eastern Orthodox church, I never took communion or went to confession until I arrived in America. I couldn't. There was no one I could trust.

My religious conversion put additional strain on an already stressful life. All my life I had tried to be truthful to myself as my father had taught me to be. Becoming more and more aware of the paradox of doing the things I had to do in working for a Godless Soviet Union and recognizing those things as immoral presented me with intolerable conflicts. For a while rationalizing helped. I told myself that surely what I was doing would help the country I loved, and I hoped it was true.

Ironically, as I was secretly finding religious solace, it became necessary to become a Communist party member. It was not a voluntary act, for I never was a fanatic believer in Marxist-Leninist ideas, and I knew that too many people joined the party primarily for career reasons. But by that time I had already worked for a few years for organizations directly related to the International Department, one of the key party organs. And I knew that I was like a white crow: I was the only employee there who was not a party member. A superior drew the attention of my boss in the Solidarity Committee to this fact a few times. Finally, I was given a choice: to leave my job, or to become a Communist party member. Of course, I understood the seriousness of the situation and submitted all appropriate papers to the party regional committee.

A year later I received the party identification card and ceased being a white crow. But for years I avoided becoming a party activist, explaining that I was overloaded by work (which, incidentally, was true).

Much later, when I was stationed full-time in Japan as an intelligence officer, I was appointed deputy secretary of the party cell of the Soviet journalists stationed in Japan. The secretary was *Pravda* correspondent Latyshev, my former adviser at the Institute of Oriental Studies and a shrewd careerist who conducted all the necessary meetings and political discussions. He was not an intelligence officer and used every opportunity his party executive position presented to improve his career. I was quite happy with that and did little work for the cell. I knew also that I would not be criticized for being lazy because as a spy, I had twenty to twenty-five clandestine meetings with my agents every month, which was a very heavy workload.

In late 1969 I was summoned to the office of the chief of the Japanese desk in the International Department. The mission he outlined for me was both interesting and surprising; I was officially linked for the first time to a journalistic post.

The International Department and the Novosti Press Agency had tentatively selected me as one of the public relations people for the Soviet Pavilion at Expo 70 in Osaka. The exposition would last for eight months, and I knew that my responsibilities would wander far afield from merely publicizing Expo 70. He revealed how right I was with his next words.

"You and Andrey Zhudro will have to organize some very large and very important meetings in the main cities of the Kansai area and aboard the Soviet tourist ships that will be coming to Osaka and Kobe. These meetings will be designed to promote friendship with the Soviet Union. You, Levchenko, will be expected to influence the activities of the Japan-Soviet Friendship Society. You must also influence the Taigai Bunko Kyokai [the Japanese Society of Cultural Relations with Foreign Countries]."

I knew what "influencing" meant. I would have to design deceptions and propaganda ploys to induce those Japanese organizations to do what the Soviet Union wanted done. And I was being told to do it, not try to do it.

He added that both Zhudro and I would be working directly under the guidance of the Soviet embassy to expand existing pro-Soviet sentiments in as many Japanese organizations as possible. "This is very important work," he continued, "and a third person will also be assigned to your office. Ivanenko, a KGB counterintelligence major, will be there to screen all of your contacts."

Aha! I thought. We're going to have a watchdog! We always did, of course, but seldom was it so open. We were to write secret reports on our activities, as always, and at the end of each week one of us would have to go to the embassy in Tokyo to transmit these reports to Moscow. Enticed by the prospect of spending eight months in Japan, a rare opportunity to learn more about the country, I accepted the assignment.

I arrived in Osaka in early March 1970 when workers were just finishing the construction of the Soviet pavilion. Strangely shaped and enormous, like a red banner flying in the wind, part of the pavilion was relatively low, while the other part rose to dominate almost all of the exposition grounds. I couldn't believe how much money the Soviet Union had spent on its construction—over a billion yen! Some Soviet specialists who had worked at previous world fairs told me that we were engaged in a major propaganda effort to win over as many Japanese as possible in that eight-month period.

The Soviet pavilion was crammed full of all kinds of exhibits. There were displays of modern farm machinery that was not at all typical of what was used in the Soviet Union. Samples of Siberian minerals had been beautifully arranged by the best designers. Spacecraft, in 1970, were good propaganda for the Soviet Union. Whole trees had been brought from Siberia to decorate the pavilion's Siberian section.

About three hundred Soviet guides were there to explain, in English or Japanese, the achievements of Soviet socialism to the visitors. This army of people from the Soviet Union spread propaganda day and night that the Soviet Union was entirely peaceful, that only American imperialism threatened world peace. One of their harder tasks was to try to portray the 1968 Soviet invasion of Czechoslovakia as a brotherly act aimed at safeguarding the Czech people. There Soviet credibility fell very, very short!

The Czech pavilion was a fairly small structure constructed in excellent architectural taste and decorated with exquisite artistry. Only a year and a half had passed since the Soviet army had invaded Czechoslovakia, and it was obvious that most of the Czechs in the pavilion were still incensed and bitter. They had their own way of getting even that infuriated the Soviets. Throughout each day, the Czechs broadcast sad, doleful music, dirge after dirge. When anyone asked why, they invariably replied, "Czechoslovakia is in mourning." The Soviets were furious, but it took months before the commissioner of the Soviet pavilion finally got the Czech pavilion to change the music. By then the damage had been done.

In our work at Expo 70, Zhudro and I found ourselves totally subordinate to Kovalenko in Moscow and his deputy, Kuznetsov. Zhudro knew both of them better than I did, because his main job was secretary of the Japan-Soviet Friendship Society, one of the very active arms of the International Department. Even so, I still had a limited amount of freedom because of the special nature of a few of my assignments, and I treasured the brief times alone.

One of my frequent visitors was Saito Nobuo, an active member of the Japanese Socialist Party and one of the key figures in the local friendship association. I remember him as a good, sincere, and industrious man who naively accepted much of the Soviet propaganda. Mr. Saito could not be called a conscious Soviet collaborator; he cooperated with the Soviets because unfortunately he believed he was doing right. Sometimes the innocent and unwitting collaborators can be the most useful agents of influence.

Those months in Osaka were draining and debilitating. Every day I felt as if I were living in two separate and very different worlds. One was inside the Soviet pavilion where, if a person didn't know he was in Japan, he would swear up and down that he was in any office in any part of the Soviet Union. The other world was outside the Soviet pavilion, outside the apartment complex. There I was lucky. I had to work with many public organizations in the Kansai area, so I had the privilege of traveling by myself, a privilege not granted to many who worked in the pavilion. I used my weekends and my rare days off to see as much of Kansai as I could, exploring museums, cinemas, and parks. This part of my life was invigorating. I loved to stop at some small restaurant for sushi, sashimi, and beer and carry on conversations with the patrons.

For the first time, I had the opportunity to really see the historical sites, Buddhist temples, and Shinto shrines in Kyoto and Nara. I was enriched by the Ryoanji complex, my first glimpse of a Zen temple. When I saw the stone garden there I couldn't believe that such a marvel was real. I lingered there for nearly two hours. Ryoanji was quiet that day, and there were not many visitors, so I could sit still and let the peacefulness take over. As I looked at the garden, I imagined that the stones were islands in the sea or perhaps the tops of mountains rising above the clouds. Gradually, my meditation on these rocks calmed and soothed me, and I began to feel serene and relaxed. I knew that I was experiencing something extraordinary, something profound and beautiful, but I have never understood why such a simple scene affected me so deeply.

The garden at the Moss Temple of Saihoji affected me also, almost as deeply as did the stone garden. The colors of the forty varieties of moss and the beauty of the trees created a fairyland. It was a place for dreaming childish dreams and thinking enchanted thoughts. I visited Nara many times and loved the surroundings of the ancient capital. Walking the well-kept paths of the park and feeding the tame deer, I absorbed the beauty of Horyuji, Japan's oldest temple complex.

In Kyoto I also saw the famous Gion festival, and it was an unforgettable experience. On that day I realized how proudly the Japanese people have preserved their old traditions and the festivities of their culture. This pride binds them to past generations, who are remembered through the resplendent customs and the culture they helped create. The festival crowds looked relaxed and happy, the women breathtakingly beautiful in their traditional kimonos and the men—some of them in traditional dress—self-assured and handsome. As I watched the sea of smiling faces, I was sad knowing that I'd probably never see anything like it again. Certainly I'd never see anything like it in the Soviet Union. Not because Russian or Ukrainian or other Soviet peoples don't have their own magnificent cultural traditions, but because the Communist party has systematically and implacably suppressed all manifestations of these cultures, robbing people of the joy of preserving and cherishing their ethnic heritages.

The most stressful part of my life was my work in the Soviet pavilion. Daily I read the Japanese newspapers—*Asahi, Mainichi,* and *Yomiuri*—and watched Japanese television. It was astonishing to me how open, democratic, dynamic, and industrious Japanese society was. People were entirely free to hold and express their own views, whether conservative or leftist, Communist or radical. Reluctantly, I had to acknowledge the contrast with the Soviet Union, where the media was strictly controlled and readers could know only what the party propaganda machinery allowed them to know. Meanwhile, I had to represent the Soviet society to my Japanese friends as a peaceful, democratic social structure that was nothing less than the best system in the world.

Working sometimes twelve to fifteen hours a day, I became physically and morally depleted. The atmosphere in the Soviet pavilion worsened as KGB officers constantly tightened security. Some of the guides were sent back to Moscow for being apolitical or because of romances with foreign women. I constantly felt that someone was watching my back. I'd be willing to bet good money that every worker in the pavilion had the same feeling. Even living in wonderful Japan was not worth this stress.

I decided to ask the deputy commissioner of the Soviet pavilion to let me return to Moscow. The deputy commissioner, KGB General Pasholikov, was known as a hard-nosed, crude individual, so I made my request simultaneously to the International Department and the Soviet Afro-Asian Solidarity Committee for which I still worked. It was granted. In June 1970, I finally ended one of the most stressful, yet interesting, assignments I had handled thus far and went back to Moscow.

After I left Japan, I had become increasingly dissatisfied. Often depressed and unhappy, I went through a period of self-examination and had to admit that I didn't like what I saw. The reasons were clear. I dealt with hypocrisy every day. I manufactured hypocrisy, traded in hypocrisy—and I hated it.

With each passing day I became more cynical, more sardonic about the system I worked for and the methods that the system endorsed. I settled back into my robotistic work as a speech writer and spokesman for the Afro-Asian Solidarity Committee. I edited speeches written for members of the committee's presidium to make certain that the correct topics were presented at international conferences and congresses: Americans were denounced as warmongers, imperialists, and fascists because of their involvement in the Vietnam War; the oppression of blacks in the United States and in South Africa was condemned. I could—and did—see the rank hypocrisy of denouncing the oppression of blacks. In our own Soviet city of Kiev, several black students had been killed for just one reason: they were seen walking with some white girls, talking and laughing with them. But my job was to denounce America and South Africa, not to point out the fallacies in Soviet logic. Besides, the Afro-Asian Committee never admitted that they knew about the deaths of the young blacks in Kiev. It simply hadn't happened.

In January 1971, I was sent with the Soviet delegation to the fourth conference of the Afro-Asian People's Solidarity Organization in Cairo as a press officer. My job was to talk to local journalists and to spread propaganda. By that time these conferences had assumed a sameness, which took away much of the pleasure I'd always found in traveling. This conference was no exception. The days followed the same routine: International Department representatives worked hard at lobbying the Asian and African delegations. There were the usual clashes among a handful of African liberation groups and a little trouble over adopting a position favored by the PLO.

The evenings were party time. We stayed in the palatially elegant Cairo Sheraton Hotel, where expenses that must have been astronomical were completely covered by the Soviet Union for all delegates and representatives. Freed from money worries, the delegates turned into conspicuous consumers—cramming the bars, calling room service, and indulging every whim that could be satisfied by food or drink, and more.

I was repelled by the custom of bribing foreigners with entertainment so that they would rubber-stamp all the Soviet Union's positions and proposals. Knowing that these feelings posed a danger to me, I looked for a way out. Very few options were open to me. I could not do what any American would do in an instant: quit the job and find something else. If I did, each personnel office would ask me the same question: Why did you voluntarily quit such a promising career? I would have no acceptable answer.

Then, seven months after I had left Japan on a bleak January day, like an answer to a prayer, Lieutenant Colonel Dolud asked me to join him for drinks in a café near committee headquarters. Dolud was with the KGB, working undercover for the Afro-Asian Solidarity Committee. It was pleasant to relax in a warm restaurant and let the tensions drain away over a drink. When Colonel Dolud, a good conversationalist, suggested that we share dinner before going home, I readily agreed.

"This may be prying," he said, a little reluctantly, at the end of the meal, "but you seem to be . . . I don't know exactly . . . you're disappointed with something at the Afro-Asian Solidarity Committee, aren't you?"

I just shrugged, saying nothing. After a pause, he continued, "I can't blame you if you are. From what I've seen, this outfit is boring, bureaucratic, and phony as hell. You need something really worthy of you, work for a real man!"

Dolud then picked up his glass and examined its contents as though it were a gypsy's crystal ball offering the answer to the problem he had just posed. Finally he spoke, and his voice altered sharply to a serious, businesslike tone. I was instantly alert and on guard. No longer was this just a pleasant, companionable evening.

"Levchenko, I'm going to be frank with you. I'm a KGB officer assigned to the First Chief Directorate, and I've been watching you. I think you have the makings of a good intelligence officer. I honestly believe that you could have a really challenging career in the KGB."

I knew, of course, that the First Chief Directorate (FCD) was the KGB's foreign clandestine service, responsible for intelligence-gathering activities.

"Now don't be surprised about this," he added with a smile, "but we've already run a check on you through counterintelligence, and the result was positive. The Second Chief Directorate has nothing but good things to say about your work with them. In fact, they are extremely satisfied with your performance. In particular, there was one job you did for them in the 1960s that impressed us very much."

I knew the job he was referring to. After I had undergone the GRU military training in 1966 and 1967, the Second Chief Directorate had given me a special assignment in 1968. (Because of my affiliation with the GRU, the KGB had a voluminous file on me with all my weak and strong points in it. I had no doubt that it contained dozens of pages of reports on me by the KGB's secret informers, or "snitches," some of whom probably were my personal friends.)

I had been summoned to the Hotel Berlin, right next to KGB headquarters. When I entered the suite, which resembled one in any European hotel, I was met by a man of medium height, impeccably dressed, who was smoking a Dunhill pipe. He introduced himself as Colonel Azizov of the KGB. Our conversation was short. Azizov told me that the KGB knew everything about me, that every step of mine had been checked out. They knew, of course, about my training with military intelligence.

"And now," he said, "we need you. We have an important assignment for you."

As he explained it to me, my assignment would be to help recruit two young Japanese diplomats who had recently arrived in Moscow. I was to befriend them, see them as frequently as possible, and report on any developments. The KGB was already working on them, studying their vulnerabilities, but they needed my language abilities and experience in dealing with the Japanese to get closer to them.

"One of them is probably a homosexual," Azizov said. "Never slept with any of the whores we introduced to him during half a year. We watch every room in his apartment"—he explained to me how it is done with the help of optics—"and we know that he doesn't even masturbate. Weird, isn't it?"

He went further, explaining that I would be a member of a team and that I might not like some people involved in this operation— prostitutes and black marketeers, for instance. But, he assured me, I myself would not be compromised. I would play "Mr. Clean," a friend. If I did a good job, my future would be assured. They would help me with my career; I would travel to Japan frequently. I hesitated, and it probably showed on my face because suddenly Azizov leaned over to me and, puffing his fancy pipe, said, "Don't refuse this offer. If you do, you will be sorry for the rest of your life. Remember, without our approval you will never go even to Mongolia."

I knew only too well what he meant. He could easily put me on the KGB blacklist, and I would never get any decent job or assignment abroad. I agreed to cooperate. In half an hour I signed a paper and agreed that I would follow Colonel Azizov's order and submit written reports on my future Japanese friends. I was to sign my reports with the code name "Arthur."

In a few weeks I was introduced to the two young Japanese. I met them many times, became their friend, went to parties in their apartment, got acquainted with their girlfriends—the KGB "swallows." One of my new Japanese friends, the one whom Azizov suspected of being homosexual, turned out to be quite straight. The way I discovered that, however, was through a very traumatic experience for me. Azizov knew I had a woman friend, a young, attractive architect named Lyuba. He insisted that I bring her into the game, and unfortunately for her, she fell in love with the young Japanese; it was a nice, clean romance between two young, single people. But Azizov wanted her to report to him regularly about everything, including every intimate detail of their personal life. After prolonged mental anguish, Lyuba refused to betray her boyfriend. Azizov threatened that she would never see him again unless she cooperated, but she still refused. Finally, one gloomy autumn day in 1969, Lyuba was approached at the entrance to her apartment building by several hooligans who told her, "You see that yellow monkey again, and you'll be dead." Without any doubt, the hooligans were KGB officers. Lyuba never saw the Japanese diplomat again.

Without Lyuba's cooperation, the KGB had to change their plans. They found out there was one vulnerability of professional interest to them: the diplomat loved to gamble and played cards for money. So the KGB decided to try to ruin him financially through gambling and then to buy his services for money.

I was asked to introduce the diplomat to an officer named Vladimir from the KGB counterintelligence. Among other dirty tricks, he specialized in cheating at cards. In some card games it takes quite a bit of time to lose a lot of money if the stakes are not too high. So Azizov gave me an order: "Get him drunk and play blackjack. Then raise the stakes and rip the son of a bitch off in one night." I was not a good card player, so I had to train with Vladimir, who gave me a crash course on the tricks and signals he used playing cards.

We went to the apartment and had a light dinner, washed down with plenty of hard liquor. Then the game started. The young Japanese lost many rubles—a lot of money by Soviet standards. The game lasted until the morning. When we left the apartment, Vladimir gave me some of the rubles and told me that it was my reward for a job well done. I asked him if he would account for the money to the KGB. "The hell with them," was the answer. "We won the money; we did a good job. They don't need it anyway."

After almost two years, I finally got out of the operation against the two Japanese diplomats and learned later, with delight, that the KGB did not manage to recruit them. I met one of them again, many years later. On a memorable day in October 1979, when I was detained and interrogated by Japanese authorities in Narita International Airport, one of my interrogators from the Foreign Office was my friend from Japan. Of course, I did not discuss his ordeal in Moscow; I did not know whether he had reported it to his superiors, and I didn't want him to feel uneasy. Questioning me was just his job. For me, however, in some ways it was a relief; he finally got even.

Ironically, that fateful meeting in the Tokyo airport could not have taken place if I had failed my interrogation and recruitment by the First Chief Directorate of the KGB. Fortunately, Colonel Dolud knew only of my work with the young Japanese diplomats, and neither of us could forecast the bizarre trail my life would take.

"Because of the quality of your work," Dolud concluded, "the door to the Soviet intelligence network is open to you, if you want it."

Dolud's seeming frankness lulled me into speaking honestly.

"I despise the Second Chief Directorate," I blurted out.

"Why?"

"How can you ask me that? My God! Just look at the atrocities the KGB's predecessors committed in Stalin's time. Come to think of it, I don't like the methods they use now!"

"Don't even think about those assholes in the Second Chief Directorate," he answered, "and don't try to compare them to the intelligence service. The two outfits are completely different. Those bastards in the Second Chief Directorate will plod along, working here inside the country with their nasty little informers and their filthy little tricks, while you'll be one of the elite, one of the best, working as a KGB intelligence officer. Just think of it, Stanislav! You'll work outside the country, on foreign territory, gathering intelligence and recruiting foreign agents. This is the most sophisticated and courageous way of helping your own people."

Then he added the one point that counted most with me. I was so tired of the deviousness of my work with the International Department and my cooperation with the SCD that this alone could have swayed me.

"This is a job for a real man," he said. "People in this line of work get hurt, they are arrested, they are declared *personae non grata,* they are constantly exposed to danger. Intelligence officers have to be quick-minded and tough. Real men!"

I'm sure he knew he had won when I asked, "What country would I work against?"

"I can't guarantee it for certain, of course," he responded, "but you are a specialist on Japan. You know the language, and you've been there many times. It seems logical that they would send you there, probably for two or three years."

My heart leaped at the prospect.

The entire conversation taxed me with the gravity of its implications. The cult of the KGB has hundreds of thousands, maybe even millions of lackeys, satraps, and servants who, from the outside, willingly or otherwise, do its bidding. But relatively few Soviet citizens themselves are ever offered full membership in this congregation, the most secret cult of the pagan Soviet religion. I couldn't quite comprehend that an invitation to the inner sanctum had actually been extended to me.

"Take two or three days to think about it," Dolud said as we parted. "Then come by my office and we'll discuss the details."

I wanted to believe that accepting this job would benefit my countrymen as well as offer me an escape from the treadmill of the Soviet Afro-Asian Solidarity Committee. I tried to think the proposition through objectively, to weigh the pros and cons with detachment, but constantly rising to the surface of my mind like bubbles in champagne was a single intoxicating idea: I could live in Japan, and all I'd have to do was change jobs!

Two days after our initial conversation I went to Dolud's office and told him I accepted his offer. He congratulated me, then handed me several dozen forms to fill out.

I'll probably never know whether Dolud even sensed my moral and spiritual emptiness as vulnerability or as ambition, pure and simple. It doesn't really matter. What matters is that, even before he had finished speaking, I had recognized where the original conversation was heading and, whether I admitted it or not, had all but decided on my response. I would take the bait and become a KGB spy.

4
Playing The Game

OUTER BANKS, NORTH CAROLINA

The shadows were lengthening as I walked on, farther down the beach away from the fishermen. Soon I felt as though all of the North Carolina shore was deserted except for the seabirds and me. I stopped to watch a flock of sandpipers. A wave swept over the hard-packed sand, and the birds raced away from the foam to stay on dry land. As the water retreated, they turned and chased the foam back to the sea. Over and over, retreat and chase, retreat and chase.

"I know that game," I told them. "I played it for years."

MOSCOW, 1971–1975

Nearly eight months passed before I was finally summoned to appear before the special board of the First Chief Directorate for a decision on my application. The questions were surprisingly routine and ordinary. Members of this special board asked simple questions about Soviet foreign policy and some elementary questions on Marxism-Leninism. I understood why, of course: their investigation of my whole life had been so exhaustive that they already knew me inside out. All they were doing at the hearing was confirming what they already knew and looking me over. As soon as the hearing ended, I was miraculously transformed into a young KGB officer.

Not far from the famous Kremlin, on Dzerzhinsky Square, stands a huge, massive, grayish building. There are no signs to suggest its purpose. In the center of the square, condemned to eternal solitude, stands a bronze statue of "Iron Feliks" Dzerzhinsky, the first chief of the infamous Soviet secret police.

When I joined the KGB in 1971, I visited the headquarters building for the first time. Everything about it bespoke gravity: the sentry who compared my face to the photo on my credentials; old, creaking elevators; long, shadowy, dingily carpeted corridors; and the grim faces of officers in civilian clothes who were generally well-groomed and polite. I was struck by the expressions on the majority of the faces: secretive, wise, enigmatic. It was a long time before I realized that those faces reflected a superior knowledge. Each of them seemed to be communicating, "I know things you will never know."

Indeed, they do know things most people will never know. When I first came to America and began making speeches to American audiences, I was shocked to learn how little is known about the KGB and the threat it poses to the free world. But then I was brought up short when another Russian who had come to the United States a few years earlier pointed out, "You can't expect them to know these things, Stan. After all, only a very few people in the Soviet Union know the truth about the KGB."

He's right, of course. Now when I address any audience, I include enough historical facts to inform them about the nature of the threat. My background briefing usually contains the following information intended for those who are curious about the Soviet system.

The Soviet secret police, now the KGB, was organized only two months after the great October Revolution of 1917 under the name Cheka (Extraordinary Commission), and it owes its existence to the personal directives of the founder of the Soviet state, Vladimir Lenin. Why did the socialist revolution need secret police? The answer lies in the history of the revolution itself.

World War I had a devastating impact on Russia. Chaos, lawlessness, and looting drained an already impoverished people; famine also took its toll. As economic conditions worsened for the masses, their resentment of the corrupt and bureaucratic tsarist government increased. The social climate became more and more volatile.

In February 1917, eight months before the October Revolution, a people's revolution took place, and the temporary government under Aleksandr Kerensky granted the people all human rights. Never before in their history had Russians enjoyed such freedom and democracy. But the new democratic government failed to end the war and to overcome the major economic and social problems. It also lacked the power to halt or control the destructive chaos and lawlessness that beset the country.

Only one political party had a clear platform: the Bolsheviks, who were radical intellectuals experienced in clandestine activities. Shortly before the February Revolution, the Communist party had split into two factions: the Mensheviks, or the minority, and the Bolsheviks, or the majority. These terms are actually misnomers because nearly 50,000 party members joined the Mensheviks, leaving the Bolsheviks with a membership of fewer than 10,000. The February Revolution caught Lenin, the leader of the Bolsheviks, by surprise, and he had to act quickly to seize power. Taking advantage of the nationwide disorder, he introduced a series of slogans, most of them very simplistic, even Orwellian, but nonetheless attractive to the masses: "Bread to the people," "Stop the imperialist war with Germany," "Away with the exploiters." The masses who supported these slogans, however, remained unfamiliar with the real Bolshevik party platform. Many of them paid a heavy price afterward for their ignorance.

After their victory in the October Revolution, Lenin and his followers faced a difficult situation. Though the Bolsheviks had seized power, they found it very difficult to retain. Lenin wasted no time in implementing the dictatorship of the proletariat over the previous

"exploiters"—the upper classes and the nonworking classes. Obviously, the Bolshevik party and its government needed a mechanism to
enforce this dictatorship. Thus the Cheka was born.

One of Lenin's closest associates, Dzerzhinsky, was named to
head the Cheka. Polish by birth, a professional revolutionary by
choice, and a veteran of tsarist prisons, he was the perfect selection.
Party members nicknamed him "Iron Feliks" because of his cold-
minded ruthlessness. His first task was to purge the October party
itself. After a thorough investigation, Dzerzhinsky came to the as-
tounding conclusion that the tsarist police (the counterintelligence
section called Okhrana) had penetrated deeply into the Bolshevik party
and had consistently done so since the early 1900s. In fact, Lenin's chief
representative in the Moscow party organization, Malinovsky, was
himself an active Okhrana agent. The editor and the treasurer of the
official Bolshevik party newspaper *Pravda* were also on the tsarist
payroll. The paranoia of the Bolshevik (and, later, the Communist)
party leaders convinced them that enemies existed within the party
itself. But these suspicions were implanted by the discoveries made in
the first few days of Cheka's existence.

The Cheka initiated a massive campaign (now known as The
Red Terror) to purge dissenters. Hundreds of thousands of people who
had opposed the October Revolution were executed. Thousands simply vanished because of their social origins, because they were the sons
or daughters of former landlords, wealthy merchants, or industrialists.
The Bolshevik party called the Cheka the avenging sword of the
revolution. As the government became more secure, Cheka began
arresting more members of the Bolshevik party itself, people who had
differed in one way or another with the leadership. By the late 1920s,
Cheka was the most feared organization in the country. Many thousands of the followers of disgraced Bolshevik leader Trotsky were jailed
or sent to prison camps. From 1937 to 1953, by Stalin's orders, the
Soviet security police staged a wave of bloody terror unprecedented in
modern history; as many as twenty million Soviet citizens perished.
During the Stalin years the name of the security police was changed
several times. Cheka became the OGPU, the Unified State Political
Administration. Then it became NKVD, the People's Kommasariat
for Internal Affairs; next, it was MGB, the Ministry of State Security.

Most important, the Soviet secret police became the main pillar
of the socialist regime. It swiftly wiped out any signs of dissent in the
Soviet Union, acting without the hindrance of restrictions or regula-

tions of any kind. It was above the law; it is still above the law. The Soviet security police became the ruthless mechanism that the Soviet socialist dictatorship uses for the subjugation of its own people to serve the interests of the new social class: the Communist party elite and members of the government bureaucracy spawned by the October Revolution.

Most Americans tend to equate the KGB with their own standard concepts of espionage organizations, concepts probably based on what little they know about the Central Intelligence Agency. But foreign intelligence and espionage is a relatively small part of the many activities of the State Security Committee known as the KGB. This huge, punitive organization employs a quarter of a million people. If the legions of secret informants from the outside are included, the number of people who work for the KGB climbs to more than a million. The world's largest clandestine operation cannot be compared with any intelligence community in the free world whose activities are legally limited and regulated. The KGB is accountable only to the Soviet Politburo and has control of almost limitless funds. The CIA, on the other hand, is strictly regulated by the U.S. Congress. One of my major reasons for writing this book is to try to tell as many people as I can reach what the KGB is, what it intends to do, and how it intends to do it. That's the only way I can repay America for my freedom—by warning the free world and by informing free people everywhere of what I know.

After I joined the KGB's First Chief Directorate, my new business concerned foreign intelligence rather than the internal and external manipulations of my previous work. One of the first subjects I had to master as a KGB officer-in-training was how Cheka first became involved in foreign intelligence and how that had developed under the KGB. I soon learned that Cheka, which began its existence as an exclusively domestic investigative and terrorist organization, moved into foreign intelligence very quickly. By the 1920s it had spread abroad, operating on two levels. First, it ran agents, mainly members of the Comintern (the international communist organization), to gather intelligence and to execute covert actions in foreign nations. Second, the Cheka busied itself infiltrating the various Russian emigré groups in France, Germany, Yugoslavia, Bulgaria, and Poland. The Cheka managed to penetrate the most active of the anti-Soviet Russian emigré organizations in Germany and France, a group headed by the famous pre-revolutionary terrorist, Boris Savinkov.

Under his leadership, these groups were sending numerous agents into Soviet Russia to collect military and political intelligence and conduct sabotage activities.

The Cheka managed to neutralize the actions of Savinkov by creating a dummy organization of phony counterrevolutionaries inside the Soviet Union, an elaborate plan that used dozens of Cheka agents. As a result of "Operation Trust," as it was called, Boris Savinkov was lured back into Soviet Russia, where he was immediately arrested and sentenced to a long prison term. A few years later the Cheka arranged a carefully staged suicide for Savinkov. In the same Operation Trust, one of Great Britain's most able intelligence officers, Sidney Reilly, was also decoyed into entering Soviet Russia and perished in the secret police's dungeons.

The Cheka expanded its foreign intelligence activities very quickly, and by the 1930s it had a well-defined external intelligence service with highly productive agents in most European countries. The Soviets placed agents in nearly all of the government offices in Nazi Germany, including the Gestapo, the Third Reich's domestic counterintelligence organization. An agent in Japan, the famous Richard Sorge, managed to penetrate the German embassy in Tokyo. Sorge, working undercover as a German journalist and correspondent, informed the Soviet leadership during World War II of the planned Nazi invasion of the Soviet Union a few weeks before the invasion took place (June 1941). I have always identified with Richard Sorge because we both worked in Japan undercover as correspondents for Soviet periodicals.

This macabre machine of the great terror, this satanic mill that crushed millions of lives and ruined the futures of millions more, was not itself immune from Stalin's purges. Stalin, the supreme Soviet dictator, tried to eliminate all Chekists who knew about his crimes against his own people. Thousands of Soviet intelligence officers vanished in the purges because they simply knew too much.

After Stalin's death in 1953, the organization of Soviet secret police was reorganized and renamed the KGB. During the so-called de-Stalinization campaign, Soviet leader Nikita Khrushchev repeatedly tried to convince the Soviet people that the purges were the product of Stalin's malice and that of a handful of his stooges in the Soviet security police. According to Khrushchev, the Communist party had nothing to do with the horror of the purges, and most party members had no idea of the atrocities committed by Stalin and his

Cheka. But Khrushchev lied. The Cheka was, and the KGB is, an arm of the Communist party, an obedient tool manipulated by the party oligarchy. No one who mattered believed Khrushchev's declarations for a moment.

I entered the Soviet Union's foreign intelligence service, the KGB's First Chief Directorate. Their offices are located far from the center of Moscow in the suburban district of Yasenevo, in an elegantly designed complex that looks for all the world like the CIA's headquarters at Langley, Virginia. Rumor has it that it was Khrushchev's idea to copy the CIA headquarters design as a joke on the Americans.

I became a student at the KGB Foreign Intelligence School, located in a four-story brick building in the forests outside Moscow. The grounds were constantly patrolled by KGB officers in civilian dress. At night they were accompanied by watchdogs. Surrounded by six-foot walls topped with barbed wire, we often felt that instead of being in a school we had opted to attend, we were really in a carefully guarded prison. The instructors used many little tricks to impress upon us the seriousness of our studies. For example, we were forbidden to reveal our true surnames. We might know our classmates, but we knew that when we finished our studies, each of us would disappear into a kind of limbo where we would remember faces, not identities. Throughout my studies, I was known as Livenko.

The routine was ironclad. Each day began with a rigorous workout at 8 A.M., classes ended at 6 P.M., and study stretched far into the night for three, four, or sometimes five hours. The basic training went on in this manner for a year. I studied rigorously, immersing myself in the disciplines of the spy trade.

Spying, like any other complex profession, must be learned, its craftsmanship mastered until it is automatic. There were many skills to be acquired. We were trained in surveillance, countersurveillance, the use of electronic devices, the use of psychological techniques, and "influence" operations. The many lectures continually reminded us that intelligence-gathering activities are always risky and difficult. We were told that our professional lives would be rigorous, stressful, and subject to considerable danger. All the instructors emphasized that each of us should thoroughly master our "trade" because once we were assigned to KGB residencies abroad, there would be no time for on-the-job training. They repeatedly told us that some skills could be learned so that they were totally automatic, whereas certain other aspects of spying required natural talents. Most people can learn sur-

veillance, for example, but finding and recruiting is much more difficult to learn. I would discover that I had that special talent, much to my
surprise, and I would spend my years in Japan on that task.

We attended lectures on the organization and methods used by
the major intelligence and counterintelligence services. The instructor
for this series of lectures, Lieutenant Colonel Khaltuyev, spoke about
the professionalism and perseverance of the CIA, of the British intelligence service MI-6, and of the French and German external services.
He also spoke at length of the skill and thoroughness of such counterintelligence services as the American Federal Bureau of Investigation and
the British, West German, and French organizations that, although
they cannot paralyze KGB activities, can effectively expose KGB and
GRU agents working in their countries.

At a lecture given by a senior KGB officer, I had my first insight
into Japan's importance as a base for intelligence-gathering activities
and why it plays such a special role in the KGB's garnering of secret
political, military, and high-technology information. In other major
free world countries, the counterintelligence services have succeeded in
arresting and expelling many of the Soviets who have been caught
gathering scientific and technological information. An especially large
number of them have been expelled from the United States, Great
Britain, France, and Italy, but Japanese counterintelligence is very
weak. As the lecturer pointed out:

> The Soviet Union can concentrate an intense effort in Japan, and it
> doesn't have to limit its effort to gathering scientific or technologi-
> cal information. We can use Japan as a base from which we can get
> anything we need. A wealth of information of political, economic,
> and military value can be gained, and it does not have to be limited
> to Japan only. With Japan as the base, all other countries of the
> world are vulnerable to the Soviet Union—and that includes the
> United States and South Korea.

This lecturer's words were later proven to be a classic under-
statement. When one sees, as I did, a shipment of scientific and
technologial equipment and data weighing a ton or more leaving Japan
bound for the USSR, and when one is told, as I was, that it's a "regular
shipment, just routine," the scope of the opportunity to exploit Japan
becomes clear.

After months of lectures, the time came when my class was
moved to Moscow to begin the practical training exercises in the city

itself. We were quartered in a large downtown residence on a side street near Zuboskaya Square. From the outside it looked like many slightly run-down old homes that had belonged to the aristocracy before the October Revolution. Inside, it was a mock KGB residency. The upper floors had been fashioned to duplicate a standard KGB residency abroad, and since residencies the world over have essentially the same floor plan to accommodate the same functions, we might have been anywhere in the world.

Each day we went out into Moscow on specific missions, making contacts and avoiding surveillance. We were perfecting the techniques we would be using in earnest in a few weeks or months. I loved it. It was exciting to pit my skills against people who were more experienced than I. More than anything else, I loved the challenge of out-thinking an adversary.

Practicing the bread-and-butter skills of any spy, we loaded and unloaded drops, signaled for emergency meetings, received radio messages from agents some blocks away, and made "brush passes" in which items were transmitted to other agents. Most of all, we practiced following a target.

We learned that there are two primary reasons for following a person. One is to keep him in sight to see where he goes; the other, intended as a form of harrassment and as an inhibition to his actions, deliberately lets him know he is being followed. The latter form of surveillance has the added value of making the target very nervous, which often causes him to panic and to do stupidly revealing things.

Keeping a subject in sight without his knowing is much harder. It is more difficult still in a city where there are many people around. That is why surveillance is usually done by teams. If one agent loses a subject or is spotted ("made") by him, another surveillance team member picks him up. Because tailing a subject is such a tricky job, we tailed each other repeatedly, all over Moscow.

We were told that when we were out on practice exercises, we might at any time be followed or observed by professionals from the Surveillance Directorate. If we thought we detected surveillance, we were told to try to verify our suspicions and, if convinced that we were in fact under observation, to "abort the meet" and return to home base. Once there, we were to report when we had spotted the observer and how and where we had verified our suspicions. If a student failed to spot a tail, he would receive a failing mark for that assignment. He also failed if he thought he was being observed when he wasn't.

Detailed reports on a student's handling of a situation, filed by both the officers posing as agents and those posing as surveillants, evaluated the student's composure and poise. It is very difficult to complete this phase of training with perfect marks. In fact, the word around school was that if a student outwitted the professionals twice, they would pull out all the stops and eventually defeat him totally.

My memories of my official outings are still clear in my mind. The first official rendezvous was scheduled to take place precisely at noon in a popular downtown restaurant. I left the house early that morning, around 9:30, and took a bus to the GUM department store. I remember trying unobtrusively to memorize the faces of all the passengers on the bus. After getting off the bus, I bought a paper at a nearby kiosk so that I could keep an eye on all of the disembarking passengers. They scattered in all four directions except for two men who were so deeply involved in animated conversation that they seemed totally unaware of anyone or anything around them. I went into the store and paused a moment by a counter to browse a bit. Sure enough, one of the men entered the store and, after looking around as though searching for someone, strode off in another direction.

I took the opportunity to do a little shopping of my own and stood in the line at the toy counter for about ten minutes. I bought a special toy for Aleksandr's seventh birthday, stood in another line to pay for it, and finally strolled out of the store. I noticed a man loitering nearby, seemingly waiting for a bus. He was the same size and height as the one I had seen enter the store, but appeared older, with gray hair, a large mustache, and glasses. Despite his disguise, I realized it was the same man.

I got on a bus going in the opposite direction from the restaurant where I was supposed to meet my contact, got off near a café where I had lunch, went to a movie, bought a loaf of bread at a bakery, and went home.

A KGB colonel questioned me at my debriefing. "I was followed, so I didn't go to the restaurant," I said. "Two men followed me to GUM; one of them followed me inside and managed to change clothes and put on a disguise. He was waiting at the bus stop when I left the store."

"How do you know it was the same man?" the colonel demanded. "How did you recognize him in disguise?"

"Easy," I answered. "He forgot to change his shoes."

A second outing was set for later that same evening. I was supposed to meet a contact at a hockey match. I rode around Moscow for three hours, using first one bus and then another, until I was absolutely sure that I wasn't being tailed. Then I went to the ice arena and met my contact. Like any two hockey fans in the world, we chatted all during the game. It was a good game and I enjoyed it. Afterward, I went home without incident. I had guessed right on that one. I hadn't been observed. As they say in the United States, I was two for two.

My third official rendezvous gave me a real scare. I didn't spot any surveillance on the way to the meet at another popular restaurant in downtown Moscow. When I sat down with the agent, however, I recognized him as Colonel Altynov, a KGB man who had suffered burnout in Japan and who now sought oblivion in alcohol. When he had finally been brought back to Moscow, some friend in an undoubtedly high position had prevented his dismissal and had gotten this job for him. Now here he was, drinking himself under the table. I was in real trouble. If I reported his drunkenness on duty, the worn-out old colonel would be dismissed. If I didn't report his behavior, and it was ever discovered, I would be guilty of dereliction of duty, punishable by my own dismissal. Even if I kept quiet, I couldn't be sure of what Colonel Altynov would say when he was sober.

No matter what I said, the drunken colonel insisted on having another bottle of brandy, and all the time he was talking, talking, talking.

"You've got to understand," he said over and over. "You've got to know what I've been through. We could've been killed." By that time he was sobbing, the tears pouring down his cheeks and dripping off his chin. "We could've killed half of Japan, and the damned KGB would've laughed."

"Come on, Colonel," I said as quietly as I could. "It's time to go home."

"Not till you know about those sons of bitches," he said fiercely. "You've got to understand."

His story was garbled and difficult to follow, but I have found out all I could discover about it since that night. It is a hair-raising account. While Colonel Altynov was in Japan, Line X, the field section responsible for scientific, technological, and industrial espionage, reported to the authorities in Moscow that Japanese researchers were conducting laboratory experiments with deadly bacteria in their search for antidotes to poisons and in their attempt to find cures for some diseases. The Soviets ordered that a sample of one particular bacteria be stolen and sent to the Soviet Union for study. Soviet scientists stipulated, however, that because the bacteria were so lethal, the sample could not be sent to the Soviet Union by plane. They were afraid that if the plane crashed with the sample aboard, widespread death would result. So the Soviet residency in Tokyo ordered Altynov and a driver to deliver a vial of the deadly bacteria to a Soviet freighter. Anyone who has experienced Japanese traffic will understand at once how stressful that was. At any second a careless driver could have hit them, and as Altynov said, many would have been killed.

Finally I got him to his feet. "Come on, Comrade Colonel," I said, "let me take you home."

He tried to pull away, and I squeezed him so hard that it's a wonder his ribs didn't break. "You bastard, they're about to call the militia," I whispered. "We are in danger. You're going home, and you're going home now, you son of a bitch!"

I got him to his house, unlocked the door, and then told him, "Colonel Altynov, when I get back to quarters, my report will mention none of this evening's events other than a successful meet."

"Bullshit!" he said as he staggered inside.

I waited in fear and trembling for his report to come in, to see what he would say. Finally, the colonel who supervised my section showed me Colonel Altynov's evaluation. I had conducted myself with "logic and poise," he had written. I had been "as insightful as an experienced officer," and he was quite sure that I could "inspire the trust of an agent."

Three for three!

For my final rendezvous I left the house at 7 A.M. to give myself a full five hours to shake any surveillants before my noon appointment. It soon became obvious that every bus I took was followed by a succession of Volga automobiles. I used every trick I knew and every evasion I had been taught. I would board a bus, jumping off at the last moment; I would dart into doorways; I would enter a store by one door, mingle with the crowd, and suddenly exit another way. Finally I saw no signs that I was still being followed, so about 11:30 I boarded a subway going in the direction of the restaurant where the meet was scheduled. The man sitting next to me was middle-aged, quiet, calm. I've since described him as having a saintly face, but any saintliness might possibly be a trick of my memory. In any case, as the train slowed for his stop, and as my fellow passenger prepared to get off, he whispered, without looking at me, "Comrade, you are under surveillance," before disappearing through the door without so much as a backward glance.

Shaken, I got off at the next stop. Was he right? I wondered, knowing deep inside that he was. He must have seen something I hadn't noticed. I knew from my training that the behavior of a surveillant is sometimes peculiar, even bizarre, when it is being observed by those not being followed. The surveillant's objective is to follow a subject without being noticed by that subject. To do that, a surveillant must remain constantly alert because his subject can see, not merely by looking straight ahead, but by using his peripheral vision. As a result, the follower might sometimes dodge, jump backward, or turn aside quickly. The one being followed might not notice, but others can, and do.

Having decided that my fellow passenger was correct, I didn't meet my contact; instead, I ate by myself and, at the last possible moment, boarded the subway to return to home base. The instant I got on that train I knew I was being watched. I can't really say how I knew, but I did. I could feel it all around me. I was blanketed in it—the feel of it, the knowledge of it.

Later I learned that the entire Moscow subway system is wired so that surveillants can contact one another on a secure line. A team can be on one train, make contact with teams placed at stations ahead of or behind them, and then disembark to be replaced by another team. In this case, which was a practice exercise, at least one surveillant was required to be visible at all times. That was part of the game. I knew that someone was watching me, but I didn't spot the stocky peasant woman with the bag of cucumbers. I remember her, but I didn't pinpoint her, as I later admitted.

When I reported on this exercise, they accepted my account. One of the officers told me, "Don't ever lose that intuition. There are times when it is more valuable than money." Because I couldn't identify a single one of the surveillants from the exercise, however, I was given a "4" instead of the perfect "5." My total was still one of the highest anyone had earned in the school's history.

My year of training for clandestine operations with the KGB had been difficult, but I had soon discovered that I had some advantages the other students had lacked. Through my GRU training, I had already had exposure to some surveillance techniques, the use of ciphers and secret writing, drops, recognition signals, agent radio communications, and the use of camera equipment. I spoke my second language, Japanese, well enough not to need special help from the language teachers. The biggest advantage I had was that I had traveled in my specialty country. Almost equal to that was that I had been trained to write.

The year of training had been as hard on my family as it had been for me, for different reasons. I was allowed to spend only Saturday nights and Sundays with my family, so Natalia had to be both mother and father to our little boy during that time. She was the one who had to see Aleksandr through colds, earaches, and other childhood ailments. She used to ask me if the KGB were going to give her a diploma in "Family."

In a way they did. Almost as much value was placed on the interviews with the candidates' families as on the candidates themselves. I nearly burst with pride at the results of the interview with my wife. The colonel in charge of my section talked with her for three hours one weekend, and she came away with flying colors. That she was very beautiful and socially charming didn't hurt, but it was her intelligence that carried the day. Natalia's perception was that the colonel was primarily interested in her emotional stability and in whether our marriage was sound. I fully agree that these are essential questions about a family that has a KGB professional in its midst. Living a normal family life when one member's existence is filled with stress and personal danger isn't easy, which no doubt explains why the divorce rate is so high within the KGB.

My final evaluation prior to graduation was a bit odd. The colonel in charge of my section was a benign, venerable, white-haired gentleman who had always treated us with the paternalism we could have expected from our own fathers. When my turn came for the final evaluation, he called me into his office, looked at me regretfully, and said, "Livenko, I need your help." I must've shown my astonishment because he smiled a little and added, "You see, I can't submit a completely truthful evaluation of you."

My mouth must have flown open at that. I know I braced myself in fear.

"You are surprised, but it is a fact. Livenko, you have a superb record in the school. You have scored well on the state examinations. In fact, I can't find a thing wrong about you, but I must. If I don't find some fault with you, my report will have absolutely no credibility. Nobody will believe what I say."

My knees felt like water as relief poured over me.

"Now, will you help me?" he asked.

Needless to say, I was flattered and pleased by the glowing report the colonel wrote. To his words of praise, he finally added two adverse comments. One was that I tended to write long, detailed reports when shorter ones would do better; the other was that when I was excited or enthusiastic about something, I would jump from point to point instead of staying with one idea. Then as I was leaving, he added, "Oh, yes. There is another thing we must add. I'm going to suggest that you be given driving lessons. You are the worst driver on God's earth."

I was a bad driver, all right, but I really wasn't any worse than most of the others. After all, none of us had ever driven cars until we entered the school. I was thus in my thirties when I learned to drive a car, a fact Americans generally think is funny; I then remind them that Soviet citizens do not grow up having much contact with the world's goods.

After my graduation I was assigned to the Seventh Department of the First Chief Directorate, the geographical department charged with operations in Japan, the Philippines, Thailand, and other Far East and Southeast Asian countries. Because I was credited with GRU training and for the experience I had gained by working with the Second Chief Directorate, I was commissioned as a senior lieutenant rather than a junior lieutenant. But on the job at the Japanese desk, I was still considered a junior and was given a case load of about twenty agents, political groups, and parties. As I was to discover, these cases were the means of rounding out the theories I had learned at school with the practical realities of what my future assignment would entail.

Just by leafing through 200- to 300-page files, I could learn volumes about the entire process of "seducing" an agent, of winning someone over to the Soviet side, and of maintaining a relationship between case officer and agent. Starting with an ordinary, even innocent, friendly contact, the case officer gradually finds the prospective agent's vulnerabilities, plays the agent much as a fisherman plays a fish until he can land it, and then pulls him in. He begins making suggestions, cautiously offers gifts, and begins to exact favors until his target is caught. The target is then an agent and must cooperate, willingly or unwillingly, with the KGB. Some of the files I studied were absolutely spectacular. For instance, there was the file on Ares, a prominent Japanese journalist who was a Soviet agent. He had been approached when he was a young journalist by Vladimir Alekseyevich Pronnikov, a case officer who skillfully shaped his political views, glowingly portraying life in the Soviet Union. Gradually, Pronnikov began asking favors until finally Ares was stealing top secret documents from the Japanese intelligence community and turning them over to his Soviet case officer.

As I dug deeper into the files, I began to see the truth in what we had been taught. Japan was indeed the treasure trove from which the Soviet Union garnered a rich harvest of intelligence information. I had to face the facts about what my eventual assignment to Japan would entail; of course, I had reservations about it. On the one hand, I wanted to go to Japan. I also wanted to undertake assignments in the field and do things on my own. On the other hand, I didn't want to hurt Japan. From the moment I realized that in order to accomplish my assignments I would have to do exactly that—harm the graceful, gracious, courageous country I had come to love—I had a nagging, guilty conscience.

To salve my feelings of guilt, I did what many others have done in similar circumstances: I rationalized that helping my own country was more important than harming Japan. Besides, I rationalized further, if Japan really cared about itself, it would enact stronger anti-espionage laws and protect itself. Instead, Japan played along, letting the Soviet Union drain it dry. The Soviet Union was consistently extracting a wealth of scientific, economic, and political data from Japan for use against both the Japanese government and people and for influencing Japanese political processes. It's sobering to realize that the Soviet Union can actually shape segments of the political platforms of one or another of Japan's main parties.

The name of Colonel Pronnikov, the man who recruited Ares, came up again and again during those months I spent studying files. One morning while I was with the Seventh Department, my boss, Colonel Kalyagin, shouted for me: "Levchenko, get downstairs! Pronnikov has gotten Ishida to give Brezhnev a car. They're uncrating it in the courtyard. Get down there before those bastards strip it before he even sees it!"

He was referring to a maroon Nissan limousine that had been given to Brezhnev by Hirohide Ishida, a former Japanese labor minister, still influential in Japan's Liberal Democratic Party, who had been cultivated and wooed by Pronnikov. Colonel Kalyagin's words revealed one of the major problems in Soviet society. No automobile in Moscow is safe from black market thieves who can strip a car to its bare bones in seconds. Even there in the courtyard of the First Chief Directorate headquarters, Colonel Kalyagin knew the car wasn't safe. The limousine was in good hands when I reached the courtyard; officers from the Guards Directorate were already there. But as I had been ordered to do so, I stayed until the vehicle was driven away.

It was Pronnikov himself that I found interesting as I studied the files. He was assigned to the Tokyo residency where he was chief of Line PR, the field section in charge of collecting political intelligence and conducting active measures. He was brilliant at his job, and his recruitment of Hirohide Ishida was a masterstroke for which Pronnikov gained both advancement and respect. Although Pronnikov might possibly have exaggerated Ishida's value, the Soviets certainly cooperated by doing all they could to emphasize Ishida's importance. When Ishida came to the Soviet Union, he was entertained by the highest echelons of party bosses. At the end of one of his visits, for instance, Premier Aleksei Kosygin personally ordered the release of a number of Japanese fishermen the Soviet Union was holding. Of course, I had known since my stint with the Ministry of Fisheries that Japanese fishermen were routinely shanghaied and held for use as bargaining chips. Nevertheless, it was reported in the Japanese press that the release of the fishermen was brought about by Ishida during his visit to Moscow as the head of a parliamentary delegation from Japan. Upon his return home, Ishida was able to report convincingly that the Soviets were reasonable diplomats. Ishida's influence in Japan was heightened, and Pronnikov's recruit became increasingly valuable to the USSR.

In 1974 the Chief Directorate decided that I should spend a year with *New Times* magazine, one of the major Soviet political weeklies. By that time I was already a case officer; this assignment was to build up my cover so that I could operate in Tokyo as a *New Times* correspondent. For about a year I worked as a journalist, writing and editing articles, doing interviews, and generally becoming assimilated into a journalistic milieu. I learned very quickly that Soviet journalism is as cynical as every other aspect of Soviet life I'd yet observed. None of the journalists believed what they wrote, and most of them knew full well that the things they were writing were deceptions aimed at Soviet readers who had no other sources for news.

When Soviet officers from the Tokyo residency were home on leave, I'd ask as many questions as I could about working in Tokyo. Usually, they would smile and say that in the intelligence business everything is tough. But then they would admit that it was possible to work well in Japan, that much information could be garnered. They explained that by using Japanese sources one could get anything that was needed about any country in the world, including the People's Republic of China or the United States of America. The KGB, they said, even had access to the Japanese Foreign Office and the Research Bureau files.

At last, the training came to a close, and my cover complete, I received my assignment to Japan. By the time I was posted I had worked for *New Times* long enough to have earned a legitimate reputation as a journalist. Articles with my by-line had appeared frequently, and I was fairly well known in journalistic circles. I knew that my colleagues at *New Times* would expect me to host a farewell party, but I really only expected twenty or thirty people of the staff of one hundred to attend. I was surprised and touched, however, when I entered the dining room to see over eighty people standing and applauding in greeting. It was a beautiful farewell party, a memory I'll always treasure.

I was also expected to give a farewell party for my superiors in the KGB, so a few nights before Natalia and I left for Japan, I invited the five colonels from the Japanese desk to join me for dinner at a popular club. In the dining room with music from a live orchestra surrounding us, we six men sitting there talking in grim tones were totally out of place, but after a few drinks, everyone relaxed and began to enjoy himself.

A surprising thing happened at the very end of the evening. One of the colonels remained behind after the other guests had gone. "I'm going to buy you one drink," the colonel said, "and I'm going to give you three pieces of advice. If you ever tell anyone I said this, I'll swear you lie. Got that?" I nodded.

"First," he continued, "in your kind of job there has to be a 'first time.' Follow the rules you've learned, by all means. They are good guidelines. But rely most heavily on your own common sense and good judgment. Second, stay away from the CIA. They are as smart as you are, and they have some enticements you've never experienced. At best, you'll waste your time. Worse has happened. Other officers trying to recruit Americans have been caught like flies in a honey pot."

He paused. "Third, stay away from Pronnikov as much as you can. He's the most dangerous man in Japan. I'll leave it to you to find out why, but don't take too long about it." He tossed down his drink and left.

I was now a full-fledged KGB officer on assignment to Japan. I was on my way to play the game. And to make a deadly enemy of Pronnikov.

5

The Hunter and the Hunted

OUTER BANKS, NORTH CAROLINA

I turned to retrace my steps along the deserted beach. Sunset was fast approaching, and I was hungry.

"Time to go back," I thought, "and find the beach path to the hotel."

I paused to watch a pelican flying parallel to the shore a hundred yards out to sea. How peaceful he looked, skimming along over the waves. Suddenly he dove straight into the water. He surfaced a few seconds later with a big fish in his bill. Flying smoothly and effortlessly, he transferred the still-wriggling fish to the pouch under his beak, but his successful dive had attracted some gulls. They fell in behind him, hoping for a share of the catch.

"That, too, is part of the game," I mused. "You are the hunter until you make your catch. Then all at once you're the hunted."

JAPAN, 1975–1979

At last, after years of preparation and what seemed like eons of waiting, I flew with my wife and son to live in Japan. We made our move in February 1975, and I don't know who was the most excited: Natalia, ten-year-old Aleksandr, or me. We had been so busy with our packing, goodbye visits, and farewell parties that all three of us were exhausted when we finally got to Tokyo. We had our little pet poodle with us on the plane, and Aleksandr worried throughout the flight because she would have to go into quarantine for the first month we were in Japan. When we landed, I was able to pull a few strings, and we got to take her with us from the airport.

Tired as we were, we badly needed a few days' rest before I began work, and I had hoped that we would be booked into one of Tokyo's many clean and restful hotels. I had in fact expected to get that kind of booking, as I had always been quartered in that kind of hotel on my previous trips to Japan. This time, though, the KGB had put us into a cheap, noisy, none-too-clean hotel within walking distance of the embassy.

"Well," I thought to myself, "propaganda trips are different, I guess. It's certain that the KGB doesn't pamper its own." To make matters worse, there were orders waiting for me. I was to report to the embassy for a briefing the next morning.

I got up early enough to get a cup of tea before walking to the embassy for my initial visit. I was a bit too early in arriving, which gave me a chance to examine the building before the doors were even open for the day. It's an imposing building, all right—vast, massive, and eleven stories high.

The first person I saw when I went inside was Vyacheslav Pirogov. He was the fellow student two years ahead of my class in college who'd play-acted at being a KGB officer when we were in school. He greeted me like a long-lost brother, obviously bursting with pride that he had reached his goal. He was a KGB officer, by damn.

"He hasn't changed a bit," I thought to myself. "He was a *stukach* in school, and he hasn't changed a bit." In college we'd all learned to spot the *stukachi* (informers) quickly. Learning who they were as quickly as possible was a survival skill. But Pirogov was harmless. Anyone as transparent as he is always harmless.

He was to be my guide on my tour of the embassy. He ushered me from the marble foyer up to the tenth floor to meet the resident, Dimitri Yerokhin, a surprisingly youthful-looking man who at forty-two was the youngest general in Soviet intelligence. He shook my hand and then abruptly dismissed me. "They tell me you're an outstanding specialist on Japan. Go and get to work."

As we left Yerokhin's office and walked out into the corridor, I saw a dark-haired, well-groomed man moving purposefully toward us. "You are Stanislav Aleksandrovich," he declared as he offered his hand. "I am Vladimir Alekseyevich."

This was my introduction to the famous Pronnikov I'd been warned about in Moscow. He was a short man, barely five feet six inches tall, but his body was hard, trim, and well-muscled.

"Please come in," he said, signaling Pirogov with a raised eyebrow that he meant the invitation only for me.

Inside his office he gave the impression that he had all the time in the world to get acquainted with me. Indeed, as I later learned, he always appraised each newcomer for himself to see how that officer would fit into his own scheme of things. If I hadn't been forewarned, I probably would have been quite intimidated by the man. Throughout our conversation he kept revealing how thoroughly he had researched me down to the smallest details. Nothing had escaped him, not even our little dog. He even knew her name.

"Tell me," he said at one point, "how did Beauty take the long flight from Moscow?" And all the time he was welcoming me to Tokyo, smilingly gracious, his cool gray eyes were assessing, analyzing, probing.

When I finally left his office, I was certain of two things. Pronnikov was both brilliant and capable and a man who had to know everything about his officers. Everything. At that time he was the chief of Line PR, or political line, and second in command of the residency. Well-informed officers in Moscow had told me that he was much more powerful than his rank of lieutenant colonel indicated. In Moscow they expected Pronnikov eventually to become the head of the First Chief Directorate. I knew that in Pronnikov I'd met a man I couldn't afford to underestimate.

Pirogov was waiting in the corridor to continue the tour of the residency, which occupied the top two floors of the embassy. The residency's hallways were lined with rooms for translation, Line X (for the theft of scientific data), radio and microwave interception, active measures (the disinformation and influence operations department), and of course, other support components. It differed little from the training residency in Moscow, except for the array of esoteric electronic equipment, the size of the operation, and the peculiar quiet.

"It's almost eerie," I remarked, "It's so quiet."

"That's because the walls, floors, and ceilings are double," Pirogov explained, "and the spaces between are shot full of music and electrical impulses. They do that to foil any listening devices."

I spent the first few days getting acquainted with the work and the officers in the residency, especially with my predecessor, Boris Pischik, a bright, handsome young man who possessed an admirable knowledge of the Japanese language. After he left to go home to the Soviet Union, Natalia and I were given his apartment, which was located in a very old building in Sendagaya. The rooms were tiny, and I found it impossible to find space for an office. My cover for being in Japan was as a journalist, and I had to be able to function as one. So when the editor-in-chief of *New Times,* the magazine I now worked for, came to Tokyo for a visit, I showed him the apartment the KGB had assigned me.

"Is this the way a correspondent for such a prestigious magazine ought to live?" I asked.

"No," he answered, "I really think something can be done to correct this. Let me see what I can do. After all, you *are* a correspondent and a damned good one. You'll earn the salary we'll be paying you."

Before he went back to Moscow, I was given authorization to rent a large and expensive apartment in Shibuya Udagawa-cho. We loved our beautiful three-bedroom apartment, and in my position with the magazine I now had the credibility necessary to support my cover.

I got acquainted with the Japanese journalists, joined the press clubs, and generally established my legitimacy as a correspondent. At the same time I dove into my real duties as an intelligence officer. In the beginning I was assigned to the Political Intelligence section of the Tokyo residency, working directly under Lieutenant Colonel Pronnikov. My assignment was to hunt for contacts in the media and political circles so that in the future I could recruit them as agents.

I was moving into a well-established program that systematically drained what it needed from Japan, a program that had emerged by trial and error from Soviet efforts after World War II. When the war ended, the Soviet Union relished the fact that Japan was powerless and emasculated. As a nation it was weakened industrially, economically, and militarily. In consequence, Japan was totally incapable of waging any kind of aggression in the Far East; it couldn't even exert enough pressure or influence to be considered a major power any place in the world any longer. For the Soviet Union, the time seemed right to move into the vacuum that had occurred in a fallen nation.

The Soviets' first plan was to turn Japan into a socialist country by creating a kind of fifth column of Japanese citizens inside the country itself. In order to accomplish this goal they focused attention on the large numbers of Japanese prisoners of war in prison camps all over Siberia and the Soviet Far East. An unprecedented brainwashing program was undertaken to indoctrinate the POWs in Marxism-Leninism. Schools were established for the POWs, Japanese language newspapers were published for them, and every possible procedure to mold them into an effective force was implemented.

As an aside here, I must note that I was taught the Japanese language by Mrs. Ivanenko who served as an interpreter in one of those prisoner of war camps. The editor of the Japanese language newspaper for the POWs was Ivan Kovalenko, chief of the Japanese desk of the International Department when I was assigned there.

Significantly, these prisoners weren't returned to their own country until 1949, though the war ended in 1945. By the early 1950s there were violent demonstrations in Tokyo and other major cities in which crowds overturned cars and chanted anti-American slogans. The Japanese government reacted by banning the Japanese Communist Party, forcing it to go underground. The Soviet plan for reshaping Japan in its own image had failed.

By the end of the decade, Japan was out of its postwar economic slump and had launched itself into a boom that rocketed its gross national product to one of the highest of the free world, leaving the Soviet Union reconsidering its tactics. By the 1960s the Soviets had decided upon a policy of establishing normal relations with Japan and of using Japan's economic might to help develop Soviet economic and military interests in Siberia and the Soviet Far East.

The Soviets faced a major drawback, however. They were fifteen to twenty years behind the United States, Japan, and other advanced countries in technological development. They hoped to buy entire plants and factories, including chemical plants and factories with direct military applications. Japan, gleefully pursuing its industrial boom by engaging in free trade with practically every country in the world, was the perfect source for such purchases. The Soviet Union was well aware that its trade with Japan would run it "into the red," but its need fc what it could secure from Japan was so great that it had to disregard that handicap. The Soviets began to cultivate contacts in Japanese political circles, among the Liberal Democratic Party and the Socialist Party, for instance, and among Japanese business circles, in order to try to pressure the Japanese government into approving advantageous trade deals with the Soviet Union.

One of the main advantages achieved by this adjustment in the Soviet approach to Japan was that they secured long-term credits, which actually amount to subsidies. In effect, the Japanese taxpayers and investors are giving a great deal of money to the Soviet Union in the name of bilateral trade. The Japanese do this to stimulate their exports and their domestic industries.

The Soviets wooed their contacts in these Japanese circles with all sorts of promises. Trade with the Soviet Union would guarantee political stability between the two nations, they said. The Soviet market doesn't have any ups and downs, they said, so it doesn't have any recessions. In return for Japan's diverting part of its trade, the Soviet Union would tap its vast deposits of essential minerals in Siberia and the Soviet Far East for Japan's use, they said. The Soviets even promised to sell oil to Japan, a deal that would have been much to Japan's advantage because it would reduce the great distances from which Japan had to import its oil. The Soviet Union later reneged on that promise, however, in the late 1970s when it was experiencing an oil shortage of its own.

It was during this period of Soviet-Japanese dealings that I entered Japan, a time when Moscow was courting Japanese business-men in whatever ways would prove beneficial to the Soviet cause. Dignitaries from Japanese business circles were often invited to the Soviet Union for lavish trips in which they were housed in luxurious hotels, served superb meals, and treated with respect and ceremony, all as part of a plan devised by the KGB specialists who were assigned to the Soviet Ministry of Trade.

A case in point was that of Toshio Doko, the president of Keidanren (the Federation of Economic Organizations in Japan), a powerful organization of the Japanese industrialists. Doko was invited to visit Moscow to meet with representatives of the Soviet trade unions. When he reached Moscow, he was informed that President

Brezhnev wanted to see him as well. However, Mr. Brezhnev was away on vacation in the Crimea, and would Mr. Doko please allow the Soviets to fly him out to see him? Mr. Doko would, of course. So he was taken at government expense to a gorgeous palace where Brezhnev was in residence for the summer. Very few foreigners were ever taken to that palace, which had at one time been a summer home for the tsars. Those who gained audience there were very high-ranking government officials and the top leaders of Soviet bloc countries, but never businessmen. By taking Doko to meet Brezhnev there, the Soviets showed him that they considered him extraordinarily important. While he was there, of course, they worked very hard on him to make him sympathetic, particularly where trade was concerned. Whether this red-carpet trip or business factors influenced him, it is still a well-known fact that for many years he was a strong proponent of trade agreements with the Soviet Union.

One small note is needed here. Whenever Japanese business representatives enter into negotiations with the Soviets, they are at a distinct disadvantage. The reason is that the KGB manages to learn the Japanese position ahead of time and forewarns and forearms the Soviet negotiators. The Soviet Union keeps such a huge number of agents in Japan in order to keep totally informed.

All during the time I worked in Japan, a pressing need was getting our hands on as many high-technology items as possible—chemical machinery, heavy machinery, computers, semiconductors, optics, radio and television equipment, anything Japan was producing that could be used for military purposes. A few years ago the Soviets really pulled off a major coup. They convinced the Japanese to sell them a dry dock of enormous tonnage and capacity, which the Soviets swore was for the exclusive use of their fishing fleet. I can't believe that the Japanese were so naive as to accept those assurances as the literal truth, because the Soviets were openly involved in a massive military buildup at the time. Surely somebody in Japan must have suspected that the Soviets would put such a dock to military uses, which is exactly what they did. In a matter of months after the dry dock was delivered to Vladivostock, the Soviets used it to repair the aircraft carrier *Minsk* and followed almost immediately by repairing several nuclear submarines.

In the summer of 1987, the free world was startled to learn that a Toshiba Corporation subsidiary had joined with a Norwegian firm to sell sophisticated machine tools and computers to the Soviet Union. This equipment will permit the Soviet military to improve submarine propellers so that Soviet submarines will move much more quietly under-water, thus making them more difficult to detect. The sale of this machinery was prohibited by both countries, but the Soviet skill in buying this highly sensitive capability is just a recent and spectacular example of the continuing successes I observed in the USSR's dealings with Japanese companies.

To ensure good results in lobbying Japan's business and political circles, the Soviets send their best-trained people to Japan. They make a clear distinction between what they refer to as clean trade mission people and those who extract what they want by clandestine means. In the 1970s and early 1980s, a prominent Soviet economic administrator was the chief of the Soviet trade mission in Japan. Spandaryan was one of the clean ones, concerned with legitimate trade agreements. But his deputy, Papushin, was a KGB colonel who had been stationed pre-viously in Great Britain. When Papushin was replaced after his return to the Soviet Union, the new deputy was also a KGB officer, Lieuten-ant Colonel Zharkov.

About fifty percent of the trade mission's workers are KGB officers; many of these specialize in scientific and technological intelli-gence because even Japan (easy as it is there to extract high technology and equipment) sometimes refuses to sell certain processes or ma-chines. When that happens, the other half of the Soviet trade mission's workers get busy. The Scientific and Technological officers try to steal the processes or samples they need, sometimes loosing a veritable army of agents to do so. When I was in Tokyo, the KGB's Tokyo resi-dency had about twenty-five full-time intelligence officers belonging to Line X, the branch dealing in scientific and technological intelli-gence.

KGB S and T officers work in places other than the trade mission or as short-term specialists. At least half of the twenty or so Aeroflot officials stationed with the airline in Japan when I was there were scientific and technological intelligence officers. Fifty percent of the employees of the news service TASS were KGB officers, and at least one of them was a Line X officer. In the Soviet embassy the scientific counselor was a high-ranking KGB Line X officer, as was one of his assistants. The GRU is also involved in high-technology theft, and many members of the GRU residency are Soviet military officers specializing in S and T intelligence.

Each officer handles three or four agents, so it's easy to calculate that the number of agents working in the science and technology field for the Soviets is at least 75, at most 100 or more. Whatever the Soviets need, those agents steal. It's a profitable business all around. For instance, the KGB might pay from $10,000 up to as high as $100,000 to an agent for stealing a particular technological process, but the cost of developing that same process would have been as high as $2,000,000. By simply stealing the samples and copying them, the Soviets save a great deal of money, and they steal a great number of samples. Even the special audio equipment used by the KGB residency to monitor radio communications between Japanese National Police surveillance teams was stolen from Japan.

In the late 1970s the Tokyo resident told us something very interesting about the Line X operations. "The proceeds from the operations these officers carry out each year would cover the expenses of our entire Tokyo residency for many years with money still left over. In fact, worldwide, technical intelligence all by itself covers *all* of the expenses of the whole KGB External Intelligence Service."

I remember a case when one of the S and T officers stationed in the Tokyo residency traveled with a Soviet technical delegation to visit a chemical plant in Japan. The Japanese hosts gave them a nice reception and then showed them the whole factory, including those parts normally treated as "off limits" to foreigners. The Japanese, of course, thought that the Soviets were going to buy, if not the whole plant, at least the technology for duplicating it. In one area of the factory the KGB officer looked at the wall and couldn't believe his eyes. There was a huge chart outlining the entire plant's technological processes.

"Start asking as many questions as you can," he whispered to a colleague. "Keep our guide distracted."

As the Soviet delegation surrounded the guide, firing questions as fast as they could, the KGB officer drew the entire chart. When he returned to the residency, he immediately sent it off to Moscow. The evaluation, when it came some two weeks later, told him that this single act of stealth had covered twelve years of expenses for the Tokyo residency.

Many specialists went to Japan on a short-term basis to check equipment that the Soviet Union was buying from Japan. They stayed for three to six months and then applied for visa renewals. In this way the number of people assigned to the embassy could be increased without changing the official numbers at all. The visa renewals allowed many of them to remain in Japan for one, two, or three years. At least half of these specialists were professional KGB S and T officers, and it's no exaggeration to say that the whole crowd of Soviet intelligence was (and doubtless still is) involved in high-technology thefts on a daily basis. Indeed, they garnered such a wealth of information that they sometimes had difficulty sending it all back to Moscow. Diplomatic couriers from the Soviet Union came to Japan twice a month, and it was not unusual for the Moscow-bound samples and technological finds from Line X to weigh as much as one ton. That was one of the reasons that the Soviet diplomatic mail was delivered from the Soviet embassy to the airport in a microbus. The boxes that filled the bus, floor to ceiling, were the gleanings of the clandestine operations of the KGB's Line X.

Logic alone tells me that the Japanese government must have known about the extensive network of S and T intelligence officers in Japan for a very long time, and why the country has done nothing to curb the thefts and to punish those who steal so openly I do not know. The United States must also be warned that it is not only Japanese secrets that the Soviets seek. Many Japanese research facilities, universities, laboratories, and corporations have close ties with their American counterparts, and there is a broad exchange of delegations, engineers, and scholars between the two countries. The KGB actively pursues the Japanese specialists who regularly visit the United States and tries to recruit them in order to obtain American technological secrets. Sometimes they are successful.

My own job in Japan, as I have said, was in the realm of political intelligence and influence, and my cover as a journalist was perfect for the assignment. The importance of S and T intelligence operations in Japan is great for the Soviets. However, as in any other country of the free world, political intelligence has the highest priority. Through it, the Soviet Politburo collects secret information on domestic and external policies of Japan and on the future plans of the Japanese government. A wealth of information is collected also on the United States, the PRC, and South Korea. I had wide latitude to move about and meet people who could be helpful. As a representative of a magazine, I could gain entry to all sorts of places that most foreigners couldn't reach. On the other hand, we KGB agents who were not counted against the embassy's limited number of diplomats did not have diplomatic immunity. If we were caught, we would not just be sent home but would suffer the fate of a captured spy.

The first professional Japanese contact I made was with a prominent member of the Socialist Party, a man to whom the KGB assigned the code name King. A soft-spoken man, he had a kind face and a disarming smile. I knew that ideologically he was very close to the positions of the Soviet Communist party and that he was an ardent socialist, but that didn't mean that he was necessarily pro-Soviet. Still, he had access to information that was potentially useful, so I carefully nurtured the relationship.

There is an American acronym that is recognized by world intelligence services as the measure of a person's vulnerability, a way to assess whether a person can be seduced into becoming an agent of a foreign power: MICE. It stands for Money, Ideology, Compromise, and Ego. Whenever an intelligence officer evaluates the weakness of a target, he always starts with MICE. Which one? Where, he wonders, is the weakness?

King didn't seem to have any of those weaknesses. He earned a fairly comfortable salary, and he lived with his wife and two children in a nice little apartment. The KGB files gave no indication that he was particularly egotistical, nor did they reveal any vices that could be used to make him compromise his beliefs. I kept on the lookout, however for something that would give me a clue as to how to reach him.

In my contacts with King, I also tried to keep in mind some aspects of the Japanese psyche. The Japanese are hard workers, deeply committed to their own culture and customs. So I tried very hard to make each luncheon or dinner with King an appealing cultural occasion. Because the Japanese hate to waste time, I would also try to give him some tidbit of information that he could use in his work for the Socialist Party. He thought I was giving him priority information on developments in the Soviet Communist party; what I was actually disclosing was information taken from *Pravda*. At the same time, I gained from him information about the Japanese Socialist Party that was sometimes quite valuable in influencing its opinions and actions.

One of an intelligence officer's most valuable weapons is subtle flattery, and I began using it on King once our friendship was established. The time came when I said, "I have to confide in you, but it's something I'm going to ask you not to repeat. The magazine that I work for is generally accepted as a 'trade union periodical,' but it's really more than that. *New Times* is a project of the International Department, which publishes a newsletter that is read by the top men in the Soviet Union, by members of the Politburo itself. Now the information I give has to be correct. I can't afford to make any mistakes with facts or sources. That's why you are such an important friend.

You are a political expert of the highest order, and I can always depend on the accuracy of what you say." ("You see, Mr. King," I wanted my words to convey, "you aren't talking to just any old journalist, but to one whose words are read by VIPs in the Soviet Union. Through me, you could influence the Soviet leaders.")

Finally, as I knew I would, I found his Achilles' heel. King wanted desperately to publish a newspaper of his own, but he needed money to get it started.

At lunch one day I asked him about the status of the newspaper. "It's not possible," he replied. "I just can't round up the money."

"Oh, I don't know," I said as casually as I could. "I think there is a very good chance for it. Please accept this in the same spirit of brotherhood in which it's offered." I placed a fat yellow envelope holding a million yen on the table; then, to cover the awkward moment, I went on talking about the help that such a publication would be and how happy I was to be able to contribute to it.

At last he reached across the table, picked up the envelope, and hastily put it in his pocket. At the end of our luncheon I said, again as casually as I could, "By the way, I'm going to need a receipt to show that I didn't steal that money. Just a signature—anything will do." He took one of his business cards out of his pocket and hurriedly wrote and signed a receipt.

That was on a Friday. On Monday I got a frantic phone call from King. I agreed to meet him for lunch. When I saw him I could tell he was having second thoughts.

"What in the world is wrong?" I asked. "You look positively ill."

"No, no," he answered. "I'm not physically ill, but I must have my business card back. My God, man, that card could ruin me, destroy my career, hurt my family if it fell into the wrong hands."

"I suppose it could be used that way," I interrupted, "but it won't be."

"Where is the card now? In the Soviet embassy?"

"Oh, no, it's in Moscow by now. We had a special courier going over on the weekend, and we just included it in the pouch."

He slumped down in his chair, utterly dejected. I did nothing to try to raise his spirits. Several months later, I gave King 3 million yen as a "contribution" to his election campaign. Although he did not become a member of parliament, his relations with the Soviets became closer due to the "contribution." King was now my man.

I was always respectful and courteous, but from that moment on, I gradually conditioned him to follow orders and directions. King proved to be a reliable agent. Whenever we tested his work against that of other known agents, he always came through.

More complicated was my relationship with one of the veteran Japanese journalists employed by *Yomiuri,* a well-known Japanese newspaper. I had been introduced to him by another KGB officer, and from the beginning, I really liked the man. We had similar tastes: the same restaurants, the same foods, the same parks, and the same ukiyoe prints. Even our attitudes toward life were similar. In almost every respect we seemed to harmonize.

A journalist in his late forties, he was the first of my Japanese acquaintances to explain in detail things I wanted to know about the Japanese culture. I often asked him about the history of Japanese literature, and he always took the time to explain fully and completely. He was the soul of patience and tact. When I asked him about some peculiarity or other of the Japanese society—the oddly nightmarish judicial system, for instance—he took pains to make sure that I understood. We could have been called real friends, except that after each meeting I had to go back to the residency and write a contact report on everything we had discussed.

I was expected to report on his financial situation, his likes and dislikes, whether he craved expensive clothing, his relationships with his superiors and his subordinates, and what kinds of decisions he was authorized to make on his own. Deputy Resident Pronnikov and Resident Yerokhin would discuss these reports in detail and issue guidelines on how to deepen the friendship, how to maneuver my friend into cooperating with me on a professional basis.

I knew I was being an even worse hypocrite as I faced myself and what I was doing. The cynical hypocrisy I had deplored for so long as the hallmark of the Soviet system was reflected in me and in my work. Sometimes, in an impulsive and absurd attempt to protect my journalist friend from my own manipulations, I'd omit data from my contact reports that I knew the KGB would find useful. My ambivalence toward the relationship was a form of mental torture for me. I longed for a friend in Japan, but in my role as a KGB officer, I had made a travesty of our friendship.

When I finally succeeded in recruiting him into the network of the KGB residency, I felt disillusioned and soiled. I couldn't sleep at night and was bitterly depressed. I felt as a jailer probably feels when he

imprisons a person he knows is innocent. Of course I knew intellec-
tually that my friend wasn't really innocent: he was knowingly cooperating with the Soviets and was getting paid for it. Still, it was I who had
seduced him, a man who should have been my friend, and that hurt.

Someone recently asked me what my profession was really like.
I answered, "Mine is the second oldest profession in the world. And it's
not much different from the first. The oldest profession seduces the
body; the second oldest seduces the soul."

I had an altogether different experience in developing a contact
with another prominent journalist who worked for the *Tokyo Shimbun*.
"Feliks" was one of the editors. I began developing a friendship with
him in the usual way, by an entirely natural sharing of interests during
conversations over lunch or a drink. I had been introduced to Feliks by
Gennadi Yevstafyev, a KGB colonel, shortly before his reassignment.

As time passed, Feliks and I discussed the troubling events in
domestic and international news, talked about books we'd both read,
and generally got quite comfortable in each other's company. Again, I
had to report on our meetings. Again, these reports were read, not only
in the Tokyo residency, but also in KGB headquarters in Moscow.

Finally, the friendship cemented and solid, the time came to see
if Feliks would cooperate with us. Over lunch one day I said that the
New Times magazine had a limited-distribution newsletter read only
by the leaders of the Soviet Politburo. "You would be welcome to
write articles for this newsletter, anonymously of course," I told him,
"especially if they provide advance information on what Japanese
policy regarding external affairs will be."

"No," he flatly refused. "I'm sorry, but I will not cooperate
with any foreign power." Then, to my surprise, he added, "I'm
saddened, Levchenko-san, that you must work for a foreign intelligence organization. You are a good journalist. I feel very sorry for
you."

Although Feliks spoke politely, that meeting in the lobby coffee
shop of the Pacific Hotel in Tokyo's Shinagawa area was our last as
friends. I'd see him from time to time at press receptions, but he
completely ignored my presence. He was among the many fine human
beings I came to like and respect while I lived in Japan; I'll always regret
that we weren't able to meet normally, as two human beings, and
become friends.

Not all my work in intelligence was so emotionally difficult,
nor was all of it fruitful. For instance, one of my developing contacts, a

once prominent journalist who now freelanced, knew I was a KGB officer. In fact, he gloried in this knowledge. Like the man who has always wanted to be a fireman and so hangs around the firehouse for vicarious thrills, my contact was a "spy groupie." He "worked" continuously, bringing me information that he'd obviously picked up in the morning newspaper. When I finally got him to see that this was not enough, he fabricated sensational, outlandish information about one or another prominent political figure. Once he came to me with the fantastic claim that Tokuma Utsunomiya, a member of parliament, and Daisaku Ikeda, the eminent religious leader, were both American agents. He said that Ikeda had traveled to the Soviet Union, spoken with Prime Minister Kosygin, and then shortly afterward had "reported the entire secret conversation to an American."

"Why shouldn't Ikeda repeat the conversation?" I asked. "What was in it that was so secret that it couldn't be repeated? After all, Mr. Kosygin is a famous man, and people do like to name-drop."

"Well," he responded weakly, "I'll bet that Mr. Kosygin asked him not to." Then, gaining momentum, my contact launched into another wild fantasy about Utsunomiya, claiming that he was a link between the United States and the North Korean government.

I finally got tired of listening to his garbage and told him not to contact me again. "If I need you, I'll call you," I said.

One of the valuable agents I recruited was code-named Vassin, and it's interesting the way he came to our attention. One of the other KGB officers was the handler for a recruit code-named Ramses. This agent reported to his case officer that he knew a man, the publisher of a newsletter, who would make an excellent agent. The KGB contact then passed along to me the job of meeting the man, sounding him out, and if he were a good prospect, recruiting him.

I phoned the man and introduced myself as the correspondent for *New Times,* told him how much I enjoyed his newsletter, and asked for an interview in order to get some answers to several perplexing questions. We met for lunch a few days later, and I was really impressed by him. A thin-faced man in his fifties, he looked as though the years had taken their toll on his health and stamina. Two things struck me the moment I saw him. He wore a jacket that was at least two sizes too large for him, and he took great care in examining everyone in the Press Club's cafeteria before coming over to meet me. This was the action of an extremely careful man and done as unobtrusively as any intelligence officer could have done it.

Our next few meetings were so amiable that I quickly became convinced that not only was Vassin ripe for the picking, he was practically ready to fall off the tree and into our hands. Meanwhile, the customary residency investigation of his background was under way. It soon became apparent that several other Soviet agents knew him and trusted his information and his judgment. By the fourth or fifth meeting, when I began moving cautiously toward recruitment, he practically volunteered to cooperate. The recruitment happened so fast that my friend in the residency who had turned Vassin over to me in the first place advised me not to report it for awhile.

"The center in Moscow will never understand that it could happen so fast," he explained. "They will assume that you made your recruitment approach rashly, carelessly—perhaps even too recklessly for you or the agent to be trusted in the future. Play it along. Spin it out a little."

As I learned later, Vassin was a veteran Communist; it was no wonder that he agreed so readily. He had been active since the early 1950s until he was expelled from the Japanese Communist party over a disagreement with its external policies. Nevertheless, he was as much a Communist as he had ever been.

In no time at all, Vassin was providing sensitive information on the Japanese government's external policy problems, on the People's Republic of China, and on other relevant political problems. Sometimes he didn't wait to be tasked with reporting requirements, but acquired and provided information on his own initiative. As I'd suspected, I didn't have to give him lengthy instructions on the security procedures surrounding our meetings. He had learned many of the basics of clandestine activities when the Communist party was banned in the 1950s and forced underground, and he hadn't forgotten a thing.

From the very beginning Vassin never hesitated to accept money for his services, though the amounts were at first fairly insignificant. No matter what I asked him to do, he never questioned my requirements. I got the impression that he had acquired a taste for games in deception and that he played them with gusto. He was an excellent agent of influence, eagerly helping me to spread sensational but very plausible stories that served the Soviet cause.

His contributions were recognized and appreciated by my superiors. If I hadn't escaped to the United States, I'm certain that the Soviets would still be using Vassin extensively, not just for collecting information, but in the operations of influence, deception, and disinformation. His was a case of a man who did what he did because of his ideology. MICE! It's where the recruiter begins and ends his quest.

I was an intelligence officer whose job was to find and recruit cooperative agents in another country. I'm often asked whether I was in great danger as I went about that business. The answer is yes and no. Trained to use the tools of the spy trade, I didn't go about Tokyo carrying firearms or any of the tricky James Bond weapons. I had been trained in the use of small arms and handguns, but the real weapons for me were caution and common sense. The main objective was to function and not get caught; I could have been put in prison.

An analogy might explain my job. When I was luring a recruit, I was the hunter, but when I had won him over from his own country, then I became the hunted. Japanese counterintelligence may be weak, but it isn't nonexistent. When I met any of the agents I handled, I always had a plausible reason to be with him. If he were a journalist, as many were, and if we were ever challenged by the Japanese authorities, the cover story was that he was trying to seduce me into saying something against the Soviet Union or that he was interviewing me. In other words, once I had caught my man, I was in danger of being caught. Yes, I was frequently in danger, but rarely in danger of losing my life.

On the other hand, a few of my experiences in the espionage trade now seem comical to me. But when they were happening, the feeling was quite different. I remember one occasion when I had to have a meeting with an agent. I left my apartment early in the morning that day, spent the usual few hours driving through narrow streets to clear my way and checking whether I had a tail. Then I parked my car in an out-of-sight place and took a taxicab to a large square where I could blend into the busy Tokyo crowd. From there I took a metro train to the meeting. Everything looked all right, and I felt confident that nobody had followed me. Suddenly I realized that quite a few train passengers were staring at me in a strange way. That was highly unusual: the Japanese are not curious people, and a foreigner in Tokyo is not a rarity.

Instinctively I checked all the buttons and zippers on my clothes; everything was in order. But still something was wrong. Finally I looked at my feet and felt as if somebody had poured a bucket of icy water over me. A ten-inch wire was hanging from my trousers— a rather unusual attachment for somebody riding on a subway train. No wonder people were staring at me! I must have looked funny, although to me the situation was not funny at all. Of course I knew I was wired; before going to the meeting the technical operations officer gave me a special device called a *yatagan*. It is a small black box that looks like a telephone beeper, but it serves a different purpose. If the KGB residency (listening to the Japanese surveillance communications, or by some other means) finds out that one of its officers is in danger, it sends a radio signal from the rooftop of the Soviet embassy, and the *yatagan,* concealed in the pants of the operative, vibrates. That means to stop the meeting and return immediately. Every radio device has an antenna, usually concealed in the trousers, that used a safety pin to hold it in place. Apparently, I had lost the safety pin, and the antenna slid down my leg, shocking the passengers on the train. I got off the train at the next station and spent some time in the lavatory fixing the *yatagan*.

Not all of my experiences were so amusing. One particularly close call occurred on a winter evening in 1978 when I had planned a meeting with a contact I code-named Edo. An administrator at one of the major newspapers, Edo was already an agent in the residency network when I arrived in Japan. I inherited him, but from the time I took over his handling I never trusted him. At each of our meetings he would claim that on the previous day he had dined with some important dignitary—the secretary general of the Liberal Democratic Party, the foreign minister, or any one of the cabinet members—and would hand me a restaurant receipt for 90,000 to 150,000 yen, asking for reimbursement. When I'd ask for written reports on those meetings, he would produce some small scrap of paper on which four or five points that had nothing to do with his alleged conversations with the dignitaries had been scribbled. Then we would plunge into a lengthy bargaining session about what part of his expenses should be covered and what his fee should be for his efforts. I was getting tired of this unreliable clown who never supplied any information of real value. I did not look foward to our meeting on that winter night.

I left my house about 6 P.M., drove to Yoyogi station, left the car in a side street, and took a train to Shinjuku where I boarded the subway for the thirty-minute ride to Ikebukuro. Leaving the subway car at the station, I detoured to the men's room before crossing the street from one of the exits to meet Edo. I was washing my hands in the restroom when I got that familiar feeling that someone was watching me. Since I knew that I hadn't been under surveillance up to this point, I knew that if there were surveillance here, it had begun here. That would have to mean that my surveillants had advance information about my scheduled meeting.

I went upstairs to the ground level and spotted Edo standing on the corner, waiting. Unable to shake the feeling that I was being followed, I went off in the opposite direction and set about thoroughly clearing my way, using several different techniques. It took about fifteen minutes for me to realize that a young man walking ahead of me, who seemed not to know where he was going, was actually performing the toughest job a surveillance team member can do: not following a target, but moving in front of him. To make sure that he was going in the proper direction, he had to stop every once in a while in shop entrances to see where I was going. Within another ten minutes or so, I'd verified that another three or four surveillants were behind me. Although I didn't trust Edo, I couldn't let them spot him. If he were the reason I was being followed, he would doubtless try again to entrap me, but if he weren't, I still had to protect him.

At a telephone I stopped and called my wife, making sure the surveillants could hear my conversation. "Where in hell have you been?" I shouted. "Did you forget that you were supposed to meet me here for dinner?"

"My God, Stas, are you in danger?"

"No, no, of course I won't wait. Good Lord, it would take you an hour and a half, and I'll bet you're not even dressed for it." Pausing as though I were listening to her, I added, "No, you go ahead and eat. I'll get something here."

"Do you need help?" she asked anxiously.

"No, no. I'm disappointed, though. Never mind, we'll do it another time."

After I had hung up, I went to the nearest *yakitori-ya,* ordered a meal, and sat down at a table facing a window so that I could watch the street. Directly across the street at a bus stop for two different routes, I noticed one particular man waiting. A bus came, a few people boarded, and the bus left. The man remained. Another bus came from the other line. He didn't leave on that one either. He was another member of the surveillance team, and I was literally blocked. All I could do was act naturally, finish my meal, and go home.

In making my routine report to the residency about the incident, I indicated my conviction that Edo was a double agent who posed a considerable threat to me. Noting that I found him to be inept and unreliable, I nonetheless recognized that he could reduce my effectiveness at best or destroy my cover at worst. I also declared my intention to test him, to verify my suspicions, or to exonerate him once and for all.

I had completed two more meetings with him when I knew for sure that he was a double agent. After one more meeting, I concluded he was of absolutely no value to the Soviets. He had become too greedy, too determined to make money. With the residency's approval, I finally let him know that his services were no longer needed.

It gave me real satisfaction to come to what I knew to be our last meeting without any money at all. When I didn't give him the customary yellow envelope, his face turned crimson. I thought for a moment that he'd have a stroke.

"You bastard!" he shouted. "You're supposed to pay me! By God, you'd better pay me, or I'll make a scandal!"

"Go ahead," I told him, "just go outside, find a policeman, and tell him you're a Soviet agent. Go on! Then we'll see who gets hurt worse, you or me."

I left the restaurant and went looking for a taxi. Edo caught up with me, grabbed my sleeve, and yelled up and down the street. "You're a thief and a cheat! You're mean and stingy! You aren't a good man!"

I put him in the first available taxi, and as I closed the door, I said, "Kindly make sure that I never see you again."

About two months later in the early hours of the morning, the phone rang. It was Edo, drunk, trying to say something but totally incoherent. I hung up and never heard from him again.

I was still a bit worried about the damage he might have caused. For several months I was especially careful in clearing my way to meetings and meticulous in maintaining my cover as a journalist. I saw no increase, however, in Japanese surveillance, which continued at the sporadic pace I was familiar with handling.

My work was clandestine, and I used sophisticated equipment such as radios, tape recorders, attaché cases that would destroy their contents if they were opened by unauthorized people, secret writing, and many kinds of cameras. Everything I did had to look normal and natural in case I was under surveillance. When I met my contacts, I had to be absolutely sure that I hadn't been followed. I was involved in the practicalities of the cloak-and-dagger game.

Generally speaking, surveillance by the Japanese wasn't rigorous; sometimes I'd go for three or four days without being tailed. But what there was of it was highly professional, and as the mouse in this cat-and-mouse game, I tried very hard not to alienate my surveillants. In fact, I managed to establish good rapport with the teams that covered the Soviet embassy. For example, sometimes when I'd park my car in a large parking lot, I wouldn't remember where I'd left it. If I knew I was under surveillance, I'd turn to the plainclothes man on duty and ask, "Do you remember where the hell I parked my car? I haven't the foggiest notion where I left the damned thing." Invariably, the surveillant would laugh and show me to my car.

On many occasions I would clear my way to a meeting with an agent by stopping first at the Press Center building in Uchisaiwaicho. No one was allowed to enter the place without a membership card, which had to be shown to the guard at the door. They were so strict about it that they wouldn't even let in Japanese counterintelligence agents. These agents wouldn't subject themselves to this rejection, which they found awkward and annoying. So, after following me there a few times, the surveillance men learned to ask me where I was going. It wasn't unusual to have one of them sidle up to me and say "Pardon me, sir, but are you on the way to the Press Center?" Many times they would leave me alone if I said that I was. They really hated the embarrassing scenes that occurred there.

In addition, they were so pitifully short-handed that they couldn't follow me or any other suspect on a regular or routine basis. That reason alone probably accounts for Japanese intelligence's spotty —though far from sloppy—surveillance practices.

There was one member of a Japanese surveillance team covering the Soviet embassy, a short little man with a round face, who didn't like me at all. I never learned why, but for some reason I agitated him. Once when I drove from the embassy to my home in Udagawa-cho, this officer followed me right to the door of my apartment and acted as though he intended to enter. There were a few tense moments when we almost got into a fistfight.

On September 6, 1976, Viktor Belenko, a senior lieutenant in the Soviet air force, flew from the Soviet Union in his MiG-25 and landed at the civilian airport on the Japanese island of Hokkaido. A furious Soviet embassy went into orbit! Despite a vigorous campaign in which they left no stone unturned trying to get Japan to return both pilot and plane, Belenko rebuffed a Soviet residency official in a relatively public encounter and refused to return to the Soviet Union. He requested political asylum in the United States. Japan allowed him to go to the United States, and the Americans had full access to the MiG and its equipment. The entire incident left all of us exhausted. Late that night as I was leaving the Soviet embassy, there was my little round-faced friend.

"Ha! Your pilot got killed!" he shouted. Obviously he didn't know that Belenko had not only escaped from the Soviet Union, but that he'd also succeeded in giving a valuable gift to the United States.

"We know all about your MiGs now!" he added.

"Go to hell!" I rejoined. That guy really got under my skin.

Since I've been in the United States, I've met Viktor Belenko, and we've become very close friends, but every time I mention the little round-faced man in Tokyo, he laughs uproariously and says, "I'm glad he bothered you! You deserved it."

He's right. I did deserve it.

Any kind of normal lifestyle is impossible for an intelligence officer. The hours are terrible. With some of the most important meetings scheduled in the middle of the night, I was rarely at home in the evenings. When I was, I'd usually be so tired that I'd fall asleep in my chair. Simple things that most people take for granted were impossible for me or, at best, a challenge. Walking out the front door to go to work? I couldn't do that because I was always on guard against being watched. Surveillance was rarely waiting for me at the apartment (the Japanese didn't have the manpower for that), but they did use the security guard to report on me. On the rare occasions when I would leave by the front door, the guard would register the time I left and make his report. For years I left through the fire exit. I just wouldn't have felt right walking out the front door as ordinary people do.

In the spring of 1977 the KGB's Eighth Directorate sent one of its communication experts to Japan on a three-month tour of duty. When he arrived, he was issued a visa that prohibited him from leaving Tokyo without first notifying the Japanese Foreign Ministry. His visit was hardly under way when I was summoned to the resident's office. The resident and the visiting officer were waiting for me when I went in.

"This gentleman needs to make a visual reconnaissance of the American base in Yokota," the resident began.

"OK," I answered.

"I don't think you understand, Stanislav," he continued. "This will be a risky mission because he's prohibited from leaving Tokyo without notifying the Foreign Ministry, and he doesn't intend to do that. You're going to have to take him."

I believe I whistled. Damn! I knew that this mission could turn nasty if we were caught by the Japanese police, and I said so.

"Well, then," the resident responded, "don't get caught. No matter what, don't get stopped by the police. You, Levchenko, are totally responsible for the security of the operation."

Double damn!

We chose the following Saturday as the best day of the week to go to Yokota. I had never been there before, certainly I'd never driven there before, and I asked for the most accurate maps and the most explicit instructions the residency could provide. My Eighth Director-ate partner compounded the problem by telling me that he needed to get as close as possible to the American installation in order to pinpoint all of their communication antennae. After I'd checked and rechecked the map and the instructions, we started. When we reached Yokota, we wound our way through the narrow streets. In no time at all, we were hopelessly lost: most of the narrow streets were not on the map.

Finally, we thought we had gotten ourselves turned in the right direction. Instead, we blundered right through the main gates of the base. "Holy shit!" my companion hissed. "We're in for it now!" The guards, hardly believing their eyes, started running after us with whistles blowing. One of them was even drawing his pistol.

I whipped the car around in a tight U-turn, screeched to a halt at the gate, forced an inane, drunken leer onto my face, leaned out the car window and said in drunken English, "I'm so sorry," slurring every other word. "So sorry, but we got lost. Damned roads aren't where they ought to be. Who moved the damned roads?"

The sentry grinned and waved us through. When I looked back in the rear-view mirror, they were staring after the car with their mouths open. The one who had waved us through was shaking his head.

For most of the time that I was in Japan—four long, grueling years—I worked twelve to fifteen hours a day. In a month I would average twenty to twenty-five meetings with agents or for developing contacts. Such a schedule violated all the rules of security, but my superiors demanded more and more of me; several of my agents had proven so valuable in supplying information that more and more was desired of them. Some days were nightmarishly exhausting. I remember one that I thought would never end.

As usual, I awoke at 7 A.M., and by 9:00 I was in the residency. At 9:15 I discussed plans with Deputy Resident Pronnikov for two meetings that were scheduled to take place that day, the first with Vassin and the second with Ares. By 9:30 I had sketched in the maps of the routes I intended to use to clear my path and had them ready to give to the officer who would be operating System Zenith, the communication system used for intercepting the messages between counterintelligence surveillance cars.

At 9:45 I left the embassy and set about clearing my way. First I went to Harajuku and pretended to shop. From there I drove to Shibuya, spending about half an hour driving through narrow side streets before making my way to Shinjuku, where I parked. For ten or fifteen minutes I wandered along side streets, stopping now and then to window-shop. All at once I looked at my watch as though I'd just remembered something important, rushed into the street, and hailed a taxi. I went by cab to Shimbashi and met with Vassin at noon in a coffee shop. Our meeting was over by 1:30, and Vassin left. I waited about ten minutes to give him time to get clear and then also left.

Taking a cab back to Shinjuku, I picked up the car and returned to the embassy at about 2:30. There I composed and filed my report on the meeting with Vassin before going to Pronnikov's office for a 5:00 P.M. conference about my evening meeting with Ares. I made arrangements with the System Zenith officer and then met the driver who would take me to the meeting site. We discussed the routes we would take and the place where we would rendezvous. Around 7:00 I stopped by my house, watched the evening news, glanced at the evening papers, and was out the door an hour later. I drove to a garden near the South Korean embassy, winding through side streets to be sure I wasn't being followed, and at 9:00 met the operational driver as planned. In his car we meandered our way to the meeting with Ares. It was 10:00 by the time we came to the residential area of Yagumo, where we circled the block to wait for Ares. After about fifteen minutes, I spotted him walking along the street and got out of the car to join him. Meanwhile, the operational driver continued to circle so that, should a surveillance team suddenly appear on the scene, he could pick me up and avoid a confrontation.

Ares and I strolled along the street, talking. Altogether, the meeting took us about twenty minutes, during which Ares passed me four rolls of film and I gave him a pay envelope. We set the time for our next meeting and said a quick *sayonara*. I returned to the car. The driver and I carefully navigated our way to a small restaurant on a side street where we stopped for a drink. Then the driver took the film back to the embassy while I returned to where I'd left my car. Finally, I could go home. I fell into bed after an eighteen-hour day that was by no means unusual.

Just as I was dropping off to sleep, I awoke with a start. I suddenly remembered that the driver taking the film back to the embassy was only a driver, and not a courier; I should have told him that the container would blow up if he tried to open it. The KGB uses special containers to transport film. These are metal boxes covered with black vinyl. Inside the box are six spaces to hold film rolls. After the rolls are inserted and the box is locked, it literally becomes a bomb. Any attempt to open it by a person not familiar with the lock ignites an explosive charge that incinerates the film inside within seconds. I myself could open the device only inside the KGB residency. Otherwise my instructions were: "If you feel any danger, or you are stopped by the police, press the trigger and throw the box out of the window of your car as far as you can." Even then, I could suffer some burns.

There could have been many innocent reasons for the driver to open the box. For instance, knowing that he carried film, he could have decided to take it out of its container to turn it over to his superior at the embassy. If he did, there would have been one hell of a fire.

It was too late to head off any possible danger. My meeting with Ares had taken place miles from the embassy, and by the time I had retrieved my car and driven home, the operational driver would have long since reached the residency. Cold-bloodedly, I decided to wait until morning. Fortunately, the container was opened by an expert at the embassy, and I didn't have to face the costs of this slip-up.

A source of another problem was the same Ares. Because he was considered one of the most valuable agents of the residency, a special electronic device had been installed in his car so that he could send an emergency signal directly to the roof of the Soviet embassy. This device was concealed in Ares' car radio. It consisted of just a few extra transistors inserted in the radio. In case of emergency, all he had to do was to turn on the radio and push a special button. Only a professional radio mechanic could recognize that this radio was unusual, and then only after taking it apart.

Ares, who liked sport cars and hated to let them grow old, was in the habit of buying a new car every three years. The KGB paid a large part of the purchase price. The day came when Ares felt he needed a new car. Within a few days after receiving cash from me, he became the proud owner of a brand new, sexy-looking car. In the past, he extracted his special radio from his old car before turning it over to the dealer, but this time he forgot. I could barely refrain from beating him up when he told me. The situation was desperate; if the new owner of the used car decided to take the radio in for repairs, within days, or maybe hours, Ares would be having a very depressing conversation with Japanese counterintelligence. Many of us would be put in jeopardy.

Keeping myself as cool as I could, I ordered Ares to go back to the dealership first thing the next morning. He had to tell the dealer a story that probably sounded idiotic: he liked his old radio, had gotten used to it, and thought it was better quality than the new one. In short, he wanted his old radio back. Fortunately, the dealer was not an overly suspicious person, and the ploy worked, but for me it was hard to forget or forgive such carelessness on Ares's part.

On the other hand, Ares recruited another agent for me, a government employee with access to sensitive information. He did it under my guidance, and everything worked out fine, but I never met that agent: all contacts with him were conducted by Ares himself. KGB headquarters, however, wanted me to produce material evidence that the recruitment in fact took place. They demanded that I be secretly present in the bar where Ares and his newly recruited agent exchanged documents and money.

To document the meeting I was provided with a special briefcase. It looked as ugly as millions of its brothers, but inside it was a hidden camera. To make a photo, I had to press a special hidden button in the handle of the briefcase. Then a small hole would open on the side of the case where the lens of the camera was mounted, and a photo would be taken within a split second. At least that's what the instructions said. Unfortunately, real life differs from books, especially in the field of intelligence.

I got the briefcase from the technical operations officer. We checked it in the residency; everything worked fine.

To conceal the real purpose of my visit to the bar, I took my wife with me to create the impression that we simply were there to have a couple of beers and a light dinner. We took a table located so that we could see every person entering the bar. I knew that Ares was supposed to meet his new agent, and I was getting ready to take their "family portrait."

Very soon, however, I realized the almost imbecilic awkwardness of the situation. The angle of the concealed camera was very narrow. To be sure I made a secret picture of the right man, I had literally to aim the briefcase at the target. How many people in your life have you seen in bars or restaurants aiming their briefcases at other people?

Soon Ares and his friend appeared. I totally forgot about my wife, turned my back to her, discreetly aimed the damn briefcase at the two men, and pressed the concealed button in its handle several times. I was very proud of myself: the tricky job was accomplished successfully, and no other patrons had looked too suspiciously at us. Headquarters would be satisfied.

But when I returned to the residency that night and woke up the technical operations officer to develop the film immediately, there was no limit to our disappointment. The film was blank. Everything in this operation was well planned, with one exception. The film in the camera was good for a brightly lit room, but not for a dimly lit beer bar where the whole action took place.

I don't know exactly when it was that I realized how miserably unhappy I was with this way of life. In retrospect, it seems to me that I realized it relatively early in my stay in Japan, but was kept so busy that I lacked the time to think about myself much. I do know that I wasn't alone in the unhappiness I felt. My colleagues often discussed the stress our kind of life caused on our families and on our mental and physical health. One man even declared that his pet cat was affected by it. With me, the impact was physical: I began waking from a sound sleep in a cold sweat. But the worst thing for me to endure was an uneven heartbeat I developed, for which the doctors were no help at all.

"It's stress," they said and prescribed Valium. I refused to take it. That's all I needed. Trying to stay alert enough while under sedation to clear a route, for example, makes a lot of sense, doesn't it?

I remember watching a nature film with Aleksandr in which the narrator signed off by saying that the law of the jungle is to "hunt and be hunted, eat and be eaten." "If that's true," I thought to myself, "then my life is a jungle. That's what I do. I hunt and I'm hunted. I'm both the hunter and the prey, and I hate it. There must be something to mankind that's more civilized than this!"

I knew in that instant that sooner or later I would have to find that better way. I was tired of the hunt and of the jungle in which I lived.

6

The Crucial
Decision

OUTER BANKS, NORTH CAROLINA

The hungry pelican disappeared into the distance, still escorted by the screaming gulls. I turned back to my homeward path, then stopped a moment to get my bearings. I was about even with the historical marker on the beach road that commemorates the wreck of the Huron, *a U.S. man-of-war that sank off this coast in 1877. I shivered a little as I looked back toward the treacherous, beckoning sea.*

"The Huron *and hundreds of other ships," I thought. "They've been coming to rest out there for three hundred years. No wonder they call these waters the graveyard of the Atlantic."*

But at this moment the sea was beautiful.

"I can understand the wrecks caused by storms," I mused. "The storms here can be deadly. But the wrecks that are caused by human error . . . those are the tragedies. God, how careful a man must be in what he decides to do."

JAPAN AND MOSCOW, 1978–1979

The agent called Ares was even more important than my narrative so far has revealed. He'd been recruited more than a decade before my arrival in Japan when he was a Kyodo news service executive, a position that provided him access to much invaluable information. Because of his personal friend in Japanese intelligence, Ares had supplied a veritable river of information. In return, he'd been rewarded at extravagant levels. Eventually, of course, the Japanese had become aware of the leak and had reassigned large numbers of their personnel to different positions, effectively neutralizing Ares's supplier. As a result, Ares had been relatively useless for the following three years, although the Soviet Union continued to pay him more than $1,000 a month. When he was turned over to me, I was told my primary task was to get him producing again.

My first step was to analyze everything I knew about him and to review the residency's files on him, of which there were volumes. Files notwithstanding, I still put him through the MICE test. I already knew about his ability to compromise his convictions and his love of money—the "C" and "M" in MICE. I also knew that Ares was a very handsome man and had an ample supply of "E" (ego). Three out of four isn't a bad place to start. Ares had developed a love of luxury and a taste for the good life, which required a great deal of money—KGB money. As soon as I realized this, the way to get to him was obvious. First, we'd cut off his payments for several months, long enough to put a decided crimp in his lifestyle. Then, when we began letting him have a little money again, I'd let him know subtly but firmly that the payments would dry up again unless the flow of relevant information resumed.

As we shall see, this tactic worked well, and Ares became productive again. Ironically, in October 1979, a few days before my nerve-wracking escape, agent Ares delivered to me an important document for which the KGB had been hunting for years.

Too bad there wasn't something as relatively simple as a MICE test to help me straighten out my personal life. I was working such long hours that I was able to see my son only in the mornings. Most nights I got home so late I didn't see my wife (at least not awake). As we'd been warned in Moscow, the demands made on a KGB agent's

127

family can strain the marital bonds uniting even the most devoted of couples. We were no exception.

A compounding factor in Natalia's growing sense of emotional isolation was where we lived: we were some six kilometers from the embassy with no other Soviet families as neighbors. She couldn't speak Japanese, either. Naturally, Natalia felt lonely and frustrated. Sometimes she felt so alone that she'd burst into tears the moment I walked in the door. I felt awful for her and for myself, too. I had to take a great deal of the blame for creating this terrible situation. In my very first interview with Pronnikov he had made it clear that if I asked him as a personal favor, my "beautiful wife" could get a job. I was too proud and too stubborn to ask. Two years after we arrived in Japan, Natalia finally got a job with the consular section of the embassy and quickly rose to a supervisory position. Her duties left her exhausted. At the end of the day she needed companionship, maybe even a little comforting. But I couldn't give it. On the rare nights I was at home, I was too caught up in my own moral and spiritual dilemma. She interpreted my brooding silences as rejection, both as a wife and as a lover.

"Don't you love me any more?"

"Certainly I love you, Natasha. Of course I love you."

"Well, why don't you show it then?"

"Oh, God, Natasha, I'm always so tired!"

Sometimes I'd try to sound her out, hinting that my frustrations with my job were getting critical. "I don't know how long I can keep this up," I'd say. "I feel so dirty, so awful about the things I'm doing to decent, well-meaning people."

"You're just tired, darling," she'd answer. "You'll feel better after a good night's sleep."

It was always at this point that I would lapse into silence. There was no use trying to make her understand. She'd been born into a family of old Bolsheviks. Her father had taken an active part in the October Revolution and the Civil War that followed. Even after his imprisonment on false charges for a period of two years in the 1930s, he'd remained a faithful Communist. He'd brought Natalia up to be very patriotic, and she brooked no criticism of the Soviet Union.

It is painful for me in retrospect to realize how little of myself I really shared with Natalia. Aside from these few hints, I never told her anything at all about my depression or of the revulsion I felt at the things I did. Never once in all the years we were married did I tell her that I had a strong religious faith. She would have been horrified, I think. When I began suffering from the sleeplessness and uneven heart rhythm, I honestly believe that Natalia thought I had brought it on myself by being a workaholic.

Of course, I clearly recognized my role in Natalia's unhappiness. After all, she knew what my job was about, though she was kept as far away from the specific details as possible. If I left the house at 9:00 P.M. and didn't return until 3:00 A.M., she didn't sleep; she worried. Not knowing is often more nerve-wracking than knowing. This is just another reason why the divorce rate among KGB officers is astronomically high.

Soon after our arrival in Tokyo, a team from TV Channel 6 prepared a painfully ironic program on our family called "Foreigner in Tokyo." Thinking that it might be interesting for viewers to glimpse the *New Times* correspondent's life in Tokyo, the Channel 6 people filmed a fine, beautifully presented program of a happy family that bore little resemblance to our situation. Naturally, they never realized that the *New Times* correspondent was actually a spy.

Natalia sometimes had to be involved in my intelligence operations. It was a condition she had, if not agreed to, at least accepted when she had first been interviewed by the colonel in charge of my section during my KGB officer's training. There were times when I had to involve her. For instance, some of my most sensitive meetings with Ares took place outside of Tokyo. To create a logical reason for traveling sixty kilometers or more outside the city, I'd take Natalia with me so that an onlooker would think we were on a family outing. She knew what those sightseeing trips were designed for, but she was never present at an actual meeting with an agent. This not only shielded her from any deeper involvement than was necessary, but also assured that only the essential people were present, which made it easier to cover one's tracks. As for the trips outside of Tokyo, we both really enjoyed them because they were the few times we could share a bit of leisure.

When our son graduated from the elementary school at the Soviet embassy in 1978, he had to return to Moscow. From then on he could only visit Tokyo in the summer months, but even then I couldn't be with him or Natalia as much as I should have. The tensions escalated. Still, I'll never forget the shock of discovering just how critical things had become. One night, very late, I'd just come in and Natalia had gotten up to get me a bite to eat. Then, very calmly, she said, "I can't take much more of this kind of life, Stas. Let's face it, we're going to end up getting a divorce."

I was shattered. Natalia was a fine, courageous woman who had always been loyal and supportive, rarely complaining about what couldn't be changed. I calmed her down, told her how much I loved her, and held her as she cried. We made up that night, but the truth was now out. Deep inside I knew that she was right. Sooner or later we would end in divorce.

One aspect of my life that I'd been warned about in Moscow needs special attention because it added much stress to an already stressful way of life: Deputy Resident Vladimir Pronnikov. My failure to ask Pronnikov to get Natalia a job at the embassy wasn't completely rooted in pride. From my very first meeting with him in 1975, I knew that Pronnikov's brilliance and lust for power created and shaped the way he manipulated his own agents and the people in the residency. Rightly or wrongly, I left that meeting knowing that I would never ask him for any favor, regardless of how small it might be, because any concession he granted anyone would have long-reaching strings attached.

Pronnikov may have been devious, but he certainly knew how to play the game. He could seem generous, expansive, and kindly, or ruthless, unforgiving, and merciless. He could seem suave and urbane or coarse and crude. But whatever attitude he assumed, he was always in control of the way he appeared to others, always adopting, chameleonlike, the stance and the demeanor that he felt best suited his purposes. When I first succeeded in recruiting King, Pronnikov was one of the first to offer congratulations, but his choice of words made his praises seem more a pat on his own back than on mine.

"Well done," he said, "my predictions have come true, and I'm so glad that I could help you. I gave you a free hand in this case, and you rewarded my judgment."

Though our relationship was adversarial, it was always professional. I think he felt that although I was always noncommittal in my dealings with him, there was something different about me, some unpredictable quality that he couldn't define. Had I chosen, I could have defined it for him easily: I didn't trust him.

I watched him ruin Resident Yerokhin about as smoothly as it will ever be done. Yerokhin had been assigned to the Tokyo embassy after completing a spectacularly successful assignment in New Delhi. From the moment of Yerokhin's appointment as resident, Pronnikov viewed him as a threat to his own ambitions. He was younger than Pronnikov, who doubtless feared that Yerokhin might therefore settle into the top seat for longer than Pronnikov could spend waiting him out.

Yerokhin had brought with him from New Delhi a trusted aide, the previously mentioned Lieutenant Colonel Gennadi Yevstafyev, to whom he'd promised a promotion. When that advancement was slow in coming, Yevstafyev became perceptibly restless, and Pronnikov moved in on him. First he hinted to Yevstafyev that Yerokhin intended to promote someone else over him. Next, he ran to Yerokhin with the tale that Yevstafyev was slandering him. Pronnikov kept going from one to the other, gradually convincing Yerokhin that Yevstafyev was suffering a nervous breakdown. At the same time he was feeding Yevstafyev's anger at what he viewed as Yerokhin's betrayal.

That the two principals in this drama never got together to compare notes is typical Soviet behavior. Soviets always fear and mistrust each other, particularly when the chips are down. It's part of the national psyche.

Finally Resident Yerokhin demanded that his superiors in Moscow "remove this madman Yevstafyev." When Yevstafyev was recalled to Moscow on grounds of mental incompetence, it turned out he had a few tricks up his own sleeve. He went straight from the airport to a KGB hospital where he demanded a complete psychiatric examination. The verdict: he was both sane and normal. In triumph, he took his clean bill of mental health and presented it to KGB headquarters, together with his own carefully prepared complaint against Yerokhin.

A Communist party commission brought charges against Yerokhin for "slander against a brother officer." Yerokhin was recalled to Moscow to await the outcome of the case. To no one's surprise, Pronnikov became acting resident. During the investigation Pronnikov wrote letters that praised both Yerokhin and Yevstafyev but corroborated the account given by Yevstafyev. Yerokhin was quietly exiled to the Border Guards; Gennadi Yevstafyev went on to become an assistant secretary general of the United Nations, a position he still held in 1985.

I thought Yerokhin's removal by such means was a vile, debased act. Rashly, I allowed others to see my anger.

"Pronnikov! The sooner he goes back to Moscow, the better off we'll all be," I said. The next day, as I was passing Pronnikov's door, he called me in.

"I've heard about what you said yesterday," he said in a dangerously soft voice. I didn't respond. "Levchenko, for those words I will never forgive you. From now on, if you want your head to stay on your shoulders, walk carefully."

He meant every word of it. I rarely saw him from that moment until he returned to Moscow to become the deputy director of the Seventh Department of the First Chief Directorate. When he left, I refused to attend his farewell party.

During all those years in Japan, I could never be the friend to my host country that I wanted to be, a fact that saddens me still. Oh how I studied Japan: its decision-making mechanisms, its way of life, its national psychology, its moral values, its culture. The more I studied, the more I loved Japan. But the sad fact is that all this knowledge and experience was a tool with which to stab Japan in the back in my role as a KGB officer.

My life was divided into four separate and unharmonious parts. The first, and of necessity the major part, was the time spent in the KGB's Tokyo residency, a place no different from the KGB headquarters in Moscow—same office intrigues, same militaristic discipline, same piles of paperwork. The second part was spent in employing all of my professional skills to induce contacts and agents to work against their own country. The third part was maintaining my cover by functioning as a journalist. Only when I was interviewing Japanese politicians or journalists for the *New Times* magazine did I feel good about myself. It was a straight job that had nothing whatever to do with my intelligence-gathering work.

The fourth part was at home with my family, the crumbling mortar that had to fit between and bind together my other three identities. All too often I had nightmares of meetings with strange, threatening people or of being caught by Japanese counterintelligence. At other times, gratefully, I'd slip into more tranquil dreams of my homeland.

We went back to Moscow on periodic visits for vacations, and the cold realities of my homeland refuted the sweet stuff of my dreams. Every time we went home, the first thing I'd have to do was report to all of my superiors at KGB headquarters. On each visit I'd hear the same litany of questions: "Why can't you recruit more? Why couldn't you get such and such information? When you get back, do this! Do that!"

Yet life outside KGB headquarters seemed even gloomier and

darker than inside. I'd look into the faces of pedestrians and be stung by the sadness, the concern, even the anger I'd see in their eyes. I couldn't help comparing those faces with the ones in Japan, which broke into smiles and laughter at little provocation. And the corruption in the Soviet Union! Each time we visited Moscow it was worse, growing like a cancer out of control.

On one visit Natalia wanted to buy some knitting worsted to take back to Tokyo with us, so she asked her sister if such yarns were very expensive. "No," was the answer, "but they'll still cost you quite a bit of money."

"Why?" Natalia asked. "That doesn't make any sense."

"Oh, you'll have to slip the clerk a bribe or she'll swear up and down that they don't have any. It's that way everywhere. You want the best bread, you bribe the baker. You want good meat, you bribe the butcher."

I found that to be true all over Moscow. I was once stopped by a policeman for a minor traffic violation, one for which I should have been given no more than a mere caution. "Oh, come on," I pleaded. "I've been in Japan for years, and this is a new regulation. Why can't you just give me a warning and let me go?"

"What will you give me from Japan if I do?" he asked. I searched around in my overcoat pocket and found one of those trick match folders that have little three-dimensional cards fastened to their backs for advertising various bars or cafés. When they're riffled, they give the effect of motion pictures. This one advertised a bar in Tokyo called the Friendly Lady and showed an innocuous winking girl. He was delighted with it and forgot all about my traffic violation.

I was furious with the Soviet leaders who had failed to establish anything close to prosperity, who never intended to establish any semblance of democracy, and who fed their people nauseating propaganda to alienate them from people in free societies around the world. Every time I returned to Tokyo, I was stirred to the core just knowing that I once again stood on free soil. Each time I returned, I was sadder and more discontented. I was filled with self-loathing and contempt at what I saw myself doing: planting stories in newspapers, spreading malicious rumors that sometimes reached (and hurt) high-ranking officials, and constantly recruiting more agents from among the Japanese.

Since the evening I watched that TV show with my son and when I admitted to myself that there had to be a better way to live, a little worrisome doubt lay at the back of my mind. Sooner or later, I'd have to face facts. When I finally got down to facing those facts, the process was unbelievably painful. I had to admit that I was by nature a workaholic; Natalia would have been the first to agree. As a result, my work had always been at a high-performance level and nearly non-stop. For the first years of my Tokyo assignment, I'd worked hard because I was convinced that what I was doing would benefit my people. I finally realized that I was indeed helping my people, but I was only helping them to become more deeply enslaved by the Soviet system. By the time I'd realized that, I was already into the job. I worked on and on like an automaton, trying not to notice what I was actually doing by the simple expedient of working harder and harder. It was stupid, no doubt, but it almost worked, for much of the time I was too tired to notice.

My KGB career had flourished, it's true, but I was nearing the end of my tour of duty in Japan. I was due to be recalled to Moscow any time after October 1979, and there were those in Moscow who had mixed feelings about me. In the first place, I'd be assigned to the Seventh Department of the KGB's First Chief Directorate, and the deputy director of that department was Vladimir Pronnikov, a declared and dangerous enemy. Feeling as he did that I was different from other KGB officers, he had tried his damnedest to slow my promotions while we were in Tokyo. I had no doubt that he would do the same or worse if I were under his command again in Moscow.

Though my KGB career was established and my professional record was exemplary, by 1977 I had grown to hate my decision to become a KGB officer. I hated having fallen for the argument that I should become a "courageous warrior and do a man's work" for the Soviet Union. Gradually, agonizingly, I admitted my eternal regret for what I'd done to Japan. Somehow, I knew I'd have to find forgiveness.

At the age of thirty-seven, I finally comprehended that I was on the wrong side.

Sometimes I still see Russia in my dreams—majestic pine groves, quiet silky rivers, magnificent old churches, icy patterns painted on the windows on frosty days. In those dreams I feel a longing for the country of my birth. But sometimes those dreams turn into nightmares in which I see hordes of people herded into labor camps and priests struggling to keep their faith and dignity in wretched prisons. I know that I'll have these dreams and nightmares for the rest of my life.

When one loves his countrymen as much as I love mine, it's a wrenchingly painful thing to decide that everything one has done to help them has been in vain. I knew only too well that what benefits the Soviet system does not benefit Soviet citizens. People are pawns in the game, as far as the KGB and the Politburo of the Communist party are concerned. Once the blinders fell from my eyes, I knew that to continue the work I was engaged in was impossible.

The next step was to decide what I could do about it. It was a long time before I could articulate it. Even to myself, I couldn't easily bring myself to say the words, "Stanislav Levchenko, you are going to have to request political asylum in the United States of America." Like anyone anywhere, I tended to confuse loyalty to a country with loyalty to the regime and therefore to wonder if the act of becoming a political refugee were not an act of treason against my people. Before I could do another thing, I had to answer that question to my own satisfaction.

At first I considered the possibility of trying to fight the Soviet system from within, as many dissidents do. But as a KGB major, I realized that what happened ultimately to dissidents would necessarily happen to me as soon as I spoke the first dissenting word. I'd be slapped into prison or locked in a mental institution. That's what they do in the Soviet Union to those who speak out against the system. The logic they use is that anyone who opposes the system is demonstrably insane. Once in the mental institution, the dissident is "treated" by means of brainwashing. If he persists in his deviant behavior, he is pronounced incurable. The treatment for incurables is a regimen of drugs that eventually reduces them mentally to vegetables.

I recalled that moment in my childhood when my father, tormented and disillusioned by the revelations of the Beria trials during Stalin's reign, had cried out in anguish over his disbelief that a Soviet leader could commit such atrocities against his own people. I remembered my early realization, never quite eclipsed by the mists of time, that the Russia my father loved—that all Russians love—and the Soviet Union were not the same thing at all. I summoned up the image, unfading, deeply alive, of the real Mother Russia, she of the courageous, long-suffering, spirited people who deserve far more than their leaders are giving. And I had my answer.

"Oh, no," I finally thought, "I'm not the one who is the traitor. If I leave the Soviet Union to live in another place, I'll not be the betrayer. If people want to know who the real betrayers of the Russian people are, let them look to the Communist party and its new elite."

I'd reached a turning point in my life, and I'd never felt more alone. Never let anyone tell you that it's easy to leave the country where you were born and raised and to go into voluntary exile. It isn't. I could confide in no one, seek no one's advice. There was nowhere I could turn to discuss my discontent. I knew that if I undertook this course, I'd have to do it alone and remain alone, never seeing loved ones and friends again. The agony of mind caused by this knowledge was so intense that I came close to deciding that the price I'd have to pay for my freedom was too high.

Aleksandr, my little son, was in school in Moscow. I didn't dare mention my feelings to my wife. As devoted as she was to the Soviet Union, it wouldn't have been safe. Our marriage had reached a point where divorce was inevitable, so I was reasonably certain that even without her extremely strong patriotism, Natalia would never have considered coming with me to the United States. My greatest concern (and justifiably, as it turned out) was for Natalia's and Aleksandr's safety in the Soviet Union should I change sides.

In assessing the situation, I considered two things. Aleksandr was a child. "Even the KGB doesn't prey on children," I told myself. Next, there was Natalia. Her credentials with the party were impeccable, both through her family's long history of absolute loyalty and her own record. I was certain the KGB file on Natalia was at least as complete as my own dossier. I also knew that Natalia would never have made a move that could have suggested any disloyalty on her part.

"Yes," I reasoned, "Natalia and Aleksandr will be safe." In all honesty, if I could go back to those initial days when I was reasoning this through, knowing what I know now about what happened to those two dearly loved people, I'm not at all sure that I'd make the same decision.

But at the time, I felt as if I was submerged in cold water. Nothing could make me feel warm even in the humid heat of the Tokyo summer. I needed tenderness, just as I had as a wrongfully punished child. And I tried to find that tenderness in brief romantic affairs with members of the Soviet theater and dance groups that visited Japan.

I had a brief affair with a woman who worked for the Soviet puppet theater, and later I reflected on the irony of the situation. She was a famous puppeteer. Her puppets made people laugh, made them sad, happy, or angry. When a puppeteer is good, many people in the audience forget that they are seeing dolls. They see the dolls as people. I reflected that I was just like a puppet, except that my manipulators were thousands of miles away in Moscow, in the KGB headquarters. Even they were manipulated by master puppeteers whose offices were located in the Kremlin.

Another romance I had was with a beautiful, tall, blond ballerina who came to Japan with an amateur group. She became very interested in me in a matter of days, and I got involved in this romance rather deeply. One night I drove five hundred miles from Tokyo to Osaka where the group was performing, just to spend a couple of hours with her. But this short-lived love left a bitter taste. I knew that my new girlfriend admired me not for my human qualities, but because she was fascinated by my profession. She was convinced that there was no better job than to spy for the Soviet motherland, and she thought I was a hero. She loved me for what I most despised about myself. Another disappointment!

Meanwhile, my professional life went on as usual. The internal intrigues in the residency had cooled down after Pronnikov was recalled to Moscow in 1977. We all hoped that his elevation to a higher rung on the career ladder would keep his interest centered in Moscow, so that we could breathe a bit in Tokyo. As we were to learn, however, his interests were everywhere. Those of us he'd left behind in Tokyo were far from forgotten. My one source of satisfaction about my problems with Pronnikov was the fact that his superior, Deputy Director of the First Chief Directorate Major General Popov, held me in high esteem and considered me to be an accomplished intelligence officer. When I was moved to active measures in the Tokyo residency, I was apparently accepted as an officer capable of implementing sensitive actions. In 1978 I became one of four or five officers in the KGB residency's think tank.

Although my tour of duty in Japan was scheduled to end in October 1979, if I had stumbled the least little bit or made some embarrassing political blunder along the way, I could have been yanked out and sent home at a moment's notice. I also knew that time was slipping away entirely too fast for me to delay much longer, but I simply wasn't yet ready to make a final commitment. Then something happened that made me realize just how short the time was getting.

I was in the resident's office one morning when his secretary buzzed through on the intercom. The resident listened a moment, then said, "Send him in."

"Shall I leave?" I asked.

"No, this will only take a moment."

The door opened to admit an officer whom I knew by sight only. I think he worked in communications somewhere.

"Come in, come in," said the resident with what I thought was a false heartiness. "We've just received a special message from Moscow, and they need you back as soon as we can get you there. Here's your plane ticket. There's a driver waiting downstairs to take you to the airport."

"What about my family? Will I be coming back? What—," he sputtered before the resident interrupted him.

"Just call your wife. Tell her you're on your way to Moscow and that she and the children will follow in a few days. We'll see to packing and returning your household effects. Now, you must hurry. Maybe you'd better wait until you're at the airport to call. You mustn't miss that flight."

As soon as he had hurried from the room, I asked, "A promotion?"

"No," he explained, shaking his head sadly, "the poor devil's in serious trouble of some kind. He just won't know it until he walks into headquarters."

I too could be returned to Moscow at a moment's notice. I'd just seen it happen to another with my own eyes. As a consequence of that incident I took pains to maintain my high level of work. I was under the sword of Damocles; I had to keep all risks to a minimum. By late spring and early summer Pronnikov was so firmly entrenched in the Seventh Department in Moscow that those of us in Tokyo were often made aware of his interest in us. I was particularly aware of his far-reaching and unsympathetic interest in me. I knew that the caliber of my work could not falter, or I would be whisked back to Moscow before I could have a chance to think through my personal dilemma. I had no intention of becoming one of the expelled officers. Even if I were to return to Moscow in the normal rotation, Pronnikov was still there gunning for me. As events unfolded during my last months in Japan, I became increasingly aware that he was just waiting to pounce.

The incident regarding agent Thomas was the final proof I needed that Pronnikov was my enemy. Thomas was a senior correspondent with Japan's largest newspaper, a successful author, and a well-received political analyst. He had been wooed by various KGB officers for about eighteen months before being turned over to me for what we all hoped would be a successful recruitment. He knew everyone of importance, including Japan's high-ranking government officials. When I took him over, I found to my delight that I thoroughly enjoyed my conversations with him. He was sophisticated and witty, cultured and urbane. He lived well, wore expensive clothes, and obviously liked the finest restaurants and meeting places. I judged early on that Thomas would welcome some additional income, so I offered him the opportunity to contribute articles to the non-existent newsletter, the same one I had used so often before to lure potential agents. "For a fee, of course," I told him. "We really need your expertise."

He accepted; this was the same man who had resisted various other KGB officers. The only way I can account for his change of heart is that I must've caught him at a moment when he needed money badly. (Money—the first weakness to look for—as in MICE.) Because I still wasn't sure that Thomas was willing to go all the way with us, I asked him to plant certain stories in the press. He did so without any questions whatsoever. The more he aided us in this way, the more I suspected that he knew he was dealing with Soviet intelligence. Then Thomas told me something straight out of a spy novel.

"The U.S. government is going to announce that the Lockheed Aircraft Corporation has paid huge sums in bribes to highly placed Japanese officials to guarantee that they will win Japanese contracts."

When I reported what Thomas had told me, my superiors were skeptical. "That can't possibly be true," one officer protested. "It's too sensational to be the least bit credible." "My God, such a scandal would cause heads to roll all over Tokyo," said another.

Several weeks later the Lockheed story broke, proving that Thomas was correct. The story behind the scandal caused political upheaval in Japan and political repercussions in the United States. During the mid-1970s Lockheed Aircraft Corporation had received large sums of money from the U.S. government in order to keep it solvent. The scandal from the U.S. point of view was that Lockheed was using American taxpayers' money to bribe Japanese officials for Lockheed's profit. By extension, the American taxpayers could be said to be bribing Japanese officials, with Lockheed merely acting as the middleman. The American government was furious, the Japanese government was embarrassed, and the Soviets, because they hadn't believed my agent Thomas, had missed the opportunity to capitalize (if you'll pardon the expression) on the scandal.

I had already been convinced that Thomas was genuine and that he could be extremely useful. After this incident I recommended that Thomas be included in the embassy's network. The new resident concurred, so I submitted a formal recommendation to that effect, and we sent it on to Moscow.

After Pronnikov's departure for Moscow, the new resident, Colonel Oleg Guryanov, had taken over control of the Tokyo residency. He wasn't from the Seventh Department; he had served as the resident in the Netherlands and, later, as the senior officer in Havana. I liked him. He was personable, clever, and capable. From the first meeting he'd had with us after his arrival, he'd established an *esprit de corps* that had been totally lacking under Pronnikov. He never mentioned the upheavals that had resulted in the recalls of Yerokhin and Yevstafyev to Moscow and that had coincidentally propelled Pronnikov into the upper echelons of the Seventh Department. It was clear that Guryanov was the kind of troubleshooter who could establish order. In no time at all, he had the residency in shape and all of us working together smoothly.

Several weeks after I'd recommended Thomas, Guryanov called me into his office. "Well, Stanislav, it's bad news. Now don't lose your temper. . . ."

"What's happened?"

"Your request for the inclusion of Thomas in the network has been turned down," he answered, "and turned down in a thirty-six-page diatribe the likes of which I've never seen in my life."

"Over whose signature?"

"Vladimir Pronnikov's."

"It figures," I answered.

I was mad as hell. That son of a bitch knew I was right. I knew he knew it, and back in Moscow he'd be sitting at his desk gloating over having put me in my place.

"Never mind," said Guryanov. "Our time will come."

It wasn't long after that incident that my high-ranking advocate, First Directorate Deputy Director Major General Popov, visited the Tokyo residency. Having met him at the center in Moscow, I was gratified that he remembered me and flattered that he took the time to look me up at the residency. After a few minutes of small talk, he adopted a serious tone. "Does all go well here with you?"

On the spur of the moment I decided to bring up the Thomas case. "Well, sir, there's something I don't understand," I began, providing him with a complete rundown on what kinds of information Thomas had supplied, the work he'd done as an agent, and his reliability in general. I finished by showing Popov the center's reply to my request that Thomas be included in the residency network.

"And look at this," I said when he'd finished reading Pronnikov's reply. "Resident Guryanov was interested enough in Thomas's reliability to research these statistics. Roughly half of the intelligence supplied by Thomas has been so valuable and accurate that it's been sent from the center directly to the Politburo."

"That damned Pronnikov!" responded Popov, almost spitting out the words. "He gave me this bloody paper to sign one night when I was so damned tired I was groggy. I did what I try never to do, initialed it without reading it. This is a terrible injustice." After he and I had both calmed down a little, he added, "Trust me to set this right, Stanislav."

When I reported the meeting with General Popov to Guryanov, he said "Let's hope Pronnikov doesn't talk him out of it once he's back in Moscow."

"I don't think he will, sir."

"Why not?"

"Because he was still calling me by my first name when he left. In the center they used to say that when Popov used a person's first name, it was a commitment." As it turned out, only a few days after Popov's return to Moscow, the center cabled its approval to include Thomas in the network and offered congratulations to me.

That happened in the early summer of 1978, just before we went back to Moscow for our last leave before my tour of duty was scheduled to end in 1979. When I arrived in Moscow, my first duty was to report to the center for debriefing by my superiors. Traditional though this visit might be, I knew that it occurred not only for reasons of protocol, but also as a visit that could have a profound effect on a person's career in many ways. If a man were in trouble, sometimes he would receive no hint of it at his residency. But when he made his call at the center—ah! Then the axe would fall.

When I got to the First Directorate building, I was filled with trepidation. I knew that the agent Thomas incident would be fresh in Pronnikov's mind. The most nerve-wracking thing of all was that he was the first man I'd have to face.

As I'd expected, Pronnikov was cool, terse, and businesslike in the preliminary conversation. As our talk was drawing to a close, he leaned toward me and said, very softly, "I underestimated you."

Here it comes, I thought. He's getting ready to move in for the kill.

"You shouldn't have gone over my head to Popov." He let the silence stretch. I didn't do a thing to break it.

"For that alone I should strike back." Another silence. "But I'm too big a man to harbor grudges." Another silence stretched on and on. Finally he added, "Enjoy your vacation."

I had survived. I got out of his office and took a deep breath. This time, I would be going back to Japan. But sooner than I wanted to accept, I would be reassigned to Moscow, and Pronnikov would be there, waiting like the spider in its web. I didn't like one little bit the image of myself as the fly.

I often think about Pronnikov because his type isn't uncommon; certainly it isn't limited to the Soviet Union. That he was brilliant and good at his job is undeniable. Equally undeniable is that he saw those who worked for him as mere appendages to his own life. When his subordinates performed well, it was proof to him that he himself—the brain of that extended body—had given the proper directions. On the other hand, when his subordinates thought, reasoned, or acted independently, they became threats to him. This attitude alone, I believe, accounts for the antagonism that existed between us. He thought I was different because I thought too much. To him, I was an enigma that he could never stop trying to solve and understand or destroy. This made him as big a threat to me as I was to him, mainly because I hadn't yet solved the puzzle of my own intentions. I couldn't let him probe too deeply because I didn't know myself what was really inside me. Until I did, I'd have to resist his probes.

Time, meanwhile, was ticking away too quickly. I was working long, exhausting hours, which, combined with my inner anguish, took a toll on my health. More and more, I suffered from cardiac arrhythmia in reaction to the stress I was under.

Even now, I can't pinpoint the moment when I knew I'd ask for political asylum in the United States. All at once, it was simply a fact, it seemed I'd intended to do it for a long, long time. Once my decision was finally made, my good health returned. Invigorated by the process of carefully planning and logically implementing my overture toward the U.S. government, I reached yet another milestone conclusion. I recognized myself as an example of the "I" in MICE, spurred by ideology to seek political asylum. I swore to myself that if I were accepted into the United States, I would devote my life to fighting the

Soviet socialist system as I never could by remaining within it—fighting for the liberation of my country and people.

I knew that when the time came to act on this most crucial decision of my life, it would have to be done swiftly and suddenly. One morning I would wake up and know that "Today's the day!" That morning came on October 24, 1979.

7
Just a Few More Steps

OUTER BANKS, NORTH CAROLINA

Darkness falls swiftly over the Outer Banks, as it seems to throughout the South, and I began to walk faster. Twilight is always the loneliest time of the day to me, and now I was completely alone, both there on the beach and with my memories—memories that even now can make my heart beat faster and my breath catch in my throat.

Then I saw it, the steep incline leading up to the steps in the cleft between the sand dunes.

It's not much farther, I said to myself. Just a few more steps and I'll be home.

TOKYO, OCTOBER 1979

Whenever I remember the year 1979, I live again the emptiness of being constantly too tired, aching with pain at the ever-widening gulf between Natalia and me, and the constant anxious wondering: "Shall I go? Will I stay? I can't bear this corrupt system! I have to go!" But once I had made the irreversible decision to request political asylum in the United States, I was the perfect KGB officer, facing the moments of danger with a coolness I had never before experienced as I went about preparing to take the final step.

In many ways 1979 was my most productive year for the KGB. Yet thanks to Pronnikov, it was the one for which I received the least credit. I expected no less from him, even though when I paid him a last courtesy call a day or two before leaving Moscow at the end of my last home leave, he seemed surprisingly cordial.

"I worry about you," he said. "They have given you too heavy a case load, much too heavy for anyone to carry without making mistakes along the way. Tell you what, Stanislav, why don't you write me a little personal note every now and again? Just let me know how you are and how things are going for you personally. Will you promise to do that?"

"Of course I'll write," I answered. "It's nice of you to be concerned."

There it was again, the Soviet approach that I've since dubbed "cynicism unlimited." Pronnikov lies to me ("I'm worried about you, Stanislav"), and I lie to him ("Of course I'll write" and "It's nice of you"); he knows that I know he doesn't give a damn about me, and I know that he knows I don't think he's nice.

Then, after all the warmth and concern he expressed, he was responsible for depriving me of the recognition that should've been mine for the recruitment of two valuable agents. By that time it simply didn't matter to me. I viewed each of my actions as merely one more inequity to add to my feelings of guilt. Resident Guryanov was very upset on my behalf. I told him it didn't matter to me at all.

I don't think he believed me, but it was true. I was completely indifferent. I no longer needed additional proof of KGB corruption. I'd long since accepted such corruption as the Soviet way of life, and my

149

own cynicism was boundless. After my experience in Moscow with the traffic cop and the Japanese matchbook, I talked with some KGB officers stationed in Moscow who told me I hadn't even seen the tip of the iceberg.

"When you were stationed here, I'll bet you never even heard of KGB officers trading in black market goods. I'm not talking about *buying*. I mean *selling* black market items," one officer remarked.

"Why, just the other day a KGB officer was arrested for selling Japanese cassettes openly on the street," another continued. "He turned out to be a full colonel."

"And I heard something else," the first one interrupted. "The people at the top are getting pretty upset, I'll tell you. I heard from a friend who really knows that the Ministry of Foreign Affairs considers this wave of corruption to be critical. He says that the American CIA is literally harvesting people from their department."

"You're telling me that corruption is that widespread?" I asked.

"We haven't begun to tell you how bad it is."

Just before leaving Moscow for the last time, I went to church—openly and honestly. I prayed for help and strength in my own crisis, and I didn't care who might have seen me.

Back in Tokyo I became more involved with operations other than my own. I knew that much of this was the result of the trust Resident Guryanov had in me, yet the increase in my workload was almost intolerable. One of the most dangerous incidents of my career as a KGB officer came about because of this extension of my duties.

One of the residency's most carefully guarded secrets was the existence of an agent code-named Nazar, who was a Japanese Foreign Ministry code clerk. Only a handful of officers knew of him: the resident, of course, and the men who handled him, Major Valeri Ivanovich Umansky and, later, Major Valentin Nikolaevich Belov, and finally, when it became essential for me to know, me (however, I never knew his real name). The KGB very rarely met with Nazar. When he had something to give them, he'd leave it in hidden dead-drop sites or transmit it by means of a brush pass with his case officer. Through Nazar the Soviet Union had access to some vital communications the Japanese Foreign Office received from its embassies around the world, including the one in Washington, D.C. There were so many messages relayed from Nazar that speedy translations were a problem, and I was called into the operation as a translator.

On top of this added load, one day I was called to the resident's office to meet an extremely agitated Guryanov. "Stanislav, I've got to ask you to do something that could be very dangerous. The worst of it is, I can't tell you a thing about it. It sounds simple because all we want you to do is to case a house and tell us whether it's old or new."

"Does it involve one of my cases?"

"No."

"Where's the house?"

"That's the problem. It's in a suburb that's way off the beaten path, one where foreigners very rarely go."

I was immediately on guard. That really could be trouble, because unlike their urban countrymen, for whom contact with foreigners is not unusual, people in the suburbs sometimes displayed a violent xenophobia. And foreigners were very easy to spot in neighborhoods where everyone was Japanese.

"Why not send Agent X?" I asked, naming a free lance photographer who had been expelled from the Japanese Communist party for his pro-Soviet convictions. An ardent Marxist, he had been quite useful on a number of occasions.

"No," he answered shortly. "This is a highly sensitive operation. It's a 'false flag' job, Levchenko—very delicate, very difficult."

I whistled under my breath. A false flag operation! The KGB was hunting a quarry this time who would never willingly or knowingly cooperate with the Soviets. The prospective agent would be met by an officer posing as someone of another nationality, representing another country's government. My casing mission would therefore involve more than merely not attracting attention in the ethnocentric suburbs, I would also have to avoid at all costs being identified as a Russian, let alone as a Soviet official. Guryanov's next words confirmed my realization.

"We've picked you to help because I think you can keep your head in an emergency. You have to get there, take a mental photograph of the house, and get back without getting 'burned.' The security of this operation depends on you."

"Do I go alone?"

"No, you'll go with Major Aleksandr Biryukov," he said.

I knew he was worried. I also knew Major Biryukov. He was a correspondent for *Komsomolskaya Pravda* and an excellent spokesman for young people in Japan and the Soviet Union.

"All right, I'll give it a go," I told him. "Sunday morning will be the best time. Most of the Japanese counterintelligence boys will still be asleep."

We met in the pre-dawn darkness of the following Sunday. It took almost five hours to clear our route before turning at last toward the outskirts of Tokyo. It was nearing noon when we finally reached the narrow, congested street that was our objective. There was room for only one car, the street was so narrow. It soon became obvious that very few cars ever passed that way: there were crowds of children playing in the street who, when they saw our car coming, called to their families. Soon our car had slowed to a virtual standstill, stopped by the crush of humanity around us. Suddenly, somebody saw that we were not Japanese and began pounding on the car, shouting "Foreigners! Foreigners!"

"Pretend that we don't understand them," I told Biryukov, "and whatever you do, don't stop. Keep pushing your way through."

We passed the target house while all this was going on, but I managed to get a good look at it. At the very end of the street, we were finally stopped completely. A group of teenagers and adults had no intention of letting us through.

"Let me try to explain what we're doing here," I said. "I'm going to get out of the car. Now don't say a word. I don't want them to hear anything in Russian."

I knew that these Japanese probably wouldn't think of us as Soviets. Their first reaction would probably be that we were Americans, so I decided to let them think that if I could. I knew that to many Japanese, English is English and that they probably wouldn't spot my accent. I fervently hoped so, anyway. Getting out of the car, I swaggered toward the crowd of people blocking the way.

"Hi, there," I said, smiling broadly, "Anybody here speak English?" An old man came forward, bowing deeply. "Hey, that's great. See, my friend and I are trying to find . . . ," and I named a landmark about half a mile away. The old man gave me directions. I bowed and he bowed. I swaggered back to the car as if I owned the world, and as we drove off through the crowd that magically parted for us, I called out, "Thanks a bunch, Papa-san."

Biryukov's hands were shaking so hard he had trouble shifting gears. We drove almost the whole way back to the embassy in silence. "Oh, yes," he said just before we got there, "was the house old or new?"

"New."

"Oh," he answered. "That's good."

At the embassy that afternoon, Guryanov was very pleased. "You forget the entire incident," he cautioned. "When you leave here, it never happened."

I never found out what it was about or why it was so important that the house be new, but—Guryanov notwithstanding—there's no way I can forget that hostile crowd around that car. The other problem was that we did not want an incident involving the Japanese police.

I'd been denied the recognition and the promotion I had earned, yet Guryanov himself demonstrated his regard for me. He called me in, handed me the registry in which all covert actions were listed and announced, "Beginning today, you are the full-time Active Measures officer." I was surprised and pleased that he had chosen this method of letting me know that he held me in high professional esteem.

"Now let us make some plans," Guryanov continued. "Your tour of duty is fast nearing an end, so the time has come for you to begin turning over your agents to other officers. I also want you to cut back on your work with *New Times*. That will free you to concentrate all of your energies on your work with Active Measures."

He was right to start planning early and to allow me to focus all my attention on active measures. I had worked with the Active Measures section on specific projects all the time I was in Japan, and I knew that being the Active Measures officer was more than a full-time job. Now, because I had reached a secret decision, I intended to make use of my opportunities to make my plans well.

I received daily orders from Moscow that contained specific directions for carrying out or initiating disinformation procedures against Japan, China, and the United States. In order to find ways to discharge each task, I had to analyze the entire Active Measures roster of agents and dependable contacts. My obvious purpose in these close analyses of those involved was to find out who could best be used to get the job done. I also had my own personal reasons for reviewing the impressive residency network: to learn whether the KGB had penetrated the American intelligence facilities in Tokyo. I could find no evidence that such penetration existed.

During that early fall I turned over all my agents to the officers who would handle them when I left and settled into working in the residency's Active Measures think tank. By chance, however, in mid-October I took part in one more major operation. The chief of Line KR, Yuri Dvoryanchikov, went home on leave, and I was ordered by the resident to take over again the handling of agent Ares temporarily. (Line KR is responsible for the penetration of foreign intelligence operations, for security services, for the enforcement of the conformity to ideological orthodoxy among Soviet citizens abroad, and for maintaining the security of Soviet embassies.)

Meeting Ares again was like greeting an old friend. "How good to see you again," he said, shaking my hand warmly. "Dare I hope that we will once again work together?"

"No," I answered, "I'm just a temporary replacement. I'm due to be rotated back home soon."

"Oh, I'm sorry, Levchenko-san. When do you go?"

"Any day, I'm afraid. I'll be gone before the end of the month."

"I'll miss you," he said. Then, laughing wryly, he added, "At first, I didn't like you. Then we became good friends. We shared danger as only good friends can, and we did much, didn't we? Yes, I will miss you."

"The life of an intelligence officer is like that," I answered. "You meet many people, and you really like a few. Then the time comes when you must say goodbye, and the good friends become memories only. It hurts."

"Will I be able to reach you?"

I should have given the pat answer of my line of work and told him that I could always be reached through my successor. Something inside me flatly wouldn't let me mouth that platitude, however; I refused to lie to him. "No," I said. "When I leave Japan, it will be a final goodbye. But we don't have to say that word right now. We should see each other several more times before I go."

"I am sad, Levchenko-san," he replied. Then, suddenly brightening, he continued. "Maybe I can give you something you've always wanted as a farewell gift."

"What's that?"

"The Directory."

I couldn't believe what I'd just heard!

The Directory was a 700-page classifed roster giving the names, addresses, and telephone numbers of most of the Japanese security officers. For as long as I'd been in Japan (indeed, for years before that), the Soviets had wanted to get their hands on a copy of the Directory. They knew that such a document would be an invaluable data base to follow the whereabouts and careers of Japanese security personnel. What a farewell gift!

The resident was as excited by Ares's news as I had been and told me to concentrate on Ares until this operation was over. I met the agent a few days later.

"I can get the Directory for you all right," he said, "But I can only have it for two hours, between 1:00 and 3:00 A.M."

"There's no way that you and I can photograph it in that length of time," I mused, stating the obvious. "The problem of duplicating it will have to be solved at the residency. Agreed?"

"Yes, but that will cut down on the time they can keep it. That Directory must be back in my hands early enough for me to place it in my contact's hands before 3:00 A.M.," he cautioned.

"God, it's ticklish," I answered, "but give me a little time to see what kind of a timetable I can work out."

The next time we met, our plans were finalized in a way that was simple yet, we hoped, effective. "On the morning of the meeting," I told him, "you be walking in front of the Japanese-French Culture Center at 1:15, and we'll make a brush pass." I'd made brush passes hundreds of times since the days (which now seem light-years away) when I'd practiced as a KGB trainee on the streets of Moscow. In those days I'd thought it was fun. Now the tension associated with it was almost unbearable because of my plans to defect.

"I'll take it from you," I continued, "and return it to you at 2:45, same place, same method." We both knew that the KGB would have its hands full. They'd have the Directory in their hands for only an hour and a half, and part of that time it would be in transit.

"OK," Ares answered, "and if anything goes wrong I'll telephone, using the usual code."

"This meeting will be our last," I added, aware of a profound sadness. "I wish you well, my friend."

Ares sounded remote and unemotional as he responded, "And good luck to you."

The early morning of the day of the meeting was starlit and still. As I approached the Japanese-French Culture Center, I felt as though my footsteps were overly loud, like a bass drum in a marching band as it parades directly in front of the onlookers. I approached the man walking toward me, stumbled, and bumped into him.

"So sorry."

"Excuse me," he responded politely, "It was my fault."

It was over. I had the package in my hands. Taking the prize one block down the street, I passed it to the driver of a waiting car and beat a hasty retreat to an all-night restaurant. The packet was taken a mile away to where a KGB officer received it and took it to the residency. There it was duplicated, page by page, at a frenzied pace. At 2:40 it was returned to me, and again I strolled in front of the Japanese-French Culture Center. It was ironic that I had achieved this intelligence coup just before I was to risk all in a defection and that I had to carry out this last important misson lest my personal plans be found out.

As I approached Ares, I was conscious only of a feeling of sadness at parting, a lump-in-the-throat bleakness. I passed the Directory to him and was on my way out of his life forever when suddenly he did an odd thing for one as professional as he was. He turned and called to me—a dangerous breach of discipline. Then he came back and shook my hand.

"Goodbye, my good Russian friend."

"Thank you, dear Ares," I said, my voice thick with unshed tears, "and goodbye."

I walked away, knowing I was saying farewell to more than just one friend. I was also bidding farewell to my beloved Japan, that precious land of gentle people and quiet courtesy.

"God help me," I prayed in my heart. "The time has come. Today is the day."

On October 24, I could not sleep until about 4:00 in the morning. Natalia was sleeping in another bedroom and, as far as I know, hadn't even heard me come in. When I got up at about 8:30, she had already left for her job at the embassy. Thoughtful to the last, she had left me a big breakfast, and while it was hard to force food down, I ate. I knew I'd need every scrap of strength I could muster for what I was going to do.

I intended to behave exactly as I always did, to appear as normal as possible until the very last moment. My usual habit was to leave the apartment near mid-morning, giving me time that I usually used to read the papers. But on October 24, 1979, I used the morning instead to consider all of the uncertainties and unanswered questions I faced.

Foremost among the questions I couldn't answer with total certainty was the one I had asked myself when I analyzed the roster in the Active Measures office: had the KGB penetrated American intelligence at a sufficiently high level to allow the Soviets to recapture me if I tried to leave? I'm not afraid to die now, and I wasn't afraid to die then. But I was afraid, and still am, of what the Soviets would do before I could reach the welcome oblivion of death. I know enough about the degradation, the dehumanization, the brutal tortures meted out to such "traitors" in Lefortovo Prison in Moscow. I remember vividly the photographs shown to us during our training of a KGB colonel, drugged and bound in a straitjacket, being hauled aboard a Soviet plane in Istanbul after he had tried to defect. He was taken, we were told, after Harold A.R. (Kim) Philby, a Soviet agent in British intelligence, had warned them in time. I wasn't going to delude myself: it could happen again, and to me, if the Soviets had penetrated American intelligence.

My exhaustive search of the residency network hadn't turned up such an agent in Japan. I didn't believe there was one. As for the CIA headquarters in Virginia, I couldn't be certain.

Assuming my reasoning was correct, another question presented itself: were the Americans sharp enough to receive me promptly, to protect me sufficiently as they checked my authenticity, and capable enough to get me out of Japan quickly? To this series of concerns, I could only shrug and say, "I'll soon know."

I had long since checked out the Hotel Sanno, the place most often frequented by U.S. embassy personnel, military officers, and various dignitaries. It was a place where people could socialize and where groups could hold receptions and luncheons or dinners. I'd known for a long time that when I made my move, the Sanno was the place I'd go. On October 24th, however, I set about first convincing anyone who might be watching that I was going about my life as usual. I left my apartment about 11:00 A.M. dressed in casual beige slacks, open-necked shirt, and a brown tweed jacket. I stopped at the Press Club and examined the wire service teletypes. Then I began weaving my car through the heavy traffic and drove into the suburbs, turning often into side streets to make sure I wasn't being followed. I went back downtown, parked, and walked for awhile, stopping occasionally to browse in the bookstores or to look at antiques. In a small café I attempted to soothe my nerves with a cup of tea.

Finally, at about 8:00 P.M. I climbed the steps to the Hotel Sanno and went in. I could've sworn there was a lump of ice in my stomach as I walked across the lobby to the desk. "The reception?" I asked, taking a wild chance that there was one.

Luck held. I was directed down the hall toward a large room where a military sentry stood posted at the door. I spotted a U.S. Navy commander in the crowd and singled him out as my target. "Would you tell the commander there that I wish to speak to him, please?" I asked the sentry.

"Certainly, sir," he said, saluting smartly before disappearing into the room. I watched as he whispered to the commander, who then looked over at me, obviously curious, before striding out to meet me. "May I help you?" he inquired politely.

"My name is Stanislav Levchenko. I'm a Tokyo correspondent of a Soviet magazine called *New Times*. I urgently need to talk to an American intelligence officer."

For a long moment the commander hesitated. Then he said quietly, "Come with me."

He led me down the corridor to an empty room. "You can wait in here," he said before disappearing. In just a second or so, two military men entered the room to take up guard positions on either side of the door. I waited. For interminable, silent, stressful moments, I waited.

"What is taking so damned long?" I wondered.

In something less than half an hour the door opened to admit an aristocratic-looking gentleman. "Wait outside, please," he said to the guards. Then, turning to me with a courteous smile, he spoke. "My name is Robert. Now, can I help you in any way?"

"I apologize," I said. "I mean no discourtesy, but may I see some credentials or some I.D.? I must know who you are, you see."

He opened his wallet to disclose his identification. In a sharp wave of relief, I said at last the words which I'd mentally rehearsed so often. "I'm not only a correspondent of *New Times*," I said. "I'm also a major in the KGB, and I formally request political asylum in the United States."

"My God!" Robert exclaimed in shocked amazement. "I've heard your name, of course, but I had no idea that you were KGB! And I'm supposed to know every KGB officer in Tokyo." He simply stood there, drop-jawed, then finally added, "Can you prove your claim, Mr. Levchenko?"

"I have no documents with me," I responded. To my own ears my voice sounded expressionless, almost indifferent. "And I have no time. I'm in danger, and we both know that the danger increases with each passing second."

"Yes. Well . . . I must report to Washington, of course. We have to be certain, you understand. Now, try to help me, will you? Who is the Soviet resident?"

"Oleg Guryanov."

"And who was the previous resident?"

"Dimitri Yerokhin."

"Who is the chief of Line PR at the present time?"

"Krarmy Konstantinovich Sevastyanov. He hates his first name, by the way. It's formed of the same letters as the acronym for 'Red Army.'"

"Does he have a nickname?" Robert asked.

"Yes. He asks his friends to call him Roman."

"Why?"

"I don't know why he's chosen that name."

"Do you know Vladimir Pronnikov?"

"Yes."

"What's he like? Describe him."

"He is the single most dangerous bastard in the KGB."

"Good! Well said!" Robert smiled broadly. "Now, I must leave you for a bit while I dash over to the embassy. Don't worry at all. I'll be right back."

The wait for Robert's return was more stressful than the first had been. Now is when I'll find out if American intelligence has been penetrated, I thought. If this Robert is a double agent, he'll take me out of here and turn me right over to the KGB. I'd be lying if I said I wasn't worried about exactly that possibility.

In about twenty-five minutes, a pretty fast trip for him to accomplish all that I knew he'd have to do, Robert was back. He was accompanied this time by a second American. I tried to read his face as he came in, but he revealed nothing. Again, he asked the guards to wait in the corridor. When the door closed behind them, Robert turned to me, his face serious.

"The United States of America formally grants you political asylum," he said with absolute formality and solemnity. My knees actually shook as relief washed over me.

"Thank you very much, of course. I'm very grateful, but I'm also concerned. We both know how difficult the Japanese can be if they decide to cause trouble. If I'm not out of Japan before the KGB discovers that I'm missing, the pressure exerted by the Soviets on the Japanese government will be indescribable. Speed in getting me away is essential. Let me just disappear. Take me to Atsugi, to your air base. Fly me out, anywhere, so long as it's out of Japan!"

"I'll try my best to get them to do exactly that, but the decision isn't mine, you understand. For now, let's just get out of here."

We left the Hotel Sanno without any difficulty whatsoever and got into an unobtrusive, unmarked car. Robert took the wheel. I liked the way he set about clearing the way, carefully and professionally. At last we turned into a fashionable suburb, and Robert parked the car. We walked four or five blocks to a large house set back a little way from the street behind a garden. A charming woman of indeterminate age greeted us.

"Come in, Robert," she said to my companion. "It's been a long time since you've been here."

"And I've brought a friend with me this time." Turning to me, he added, "This lady is our friend, and a good one she is, too."

"Dinner is almost ready," Robert's "good friend" told us. "You've just time to wash up and have a drink beforehand. Come along, and I'll show you to your room." She led the way to a comfortable room with a bath, saw that we had towels, and went away after telling us to come down when we were ready.

Later we were given aperitifs and an excellent dinner; then the lady disappeared. I never saw her again.

Soon the American who had accompanied Robert to the Hotel Sanno arrived. "I've hidden your car," he said to me. "It's to-hell-and-gone on the other side of Tokyo. Do you want your keys back?"

"I won't be needing them."

Both Americans laughed. "You're OK, Stanislav," said the second American, who then told Robert, "So far everything's going well."

It was a tense night. Robert was on the telephone almost constantly, talking in code to the American embassy. Around 3:00 A.M. he came over to where I was slumped in a chair. "I'm going to have to go over there for a little while. I don't know what it is," he said. "Something too ticklish to discuss on the phone, even using double-talk." He must have seen the alarm in my face because he added quickly, "Now quit worrying. You're ours now, buddy! My friends and I will never give you back. Never! And that's a promise!"

When Robert returned at daylight, his news was extremely disturbing to me. "Washington has turned down the proposal to let you fly out on a U.S. military aircraft."

My heart sank. I knew I wasn't yet safe and that the long tentacles of the KGB could still pull me back in.

"If they knew as much about the KGB as they ought to know, they'd realize how much danger they're putting me in this way," I burst out. "The safest way out for me is on an American plane. That way I could just disappear."

"Stan," said Robert, quietly and reassuringly. It was the first time anyone had ever addressed me with the Americanized nickname of Stan. No one ever calls me by any other name now, and I've gotten used to it. "Now, Stan, it's going to work out OK. It really will. Look what's been done. Here's your passport back, officially stamped, with your visa. Here's a first class ticket on Pan Am for a flight leaving today. And here's my ticket. I'm going with you. It's an honor to be your escort."

"There will be trouble at the airport," I predicted morosely. "There'll be trouble."

When we got to the airport several hours later, we checked in and cleared customs without incident. With the first-class departure lounge in sight, it seemed as though my fears were groundless. Then it happened. With only a few feet to go, I came face to face with two Japanese counterintelligence officers. I recognized them at once, and they certainly recognized me.

"We're in for it now," I told Robert. "Those two will alert all of their forces. They'll notify the Ministry of Foreign Affairs, and you can bet your life that as soon as the ministry knows, the KGB will know, too."

"OK," said Robert. "So we're in for a spot of trouble. Just stay calm, and we'll handle it. You've coped with worse."

I wasn't sure that I had. If the KGB succeeded in getting Japan to hand me over to them, I was a dead man.

In no time at all the first-class lounge was jammed with a dozen Japanese, quickly followed by five or six more. One man, obviously the senior officer in the group, approached Robert and spoke to him in English.

"I must speak with the gentleman with you, sir," he said.

"I'm sorry," Robert replied, "but we have no time. We are leaving in ten minutes for the United States."

"We must speak with this gentleman before you can leave," the senior officer repeated.

"Why?" demanded Robert.

"Official business," the Japanese officer answered.

"I'm traveling with a valid American passport, and my friend is traveling with a valid U.S. visa. There are no irregularities, so there's absolutely no reason for a delay."

"So sorry." The Japanese official bowed politely. "I'm sure that you do not need to be reminded that this is Japanese territory, sir. Excuse me, also, but we mean to question him alone. You may neither listen nor participate."

Without my quite realizing how it was done, I was suddenly effectively blocked in by Japanese men while Robert and another American were inexorably backed across the lounge and into the remotest corner.

"You will be seated, please," the Japanese officer ordered. It was politely done, but it was an order all the same.

"Just one moment," I spoke angrily. "I'm not going to talk to you or anyone else until I know who you are."

"Some of us are from the Chiba Prefectural Police Headquarters, and some of these officers are security officers whose duty it is to protect you."

"Am I being held as a witness to a crime of some sort?"

"You are not being held at all. We merely want to ask you a few questions."

"Am I accused of a crime?"

"No, no, of course not."

"Has anyone threatened my life?"

"Not to my knowledge." The officer was beginning to show his annoyance.

"Well, then," I said in as reasonable a tone as I could muster, "there is no reason why I should talk with you at all. You are all policemen or security agents. You have interfered with me while I'm trying to conduct my personal business. I'm not a criminal. I have neither committed nor witnessed the commission of a crime. And since you say no threats have been made against me, I think I can take care of my own security."

"I sincerely apologize for the inconvenience," he said, still maintaining his polite stance, "but if you wish to leave Japan, you will talk to us. Who are you?"

"You know who I am."

"What is your job?"

"You know that, too. I'm a journalist, the correspondent for *New Times,* a Soviet publication."

"Are you a KGB officer?" he demanded.

"I'm a correspondent for a magazine. I'm going to the United States with the permission of the American government, and you have caused me to miss my plane. It's just left."

"I'm sorry, but you aren't suffering in any way. You are sitting in a luxurious lounge in all comfort, and there are other flights today. So, to proceed . . . who are you?"

That was the pattern. Over and over, the same questions were asked. Meanwhile, the first plane had gone, the second plane took off, and the seconds kept ticking past. Finally I exploded.

"I insist that I be released or arrested!"

"There is no question of arrest in this case," I was assured. "But we have a consular agreement with the Soviet Union. We must guard against offending them. We must notify them and give them the chance to meet with you and talk with you before you go."

All the time the questioning had been going on, the lounge had become increasingly crowded. I noticed a number of American businessmen waiting for flights to the United States, and though we had begun our session in a somewhat isolated corner of the lounge, more and more people were now within earshot of my interrogation. One little Japanese man in particular was close enough to hear every word, but with characteristic good manners, he appeared not to hear anything at all. I turned my attention back to the senior officer.

"I find that very interesting," I said as sarcastically as I could. "I had no idea that it was the function of the police to guard against hurting the Soviets' feelings. I really thought that was the function of the Ministry of Foreign Affairs."

He reddened at that. "People from the ministry are on the way," he said sheepishly.

"Then you can damned well let them do their own questioning," I said. "I'm going to the restroom."

Four or five Japanese escorts surrounded me. "Damn it to hell! I don't need any help from you. By God, I do think I can manage to urinate all by myself!"

They came along, nonetheless. Robert came into the restroom while I was there. By that time, he was seething with anger and openly dared the Japanese to interfere.

"Our embassy is calling the Japanese deputy foreign minister right now," Robert whispered, "and he's threatening Japan with mayhem. Keep up the good work, now. You're doing a super job!"

I pulled one nasty little trick of my own on my captors. Knowing that they couldn't drink while on duty, I later ordered champagne and made an elaborate show of enjoying every ice-cold mouthful. But I really tasted nothing. It could have been day-old tea as far as I was concerned. I won't lie about it: I was getting more scared with every passing moment.

When we went back into the lounge, there was a party of people from the Japanese Ministry of Foreign Affairs, and I could almost feel the relief of the Japanese official who had kept the interrogation going until they got there. "Ah," he said when he saw the ministry representative, "you can't object to official questioning now." "Oh, can't I?" I thought. "I object like hell." Sure enough, the same old pattern was repeated.

"Who are you?"

"Now I've told you people that until I'm blue in the face, and nothing can change anything I've said. When you ask me something new, I might answer you, but I'm not going over that old ground any more."

"You are in no position to tell us what you are going to do. This is my country, not yours, and you do not make the rules." He had obviously decided to get ugly.

"One of the things I've always admired about Japan is that you have laws here. What you are doing right now isn't lawful, I don't think. At least these other gentlemen were polite, which is more than I can say for you," I retorted.

About that time an attendant from the Pan Am desk approached us and, calling the most recent interrogator by name, said, "Excuse me, sir, but there is a telephone call for you. You can take it right here," she said, plugging an extension phone into a jack near one of the overstuffed chairs. If I had to describe the way he walked over to the phone, I'd say he marched.

I watched him as he listened, but I couldn't tell who was calling or what was being said. It was obvious, though, that this smart-ass foreign ministry officer was being humiliated and chagrined. He put down the phone, muttered something to an aide who was standing beside him, then turned to me. "You may go," he fairly barked at me. "You are free to go."

"Thank you very much," I said mildly.

Surrounded by twenty or so Japanese policemen, Robert and I were escorted from the terminal, across the tarmac, to the waiting plane, Flight 2 on a Pan Am 747. As we left the lounge, the group of

Americans whom I'd noticed for the last four or five hours seemed to decide that they weren't waiting for a plane after all. Most of them left. A few unobtrusively joined the crowd of Japanese around us.

As I mounted the last step of the boarding platform, I felt a wave of relief that left me weak. I was on my way to a new land, and all I owned in the world were the clothes I was wearing, about $30 in yen, and $100 that one of the Americans, who had pushed through the crowd of Japanese, had pressed into my hand. "That's for luck," he called to me. "You're a brave son of a gun, Stan. Good luck and God bless."

All the way across the tarmac and as we were getting on the plane, one Japanese policeman kept calling, "Please, sir. Please don't go until you tell me. Please, who is the KGB officer who is working against Japan? Please, who is it? Don't go until you tell. . . . Please, sir. . . . Who is the biggest threat to my little country?"

Once we were safely aboard and just before they closed the door, I leaned out, and there he was, still pleading, "Please, sir. . . ."

I called to him: "Hey, you want to know who's the biggest threat to Japan? It's that bastard Vladimir Pronnikov!" The last I saw of the policeman, he was running down the tarmac after the plane, saying "Thank you, thank you, thank. . . ."

Standing inside the plane, I looked at Robert. "That was close!"

"Yes, sir, that was a bit close all right!" Then, with his quick, friendly smile, he added, "But look at it this way—you're home free!"

Those words were the first of many American slang expressions I was to learn. But to me they are neither slang nor colloquialism. I learned that they refer to a children's game, hide-and-seek, where one player is the "seeker" and must find all the other players who are in hiding. If one of the hidden players manages to slip back to his home base without being caught, then he's immune from having to be the seeker next time. He is "home" and "free."

How apropos! How neatly the phrase fit me. Just a few more steps, and I, Stanislav Levchenko, former KGB officer, would at last be "home free."

8
Journey's End

OUTER BANKS, NORTH CAROLINA

The homeward path was longer than I'd thought. The cleft between the sand dunes was steep, and climbing up through the loose sand took a lot of effort. The wind was freshening, and the dry sand from the dunes sifted in lacy patterns onto the hard-packed beach. For no reason at all, I thought of rush hour in Tokyo and the countless faces in the crowds, just like the sand on this shore.

"Yes," I thought, "We are like these grains of sand. We humans try so hard to control our lives . . . but too often we are just pushed along by things we can't control."

I brought my thoughts back to the pathway. I didn't want to stumble over some hidden obstacle. I had come too far to fall just when I had reached my journey's end.

THE UNITED STATES, 1979–1981

I can't begin to describe how tired I was when Pan Am Flight 2 landed in California. I know that I was damned near exhausted from the stress and the lack of sleep. It was 11:25 A.M. local time on October 26, 1979, but in elapsed time it was nearly twenty-four hours since the government of the United States had acted so quickly in granting me political asylum and since I'd told Japan goodbye. I hadn't actually slept in the last forty-eight hours except for a few naps, a few minutes on the plane, a few restless catnaps in the early hours of the morning in the Tokyo apartment. I felt giddy, dizzy, disoriented, and bewildered as I left the airplane. Too much had happened, too many ordeals had been endured.

Despite all the dizziness and feelings of unreality, I was elated. At last, I thought, I'll be free. It was a heady idea. At the same time, I was a little apprehensive. Would I be accepted in this new country, I wondered. Would I be trusted and believed? Would I be able to adjust to this new life in an unknown society? I was excited and happy—and scared. Most of all, I just felt tired. I wanted to stretch out on a bed somewhere and sleep forever.

We were the last people to disembark that morning. Just ahead of us were the four or five American businessmen who had boarded with us in Tokyo. When we entered the lounge area leading to customs, I saw several of them chatting or buying newspapers. A couple were waiting for phone booths to empty. When we walked out of the exit tunnel, a man got up from one of the seats that lined the lounge area and came to meet us. Extending his hand, first to Robert and then to me, he spoke. "Robert? Mr. Levchenko?" After he and Robert had exchanged I.D.'s, he continued, "I'm Mac, and it's a privilege to welcome you to the United States, Mr. Levchenko."

Mac was a U.S. government official. I was struck at once by his easy manner and friendly smile. From that very first moment, I never found him to be anything but considerate and thoughtful.

"Do we have to go in there for anything?" Robert asked, nodding toward Customs.

"No, we're all clear. Let's get you two checked into a hotel as fast as we can. Mr. Levchenko, you look absolutely exhausted."

"Call me Stan," I said, "Robert does."

In a surprisingly short time our escort had taken us to a major hotel in downtown Los Angeles. Robert and Mac came up to the room to see that I was settled and comfortable.

"Stan, you can do whatever you wish. There's no schedule for you at all. Call room service if you're hungry or want a drink. Take a long shower. Go to sleep. Take a walk. Whatever. Your time is your own here, so enjoy yourself. Get used to things," Mac smiled again and gave a mock salute. "Just remember, if you need anything, call Robert or me."

"Call Mac if it's in the next five hours. I'm going to hit the sack," said Robert as he yawned and stretched.

"He's going where?" I asked Mac.

"He means he's going to bed," Mac told me. "It's slang."

"Will you be OK, Stan?" Robert asked.

"Yes," I answered, "I'm going to hit the sack, too."

They laughed. "Yeah, I think you're going to be all right!" said Robert.

They left me and went off to their own rooms. It was the first time I'd been alone in almost three days. I ordered a quick lunch and took a warm shower while I waited for room service to deliver it. I walked around the room while I ate, looking out of the hotel windows for glimpses of this internationally famous city. Finally I put my tray outside the door, hung out the *Do Not Disturb* sign, and fell into bed. I don't think I even straightened out before I fell asleep.

Suddenly I awoke in a cold sweat, the sheets clinging to my skin. Then I realized where I was—in the United States, in the city of Los Angeles, in a luxurious hotel—and the terror receded. My head ached with a dull, heavy throbbing. I decided to take a walk, to breathe some fresh air, and get a little exercise. I'd been told that I was free to do what I chose, but when I left the hotel, I couldn't shake the suspicion that I was being followed. Instinctively, I set about clearing the way. After a mere ten minutes I was absolutely sure that I wasn't being tailed. I was suddenly cheerful. I wanted to dance and sing, to shout from the rooftops, "I really *am* welcome!"

Nobody bothered me the entire free time. While I was walking around outside the hotel, I bought a change of clothing, a toothbrush, a few toiletries, and the necessities to get me to Washington. Everywhere I went, the salespeople were smiling and helpful, and after every transaction, they would say, "Have a nice day." I had never heard that expression before, and at the time I thought it was a nice thing to say. For me, still disoriented from my long ordeal, seeing these busy, happy, smiling people was like seeing a zoo from the inside out.

Robert and Mac had given me their room numbers; otherwise, however, they neither hovered over me nor made any demands. We three met for dinner, but the conversation was lighthearted. I think they knew that I needed to have my feelings perked up a little at that point. Anyway, neither Robert nor my new friend pressured me or asked probing questions. When I went to bed that night I was at ease and relaxed, and I slept a long, untroubled sleep.

On the morning of October 27, Robert and I took a TWA flight to Dulles International Airport in the northern Virginia suburbs of Washington, D.C. Again, Robert and I were met, this time by three officers who took us to a large apartment complex in Virginia within easy reach of downtown Washington. I was taken into a well-appointed three-bedroom apartment and told to make myself at home. Then we were briefed on what to expect of the next several days.

Robert would stay in the Washington area for three or four days to take care of some official business of his own and to make sure that I was going to be OK. Two of the men who had met us were going to stay with me, and the third was to be my courier (more or less).

"This is your apartment," the third man said, to my amazement. "It's been rented by the U.S. government especially for you during this adjustment period."

One of the men, who introduced himself as John, said, "Now, Jeff and I are going to be living here with you for awhile, and we don't want you to think it's to keep an eye on you or to control you in any way."

I liked them both. John was about thirty-five years old, quick-witted and intelligent; Jeff was about fifty-five, with a dry sense of humor that could go right over the heads of people who were more obvious.

"That's right," Jeff said, "The only real reason we're going to stick around is to guarantee your personal safety. Just think of us as the Friendly Bodyguard Service."

"After all," John added, "we do have a sneaky suspicion that the KGB will be trying frantically to locate you."

"Yup," Jeff said, hitching up his pants in an imitation of Gary Cooper, "and some of those fellers are used to this here range."

It was harder than I'd expected to say goodbye to Robert when he left a few days later to go back to Japan. In the short time I'd known him, we had become friends, and much to my surprise, I'd really come to depend on him. Jeff and John told me later that it's not unusual for that feeling of dependency to occur. The trauma of leaving everything one knows for life in another country leaves a person rudderless, and the sponsor who helps in those circumstances becomes very important very quickly.

For the first few days I stayed close to the apartment, almost never venturing out. I rested, ate, slept, and regained strength each day. I was, in fact, exactly like a patient who is recuperating from a prolonged fever. Jeff, John, and I spent hours just talking. I knew they were trying to introduce me to the United States in as much detail as they could, and as I began to bounce back, I had considerable interest in the information they offered. Curious about everything, I asked questions about things ranging from Social Security to shopping and far, far beyond.

My new roommates were friendly, easygoing men. During my years as an intelligence officer I had developed a kind of sixth sense about people. After only a few hours I could tell whether a person is sincere. Both Jeff and John were genuine, caring people. After I began to get some energy back, Jeff and I would sometimes go out for a drink in the evenings or drop into a neighborhood movie. Sometimes we'd go into Washington to the theater. Gradually we became friends, and as I slowly "came back to life," as John called it, it began to dawn on me that the process of discovering America for myself wasn't as painful as I'd feared. Everything was new and different, and I was fascinated by it all: the department stores, the supermarkets, the traffic on the streets—everything. On weekends we strolled through the parks, and I visited the wonderful National Zoo.

"The hit of the year, our zoo," John said. "Everybody in the world is beating a path to our zoo to see the Chinese pandas and to lay down a bet on whether Ling-Ling is pregnant." They were pretty creatures, those giant pandas, like huge overstuffed toys, but the thing I most enjoyed about the zoo was people-watching. I watched happy, laughing children and families having fun. I think my first impressions of the American family came from those early trips to the zoo.

On Sundays, Jeff or John would take me to visit the various churches in the Washington area. I went to services in Protestant churches and in Roman Catholic churches. I went to the National Cathedral and to the Greek Orthodox Cathedral in Washington, D.C., and the people in all of them were like those I'd observed so long ago in the Eastern Orthodox Cathedral in Moscow. They were joyous in the practice of their faith and at peace within themselves when they left their churches after services.

The time came when I had to deal with the business of my position as a political refugee. I understood, of course, that in return for asylum in the United States and in order to establish my credibility, I'd have to undergo extensive debriefing. I'd have to answer truthfully questions about my life, my career, and my reasons for requesting political asylum. I was prepared to do so within limits. On the very first day I arrived in Virginia, I made those limits quite clear to the government official who had referred to himself as the courier.

"I'm requesting political asylum in America because I can no longer tolerate the policies of the Soviets' socialist regime," I told him. "But I won't betray the decent officers that I worked with, and I won't betray any of my agents in the Tokyo residency. Also, I will not take any money from the Central Intelligence Agency."

"That's an admirable loyalty, Mr. Levchenko, for one who is so ideologically opposed to the Soviet system and their policies," the courier remarked.

"I can't betray those people. I absolutely cannot. I'm obligated to them, personally and morally," I declared. "And I feel this so deeply that I demand an official pledge that any information I might provide will never be exploited to harm a single individual."

The courier chose that moment to tell me the name I should use in addressing him. "I've got that, Stan. I can call you Stan, can't I? And you call me Bob."

"I mean this, Bob. I'll want the assurance that no individual will be hurt by the information I give. If the United States can't or won't give me that pledge, then I'll appeal to the United Nations and request its aid in placing me in another noncommunist country."

Bob didn't even bat an eye. "Anything else you want me to tell the office?"

"Yes, I want to meet with a Russian Orthodox priest. I want a chance to seek his counsel and to make my confession."

"Of course," he responded. "We'll have a priest here before the day is out."

The Russian Orthodox priest became a frequent visitor. Christian though I declared myself to be, I'd never taken any of the sacraments, never been baptized, never even made confession. When I told the priest that I didn't really know how to pray, that I'd merely composed business letters to God, his eyes brimmed with tears.

"My poor boy," he said, "let me introduce you to the God I know. He doesn't want formal letters from His children. He wants you to talk with Him."

Of course, I had to learn the rituals, too, so there I was, a man in my late thirties, taking catechism, and loving every minute of it.

The time finally came when Jeff and John broached the subject of my meeting with some U.S. government officials. I agreed that it was time to start the debriefings. I knew that I was physically and mentally strong enough, but I'll always be grateful for the tact these two men showed when they asked me.

"If you don't mind doing it, Stan, they really need to talk to you," said John.

"What's your reaction?" Jeff wanted to know.

They made me feel that it was all up to me, and me alone. I knew it wasn't, but their making me feel that way was reassuring.

"I think it's time to meet," I said.

I went through a few weeks of debriefings and discussions, and to my relief, I never detected any ill will or hostility toward me from the people I met and those with whom I talked. But, while I felt that they trusted me personally, I understood professionally that certain questions had to be posed in such a way that the answers could be checked, rechecked, and verified afterward. I recognized that this was absolutely necessary in their questioning, and I knew the seriousness of the matters under analysis.

I think that the officers with whom I talked thought I was too idealistic, perhaps even naive, in the position I'd taken. I know they found it difficult to reconcile my hatred of the KGB and of the Soviet system with my determination to protect those individuals I felt were undeserving of censure.

In any case the questioning was conducted with as much diplomacy as possible, even though in some ways it was a bit distasteful, both to me and to them. For example, I was required to take two polygraph tests, spaced several days apart. This, of course, was a good way to check the consistency of what I'd told them and to verify information I'd given them. I hated having to take the tests, but afterward I was glad that I had. When they were completed, the examiner said, "Well, these are about as clear-cut as any two tests I've ever administered. They prove conclusively that the subject has told the truth."

The two caseworkers who were assigned to me were known to me only as Rob and Mr. Binns. Rob was with me every moment during questioning, and we became friends. (We still visit each other often and stay in touch by phone.) I was given a full battery of tests and examinations, including an I.Q. test. I was also given a vocational aptitude test, and I get a lot of fun out of my friends' reactions when I tell them the results of it. Rob saw the fun in it when he first read the conclusion it reached.

"Hey, Stan," he said, "do you know what your mistake was in choosing a career? You didn't choose the right thing, that's all. KGB officer, indeed! Hell, according to this, you should have been either a teacher or a priest!"

An official psychiatrist and his colleague, both with top-secret clearance, characterized me as "highly intelligent." Rob and Mr. Binns saw me as a profoundly troubled, but deeply moral, person. They went even further, I think. I believe that they both viewed me as a Christian who had been spiritually strained to the breaking point by the years of hell from which I'd just escaped. I'm positive that they read me accurately when they urged that I be given time to consider and rethink my situation. They knew that any sign of coercion by U.S. authorities would cause me to rebel, that my full cooperation would come of my own free will or not at all. The authorities finally agreed to the terms I'd insisted upon, and Mr. Binns said, "Stan, we'll welcome any help that you can give us. Tell us as much or as little as your own conscience dictates. We ask no more, no less."

The day-to-day problems of living in the Washington, D.C., area, one of the most expensive places in the world to live, became obvious very quickly. I asked that the officers and bodyguards who had been assigned to me and to the Virginia apartment be withdrawn. The government was reluctant to do so, but knowing how essential it was for me to feel as free as possible, they finally agreed. My problem with money remained. They could provide an apartment, stock it with food, drink, newspapers, records, toiletries, and such, but without money of my own, I was still virtually a prisoner, little different than people who find themselves under house arrest.

One day Rob came in with a proposal.

"Stan, stop being so stubborn, damn it! The government of

these United States hires consultants all the time at fees ranging from $50 to $200 a day. You can check that out for yourself if you want to. Meanwhile, what the hell do you think you're doing right now? You're working as a consultant, that's what, and you're more effective than most of them. Now, be honest. Is there any reason on God's green earth why you shouldn't be getting a fee?"

Reluctantly I finally agreed to accept $50 a day, and when I got my first payment of $250, I gave $100 of it to Rob.

"I owe this to an American in Tokyo," I said. "Would you see to returning it to him? Tell him that I thank him and that I'm returning not only the money but also the blessing. The blessing he gave me has helped me very much, and I hope mine will be helpful to him."

Rob took the money and turned away, smiling.

By mid-December 1979, my debriefings were nearing an end. The wheels of the American intelligence community were already in motion, checking, rechecking, and verifying what I'd revealed. I was getting eager to get away, to find a job, and get settled into a new life. The story of Stanislav Levchenko, former KGB officer, had finally reached its end, I thought, and I longed to close the chapter and move on to a new one.

It wasn't over, however, thanks to the actions of the Soviet embassy in Washington and the U.S. Department of State.

When I'd first reached the United States, I was told that I didn't have to see anyone from the Soviet embassy.

"You are a free man," a government official told me, "and you are not under any obligation at all to see any of the Soviet personnel that might be assigned to the United States."

"But other countries do make that requirement, don't they?" I asked.

"Yes, there are some countries that require anyone who asks for political asylum to meet with representatives of his native land, but in this country, we give people the chance to, but it's strictly voluntary in most cases. If you decide to see them, you certainly can do so. If you decide you don't want to see them, you don't have to."

"Then I refuse to meet with anyone from the Soviet embassy. I never want to see anyone from the KGB again in my life, if I can avoid it. If it's up to me to decide, then I most certainly refuse."

What happened next amazed me. I didn't think I was important enough for the Soviet Union to approach the president of the United States about me, but that's almost what happened. Ambassador Anatoly Dobrynin went first to the U.S. State Department and formally demanded access to me from Secretary of State Cyrus Vance. (Having served as the Soviet ambassador to the United States for a little more than twenty-five years, from 1961 until the spring of 1986, Dobrynin is now the secretary of the Central Committee, the chief of the Soviet Communist party's department that is responsible for all of the Soviet Active Measures.) When Dobrynin spoke with the State Department, he even went so far as to hint broadly that should Vance fail to provide such access, he, Dobrynin, would go directly to President Jimmy Carter. My case had attracted attention from the rarified atmosphere of the top offices in both countries.

Shortly after Dobrynin's call to Cyrus Vance, I was invited to the Department of State. When I asked Rob what this invitation was all about, his answer was ironic and a little bit sarcastic.

"Well," he began, "it's an invitation in the way it's worded, but it's supposed to be interpreted as a command performance. Understand?"

"No, I don't understand. What's a command performance? Who's performing? Not me, that's for sure."

"No, no, Stan. It's just an expression. When kings and queens wanted to see a theater performance, they would 'invite' the performers to give a show just for them, and of course the actors or dancers or whatever never refused. That's what the expression really means, that you are being asked to go somewhere, and they expect you not to say no."

"Can I say no?"

"I guess you could," he sounded dubious, "but it would be very rude if you did."

"I have to go, then?"

"Yeah," he said with a wide grin, "when the chips are down, I guess you do."

So I accepted their invitation, and Rob and I went together to the State Department. In fact, Rob stayed with me throughout the entire merciless and grueling session. We were shown into the office of a deputy undersecretary. He was a young, impeccably dressed man, obviously a "man on the way up," the very model of the stereotypical bureaucrat (with a capital "B"!). Even his first words to me were arrogant.

"Levchenko, we have been informed of your reluctance to meet with the representatives of the Soviet Union. May we ask why?"

"Holy shit!" Rob said under his breath, "He uses the royal 'we.' The supercilious bastard!"

The rudeness and arrogance of his manner certainly didn't escape me, either.

"Do you realize what you are doing?" he continued. "The Soviets will retaliate, you know. They won't sit still for this. Because of you and your uncooperative attitude, Americans in Moscow at this very minute are vulnerable to all sorts of retaliation."

By that time I was so angry I absolutely refused to speak. I've never come so close to diving across a desk and hitting a man in my life. In fact, Rob told me later that he thought I was going to do just that. Meanwhile, warming to his task of applying pressure, the junior, self-important deputy undersecretary went on: "Americans in Moscow will be beaten, imprisoned, subjected to unspeakable humiliation, and all because of you and your stubbornness. You, Levchenko, are morally responsible for everything that happens to those people and don't think for one minute that we will forget it."

"For Christ's sake!" I burst out. "Do you really think I don't know the Soviets? My God, I asked for political asylum because I know them too well. Retaliate? Of course, they will retaliate. They don't need any other excuse than this: Stanislav Levchenko, a KGB officer, dared to leave the Soviet Union and ask for political asylum in the United States. You dare to charge me with 'moral' responsibility for what happens to Americans in the Soviet Union? Well, I would remind you that they are there voluntarily, but by God, I have a family there. Now, I go from your office. I will never accept another invitation to come here."

I left.

Rob caught up with me at a run. "Slow down, Stan," he said. "You've made your point. My God, but you *did* make your point!"

We walked the rest of the distance to the car in silence. We rode together for long, oppressive minutes, still in silence. Finally, visibly shaken, Rob spoke, "God, Stan, you don't know how sorry I am this happened. . . . But I feel compelled to tell you something I believe with all my heart. The United States is still the best country in the world to live in. American democracy, for all of its shortcomings, still works. Just don't expect it to be perfect. It isn't. And as you have just seen, we have our share of sons of bitches, too."

"Yes," I said, "so does the USSR. I knew one named Pronnikov."

Before that day was out, a report of the incident was made to then CIA Deputy Director Frank Carlucci, who later became the National Security Adviser to the president in January 1987. Carlucci immediately issued a specific directive in which he stated that the political refugee, Stanislav Levchenko, would henceforth be immune from any and all pressures from any branch of the bureaucratic hierarchy.

On my own initiative, I finally met with the Soviets. I had become more and more uneasy over the fates of my wife and son, and as time went on, it became clear that the Soviets had to be convinced that I would never return to the Soviet Union and that their pressuring me to do so was absolutely useless. So, in January, some ten or eleven weeks after my arrival in the United States, I met with high-ranking officials of the Soviet embassy for the first time. We met in a dreary basement room at the Department of State, a cheerless setting for a dismal confrontation. I had expected to be questioned by a tough KGB professional; instead, they sent the embassy's minister counselor, Aleksandr Bessmertnik, a smooth, urbane diplomat, who in 1986 was made the USSR's deputy foreign minister. The interview was understated and brief. There were no attempts by Mr. Bessmertnik to intimidate or threaten, which is not to say that I wasn't both threatened and harassed all the same. It was very subtly done.

Mr. Bessmertnik handed me two letters from Natalia; both were unsealed. The words painted a grim picture of life for her and my son, but most of the texts were pleas for me to return immediately, to help make things right again. It was patently obvious that these letters had been written under KGB pressure.

I read the letters, then I made a brief statement:

> This statement has been prepared so that there can be no doubts about my reasons for coming the United States or about my future intentions. I came to the United States for personal reasons. I was not coerced into coming here. I came of my own free will and because I voluntarily chose to do so. I want the USSR and its officials to know that the decision is irrevocable and that there is nothing that they can do to change my mind or alter my decision.

Mr. Bessmertnik listened quietly to my statement. The meeting ended quickly thereafter.

Shortly after that meeting, I got two letters from Natalia, letters that she had obviously sent without the knowledge of the KGB. In the messages and the two telegrams that quickly followed, there was some concrete information about the way things were going with my wife and my son. I was shaken and dismayed. In the first letter she outlined the situation from Aleksandr's standpoint.

"Poor little boy," she wrote, "he is so miserable. He's having a terrible time at school. The KGB has put his teachers under orders, of course. How else could they be so cruel and unfeeling? The other day, he came home, rushed into the bathroom, locked the door, and threw up. A neighbor from across the hall came and told me, and we stood outside the door for half an hour, begging him to let me in. When he finally opened the door, he was so pale I was frightened for him. When he talked to me later that night, he told me that each day his teachers try to make him write compositions on his thoughts about people who leave their motherland. Today, one teacher took him by the shoulders and shook him. 'What do you think about defectors, eh? Why don't you tell us?' she kept saying. Aleksandr refused to say anything."

In the second letter, Natalia told me that the KGB had made life so impossible for Aleksandr that she had transferred him to another school, but that the new school was even worse than the first one. "The KGB has been at work in this school, too," she wrote. "The environment is so hostile that I don't know how long he will be able to take it."

About herself, she wrote, "Stas, I can't begin to describe it. The KGB is everywhere. I'm followed every time I leave the house, and at least two times a week I'm summoned to that godawful Lefortovo Prison for interrogation. I'm always afraid that one day they won't let me leave at all, and I fear for Aleksandr."

Both telegrams said the same thing: "We want to join you Stop Start proceedings your end Stop Natasha and A." My God, had I ever miscalculated!

When I'd come to the final decision to leave them behind, I'd considered every eventuality, I'd thought, and had logically opted for the course that would hurt them the least. They knew nothing at all about my plans to leave. Natalia would never have agreed to escape with me, so I'd never broached the subject to her. In the first place, she was too patriotic to even consider joining me. Besides, had I told her what I was thinking, the mere hearing of it would have made her a criminal, and I knew it. By law, she would have been obliged to turn me in; I knew her well enough to be sure that she would never do that. When push came to shove, I had felt almost certain that, when the

KGB learned of our marital problems and that she and I had decided on a divorce, Natalia wouldn't be held accountable for any of my actions.

I also knew that those who cooperate with the KGB are not as viciously treated as those who don't, and God forgive me, I'd thought that Natalia would denounce me and be spared. I'd even been certain that once the KGB was convinced that Natalia and Aleksandr knew nothing about my intentions and that they had no part in my ideological insurrection, it would leave them alone.

I was wrong. Wrong in thinking that the Stalin mentality no longer exists in the Soviet Union, wrong in thinking that innocence is a protection against the evil of that mentality. I'll live the rest of my life with the knowledge that my miscalculations caused pain and horror for my wife and my son. I swear that I will never again underestimate the limits of the evil that the Soviets are capable of perpetrating.

In early January 1980, I managed to get a telephone call through to Natalia. I timed it for the early morning hours, Moscow time, because I knew that it was the time when the KGB's activities would be at their slowest. The conversation showed me once and for all that Stalin-like barbarism still flourishes in Moscow. My wife and son were living in abject poverty. Natalia was denied employment except for a part-time teaching job that paid less than half of a living wage. Our son, victimized by organized harassment, had developed high blood pressure and a stomach disorder, probably ulcers.

"Stas? Is it really you? Oh, it's so good to hear you speak," Natalia said when she recognized my voice. "Stas, we're so alone. . . . We've lost everybody. . . . I'm so scared. . . . No one talks to us but my poor old mother. What? . . . No, we haven't received anything. . . . No, no letters, packages, money orders . . . nothing." Then she added, "They say that we're all three guilty under the law."

When I'd hung up the phone, I cried. For the first time since my father's death, tears flowed, and the pain of all the years of my life was in them. The lonely little boy in the Moscow streets was still there in the lonely, bereft man in America. As I dried my tears, I realized that I still had a great deal to do. I knew in that moment that I'd do everything in my power to avenge my family, that I'd tell everything I knew to anyone who'd listen.

Rob was with me when I talked to Natalia, and he knew how downcast and depressed I was. Indeed, that was one of the darkest periods of my life.

"You really need a change of pace, Stan," he said a day or two later. "Have you gotten to meet Viktor Belenko yet?"

"No, but I was in Japan when he flew his MiG-25 into Hokkaido."

"I want you to meet him," he said as he was leaving that night. In less than a week Rob had arranged for me to meet Viktor, but more than that, he'd gone against all existing procedures and, without notifying his superiors, had set it up for me to take a trip across the United States with Belenko.

I liked Viktor the first time I saw him. He has a wonderful personality—intelligent, animated, bold, and irrepressible. Viktor has blended perfectly into American life. When we started out on the long journey, I asked Viktor what this trip was supposed to accomplish.

"Oh, that's simple," he answered. "I just want you to see firsthand what you've traded for. Every step of this trip, I want you to be making comparisons with the Soviet Union."

I was certainly in a position to do that. After all those years of showing the Soviet Union to visitors, I knew what to look for. When we drove through the Midwest, I saw fertile farmlands and neat, prosperous-looking farm buildings and homes, and all of these were real, working farms. There were no Potemkin-like false fronts or make-believe models such as those I'd shown in the Soviet Union. And even in the most rural sections there were private automobiles parked in front of the houses, trucks and heavy farm machinery at every farm, and all the homes seemed to have electricity and water. Mile after mile, we drove past huge plantings of wheat and grain, corn and vegetables. No wonder the Midwest is called the breadbasket of the world.

The livestock was incredible to me. Throughout the Midwest there were huge dairy herds, pigs in countless numbers, turkey and chicken farms with well-tended buildings and poultry runs. On the West Coast were the sprawling cattle ranches, and in beautiful California, I saw the lush green valleys where food crops, vineyards, and flowers are everywhere. At one point in the trip, I wrote a note to Rob in which I called this country "beautiful and diverse." It is truly "America, the Beautiful."

I also enjoyed getting to know Viktor. He has a wonderful sense of humor that kept me smiling nearly the whole way. This was despite the fact that no matter where we went or what we saw, the plight of Natalia and Aleksandr was never far from my mind. I managed to get another call through to her several weeks after the first, again around 2 A.M. Moscow time, again when the KGB controls were the weakest.

"Things are about the same," she reported. "Certainly they're no better."

"Has Aleksandr gotten better?" I asked.

"Well, no, Stas. He's been expelled from school for fighting, and his blood pressure is still very high. Whatever it is that's wrong with his stomach is making him vomit two or three times every day."

"And you, Natasha? How are you?" There was a long silence as though she were debating how much to tell me.

"Natasha, what's wrong?" I demanded.

"I'm okay, I guess, I've. . . . I've lost some weight. . . ."

"How much weight? Tell me the truth, Natasha."

"I weigh about ninety pounds, Stas."

"Oh, my God. . . ." Natasha had been a beautiful 130 pounds in Tokyo.

"I still haven't been given decent employment. . . . The KGB still follows me everywhere. . . . The other day I was even caught by what the police called 'a gang of thugs'; I think they were KGB, though. . . ."

"Natasha, how badly were you hurt?" I interrupted.

"Not too badly, Stas. I was hit a few times, and they kicked me once when I fell down."

She sounded so tired, so weak.

"My situation is very difficult," she said with a sigh of despair. "It's near the end, I think. I'm quite without hope now. . . . I feel like a grain of sand and . . . nothing more." Her words still haunt my dreams and echo in my ears.

When I told Viktor about the conversation, I was distraught. "How could I have been so wrong?" I burst out. "So stupid! How could I have been so idiotic as to think there's even a trace of humanity in the KGB?"

"Damn right, Stan! You of all people ought to know the KGB better than that." Viktor fired the words right at me. "And if you did think so, you were just fooling yourself. You know perfectly well that you can never make peace with the KGB. All you can do is fight them."

He was right. Then and there, I vowed a personal vendetta against the Soviet system—to fight for the rest of my life, if need be, for the freedom of Natalia and Aleksandr and of the Soviet people, no matter how long or how hard the war might be.

Immediately after that conversation and as soon as I got back from the trip with Viktor, I went to the Department of State and filled in several copies of what's called the "invitation," the document that people who have relatives in the Soviet Union can send to them so that they can apply for exit visas. I heard absolutely nothing from anyone regarding any action on those invitations.

My second meeting with representatives of the Soviet embassy was in the spring of 1980. At that meeting I delivered a subtle, carefully worded ultimatum. So far, I'd stuck to my initial position that I would give to the United States no information that could adversely affect individuals in either Japan or the Soviet Union. I let the Soviets know that I would continue to follow my own rule provided the mistreatment of my family ceased. Then I gave them copies of the invitations for my wife and son, which they promised to deliver. They lied; neither Natalia nor Aleksandr received any copies from the Soviets.

My next move was to send invitations through my own private channels. My wife took them to the Soviet emigration officials and put them on the desk herself. The officer on duty refused to pick them up. Instead, he informed her curtly, "Madam, I advise you to give up all hope of leaving the Soviet Union."

During 1980 and 1981 I was still able to phone my wife and son, and the conversations revealed that my ultimatum had done absolutely nothing to force the Soviets and the KGB to stop their mistreatment of my family. I considered that to be a kind of dare, a challenge to me to hurt them if I could. It was a dare that I relished taking, and the actions and reactions of the Soviets subsequently proved that I did indeed at least sting them quite a bit. But more about that later.

In one of the conversations in late 1980, my wife told me, "They are preparing to try you in absentia, you know."

"I've been expecting it for some time now," I answered.

"It's to be a military tribunal," she continued, "and I have been approached several times by people who want me to provide them with defamatory information about you."

"When did you have the last visit?" I asked. "And are they getting nastier each time?"

"Three days ago . . . and yes, they are. I told the colonel that there was no use asking me," she said. "I told him, 'Sir, there is nothing negative I can possibly tell you. I will not help you to prosecute him or make it easier for you to persecute us!' I'm not going to lose my nerve!"

"Natalia," I pleaded with her, "please divorce me. Please, Natalia. Cooperate with the KGB. Do anything they want you to do. I can't stand knowing what they are doing to you and your lives. Natalia?"

"No," was her only answer, "I can't bring myself to do that."

They tried to force Natalia and our son to hold a press conference to condemn and denounce me. Again she refused to cooperate with them.

Finally I had to accept the facts. The KGB and the Soviets were holding my wife and son as hostages in their attempts to force me to return to the Soviet Union.

In the summer of 1981 I had my third and last meeting with Soviet officials. Again we met in the gloomy basement of the State Department building. The chief of the Soviet group was Yevgeniy Ponomaryov, a KGB counterintelligence officer. Without waiting for the formalities to begin, I said, "I am not going to listen to any more demagogic statements from anyone. This meeting will be over as far as I am concerned when I have presented my own prepared statement. Here it is:

To the Soviet leaders:

I despise and abhor the Soviet government. I despise and abhor the morally corrupt, expansionist Soviet system. I hold the Soviet government and the Soviet leaders in contempt for their treatment of an innocent child, my son, and an innocent woman, my wife. From this moment, be advised that I will openly fight this government and its leadership.

This is my formal declaration of my personal war against the Soviet system, its leaders, and the KGB.

Ponomaryov looked as though he were having a stroke. The further I went with the statement, the redder his face turned, going from pale pink to tomato red. When I had finished he shrieked, his eyes radiating hatred, "I didn't come here to listen to Levchenko's treason!" He was still yelling as I left the room.

I never meant anything more in my life than what I said in my personal declaration of war. I knew that I'd reached the point of no return on the night Viktor Belenko told me, "You can't make peace with the KGB. All you can do is fight them." Everything that has happened since my arrival in the United States has served only to reinforce the moral outrage and righteous anger that sent me that October evening to Tokyo's Hotel Sanno to ask for political asylum. I knew I was right then, just as I know I'm right now. I am at my journey's end, and I am fighting a war as real as any that's ever been declared by nation against nation.

Of course, the Soviet Union has struck back. I was tried in absentia by a Moscow military tribunal three years after I left Japan. The sentence? Death.

9

No Separate Peace

OUTER BANKS, NORTH CAROLINA

I trudged the last few steps through the sand until I reached a flight of wooden stairs leading up to the beach road. I was weary and out of breath when I got to the top step; I had walked a long way, longer than I'd thought. I sat down to shake the sand out of my shoes.

In the deepening dusk the sea was wine-dark, as the poet Homer said, and for a moment I felt a kinship with old Odysseus. What must he have felt when he reached home at last at the end of his journey? He was home finally, but did he feel at home?

Probably not. He probably knew that the call of that beckoning sea was the summons the gods meant for him to answer.

"Like me," I thought. "I too have a call to answer and a war to fight. And I'll do it, wherever the job takes me. There will be no separate peace for me."

THE UNITED STATES, THE 1980s

My emotional catastrophes weren't over, even when I finally resorted to declaring a personal war against the KGB and the Soviet system. I lived under a constant strain caused by the fear and uncertainty of what was happening to two people whom I love dearly. I never knew from one moment to the next what the KGB might do to try to force Natalia and Aleksandr to comply with their wishes, and it was almost impossible to get news of or from them. As the days went by, I came to realize that the cord between me and the land of my birth had not been swiftly cut and safely tied off. Instead, there were raw ends that left me bleeding inside. I talked about this feeling of constant pain and worry with Viktor Belenko.

"The KGB keeps me always on the alert, always on guard," I said. "I never know from one minute to the next what new harassment they will impose on Natalia or Aleksandr."

"I know," he answered. "That's their way of trying to whip you back into the corral, as they say out west."

"Did they do these kinds of things to you and your family?" I asked.

"Oh, sure they did. It's their way."

"How have you managed to adjust to it?"

"I haven't, Stan, old friend. You can't ever adjust to it. You live with it, like you live with a toothache."

Viktor Belenko and I had some amazing similarities, and I'm not proud of the part I played as a KGB officer when he landed in Hokkaido, Japan. The plane he flew, the MiG–25 interceptor, had two top-secret electronic devices on board. When the Tokyo residency got its first messages about the plane, Moscow's primary concern was for us to find out whether the pilot had pushed the destruct button to demolish those devices. We cabled back that they were intact and that the Americans were already examining them with a team of their own electronics experts. Moscow was in a tizzy, and the residency wasn't far behind. In a matter of hours a special courier flew in from Moscow with a letter the KGB had manufactured that was supposed to be from Belenko's wife, begging him to come back and rescue his loving family. There were photographs of a tearful little woman cuddling a

193

three-year-old boy and captions for the photos that read: "Grief-stricken wife and tiny son of defector Belenko." Chief of Line PR Roman Sevastyanov gave me the job of getting the letter and photos in print in the Western press. "I don't give a damn how you do it, but I want this in print within twenty-four hours," was his instruction.

Well, that was my job. That's what active measures was all about—planting stories, spreading disinformation, circulating forgeries, engaging in subversions when necessary, and as perhaps the most important function, manipulating public opinion. I called a young American who was connected with the Associated Press. I knew that he would have given his left arm to become a regular A.P. staff member. Meeting him at a coffee shop, I translated the letter for him and showed him the photos.

"That's a bunch of crap," he said after he'd thought it over.

"True," I agreed. "But no one else has this particular 'crap.'"

The next day newspapers in Japan and the United States printed an Associated Press dispatch in which excerpts of the forged letter, finishing with the words "hugging and kissing you, your son Dyma and Lyuda," were given prominent play. No doubt many readers felt compassion for that pitiful, abandoned little woman. But the truth was a great deal different from the picture the A.P. dispatch created.

"My wife absolutely despised my career in the military," Viktor told me. "She hated and resented my flying. Every time I had to go on a mission, she had a temper tantrum. I came back from a long flight not long before I flew out to Japan, and she told me that since the only thing I really loved as much as flying was my son, she planned to get even for everything I'd put her through. By God, she'd take my baby and go home to her parents thousands of miles away from where I was stationed, and I'd never see him again. She'd see to that, she said."

"And our Active Measures press release made her look like a martyr," I said. "You must have hated our guts."

"No, I know how things like that are done and why," he said. "But I got quite a laugh out of Lyuda's little touch of 'hugging and kissing' me. From the moment she announced her decision to take my baby away, she never said another word to me, kind or otherwise."

"Now let's be fair," I said. "She probably had nothing at all to do with the wording of that letter. The KGB did it." I was thinking of all the pressure that was put on my Natalia and how bravely she refused to cooperate.

"But she posed for the damned pictures!" He had me there.

In my first two years in the United States, I managed to get a few phone calls through to Natalia, probably thanks to a system of direct dialing that Moscow was using. Each time we talked I was torn apart by learning what things were like for her and Aleksandr. In one of our last conversations Natalia told me, "Stas, did you know that you have been tried? It was a military tribunal, as we thought it would be, and a secret trial, of course."

"When did it take place?"

"At the end of August 1982. Why in the world would they wait nearly three years after you went to the United States?"

"I don't know, Natasha. I just don't know. Maybe they had a hard time finding anything derogatory about me." I laughed a little at my own weak joke, but there was quite a bit of truth to it. Three years to prepare evidence? They had trouble, all right, and much of their trouble was due to the fact that they were unable to find proof that I had not done my job well when I worked for the Soviet Union. All they could truthfully charge me with was having requested political asylum in America. Perhaps they still hoped to lure me back.

"What was the verdict?" I inquired.

"You know, Stas. What else could they let it be? They've sentenced you to death for crimes against the Soviet Union."

She was right, of course; what else could they possibly have let it be? So they had reached a quick and simple verdict: I was sentenced to death. Not bloody likely, I thought, and you sure as hell will have to catch me first.

No, I wasn't scared by this verdict. On the contrary, after hearing this news I became even more active. All of my time and energies were concentrated on my fight against the Soviet system. I even took great pride in knowing that the Soviet Politburo had sentenced me to death, because the sentence constituted an admission that in their eyes I was a dangerous enemy.

In 1982 the Soviet authorities suddenly discontinued the system of direct dialing from overseas to the Soviet Union and put every phone call from abroad on operator control. Whenever I tried to call Natalia after that, the operators refused to connect me. I was totally isolated from my family. Finally I gave up all hope of ever being able to get them to the United States.

In 1983 I was invited to appear before the Intelligence Committee of the House of Representatives, an invitation I accepted with much pleasure. I was introduced to the congressmen by senior CIA officer Portman, who stated in his introduction:

> The information that he [Mr. Levchenko] has given to us has been checked out in a number of different ways, and we are satisfied that he has told us the truth. Not only are we certain that he has been truthful with us, but we are also grateful for the scope and extent of the information that he has provided. We know from our own knowledge that the information he has given us has proved so damaging to the Soviet cause that it would be inconceivable that he might be under Soviet or KGB control.

I met with that committee on July 13th and 14th when I was asked to be a witness addressing the subject of Soviet active measures, about which, in all modesty, I can certainly claim to be an expert. I was glad for the chance to meet with the congressmen, the members of the House Intelligence Committee. I was even happier to answer their questions, which proved to be probing and provocative.

The closed-door hearing continued for two full days. A declassified version of the hearing transcript was published in December 1983, and I sincerely hope that little pamphlet has been helpful in informing people about the enormity of the whole KGB and about how the huge machinery of Soviet Active Measures actually works. As time goes by, I'm more and more certain that only through awareness can people counteract the KGB.

I still had to wait a few months after that testimony for the Intelligence Committee before I could start appearing in public. I had a commitment to Reader's Digest Press not to make any public statements regarding my life's story before John Barron's book, *KGB Today: The Hidden Hand,* was finished. While still in Tokyo in 1979, I'd read *KGB: The Secret Work of Soviet Agents* by Barron, a senior *Reader's Digest* editor and one of the world's foremost experts on KGB affairs. From the book jacket I learned that Barron lived in the Washington area, so about a month after I got to the United States, I called the magazine's Washington bureau and asked to speak to him. To my surprise, he came on the line right away. I introduced myself, then said, "Mr. Barron, I read your book, *KGB: The Secret Work of Soviet Agents,* and I just wanted to call and tell you that it's superb. You are deserving of your reputation as an expert on the KGB."

"Thank you very much," he said. "Considering your background, that's quite a compliment."

"I realize that this is presumptive on my part, Mr. Barron, but I'm very much in need of someone to talk to, someone who really knows what my background is like."

"No presumption at all," he said warmly. "You must come to visit at once; tonight, if possible."

We settled on a date for me to visit him at his suburban Virginia home, and on a rainy night in late November 1979, I went out to meet him. John was cautious at first—I was too, I suspect—but we gradually got acquainted and have become friends as time has passed. That night we merely visited and listened to music from his excellent collection of records. I left his home around 1:00 or 2:00 A.M., feeling pleased and relaxed.

He and I didn't discuss anything of a business nature that first evening beyond mentioning that a new book on global KGB activities needed to be written. "Your insights ought to be in it," John said, and I agreed to the inclusion of whatever would make the book effective.

After my formal U.S. government debriefings were completed, John and I were both eager to get to work on the new book. In order to lose as little time as possible, he suggested we find someplace that was quiet and where we would have a minimum of interruption. I envisioned someplace on the East Coast, but John's proposal for a work place was much more glamorous. "Let's go to Hawaii," he said. "I know of a hotel there that's absolutely perfect." I'd heard about the Hawaiian islands and had seen pictures of them in some documentary movies, but I'd never seen them with my own eyes. I didn't demur one bit about going.

"Of course," I said. "Let's go to Hawaii."

May 1980 found me on one of Hawaii's most beautiful islands, Maui. The perfect hotel John had talked about was exactly that. Perched on a high cliff with a stunning view of the Pacific Ocean, it had everything conducive to good work habits. We had time to work and to relax, and I never tired of watching the colors—alternately azure, turquoise, and dark blue—of the water. John wrote the first pages of the book in that gorgeous setting.

As I worked with John, I learned a new kind of journalism, one that isn't practiced in the Soviet Union. I had made a reputation for myself as a professional journalist, but I'd never learned even the most fundamental facts about real journalism. In John's world, everything to the most minute detail had to be precise, checked, and rechecked for accuracy and truthfulness before going into print. I experienced a great joy, an elation at being free to spill out the truths I'd kept inside for so long. As we worked, a magnificent realization dawned on me: like John, I too would be free to use whatever skill I had in writing to tell the truth about the KGB and the Soviet system. I can never thank John Barron enough for opening that door for me.

John worked very hard on that book for almost three years, and the finished product, entitled *KGB Today: The Hidden Hand,* was finally published in the United States in May 1983. Because of its descriptions of KGB operations around the world, it has since been translated into many languages, including Japanese. The revelations in the book were eye-openers to people all over the world, and I'm proud that I had an early role in its effectiveness.

I waited impatiently for it to hit the bookstores all over the United States and in Japan. I felt somehow that the book would in a small measure help me to repay a moral debt to the Japanese people by disclosing the KGB operations in their country and by revealing the Soviet goals and targets in Japan. That the book succeeded in raising questions in Japan is a matter of record. I held a press conference in Washington, D.C., on December 10, 1983, for foreign journalists, most of them representatives of Japanese media. Many of them expressed dismay and consternation at the treasures that the KGB had found in Japan.

Since then, the so-called Levchenko case has received wide publicity in the Land of the Rising Sun, and this publicity has to a large degree helped me to achieve the objectives that were the reasons for the book's publication in the first place. I wanted to show the Japanese people that the Soviet threat to Japan is very real and very serious. I wanted to make them aware of what the KGB is doing to the country—and what it has been doing for years—and to show how the KGB is going about the job of exploiting Japan. I wanted to warn the Japanese people of all walks of life of the KGB's penetration of their journalism and their visual media, of their political parties, and of their government offices. Listing the names of Soviet agents in Japan was never my intention. I finally decided to name a few, however, difficult though that decision was, because without giving examples I couldn't adequately prove the KGB's methods in Japan. I have explained this many times in talking to representatives of the Japanese mass media.

In general, the reactions of the Japanese newspapers, magazines, radio, and television were positive and objective. Not unexpectedly, considering the accusations I'd made and the Soviet influence that lay at the root of those accusations, some publications and certain journalists tried very hard to destroy my credibility. The bizarre and libelous methods they used actually served to validate what I'd written.

One of the ugliest of these stories was the unsavory statement that John Barron and I had a homosexual liaison and that we'd "lived together" while he wrote the book. I recognized the ploy, since my own work with the KGB had included similar attempts to manipulate public opinion in order to spread disinformation. The fact that the *KGB Today: The Hidden Hand* told how the use of sexual innuendo was one of the KGB's favorite ploys was certainly supported by this obvious attempt to defuse an explosive situation.

A few Japanese journalists lacked the courage to admit that Japan's attitude toward the Soviets was feeble and servile. Instead, they chose me as their scapegoat. They vented their anger and frustrations by criticizing my actions and totally ignoring those truths that, sooner or later, Japan must face.

I'd expected all of these reactions. I knew that what I was doing was right and that all thinking Japanese citizens would understand my intentions. The course of later events proved me correct. It has been gratifying that high-ranking Japanese officials have endorsed what I have said. "Timely and essential" was the judgment of Masaharu Gotohda, then chief secretary of the cabinet. "Mr. Levchenko's statements are credible as a whole," said Akira Yamada, then the National Police Agency public safety chief.

As a result of all that I'd revealed, the KGB residency undoubtedly lost a large part of its network, and it will take years for them to recruit new agents and to rebuild to their former level of strength. More important, large numbers of the Japanese public are now aware of Soviet intelligence methods and their strategic aims in Japan, and it will be much harder for the KGB to make new contacts in the country. I'm proud to know that I was the instrument for giving the alert to Japan, for warning them of the dangers, because Japan is a country that I care deeply about and miss terribly.

I miss so many things about living in Japan. Lake Hakone, encircled by emerald mountains. Meiji Park, where I strolled with my son, watching schoolboys fly their kites of all shapes and colors. Tokyo's saunas and getting scrubbed completely clean, then relaxing in the dry heat. Japanese television—very educational, Americanized to some extent, but still essentially Japanese, with a wide range of serious, well-directed programs.

I even miss the crowds of office workers hurrying to their places of business in the morning. The morning crowd in Japan is unique: men in business suits and crisp white shirts, women in neatly ironed skirts and blouses, schoolboys in dark blue uniforms—the Japanese in the mornings look like a huge, uniformed family. All of them wear the serious expressions of athletes psyching themselves up for the competition. Even as a foreigner in that crowd, I always felt charged up for the long work day ahead. Americans are hard workers, but not as hardworking as the Japanese. The Japanese are totally devoted to their work and spend most of their waking hours doing it.

The walls of my home in the United States are covered by the woodblock prints of Utamaro and Hiroshige. I drink my Japanese green tea from a beautiful Kutani-yaki teapot and cups given to me by a friend who recently came back from Japan. I listen to my sophisticated Panasonic radio, which picks up a couple of Japanese stations, and I practice my Japanese with them so I won't forget colloquial Japanese. I try to hold on to the things I learned to love about Japan. But whenever I open my bedroom closet, I'm reminded that I'm now a free man living in the United States.

In that closet I keep the brown jacket, beige slacks, and short-sleeved shirt that I wore on my dramatic flight from Tokyo to Los Angeles. I keep that outfit of clothing in plain view to remind me of my reasons for being here, and in my safety deposit box, I keep the last notebook in which I scheduled meetings with KGB agents in Japan. My memories are still poignant, but I've also blended into American life. After all, I've lived here for more than eight years, and America receives its adopted children very warmly.

In my interviews with American and European journalists, in my lectures, articles, and research papers, I expose to the public's eye the machinery, and the operation of that machinery, of the most powerful weapon in Soviet hands—the KGB's Active Measures. Since 1986, when Anatoly Dobrynin was recalled to the Soviet Union after serving as the Soviet ambassador to the United States for twenty-five years, I have requested these audiences to ask themselves why Dobrynin is now the head of the Soviet Union's Active Measures Department. Could it be because he so well understands America and Americans?

I'm gratified to know that partly as a result of my activity, more and more people on all continents are becoming aware of the scale of the clandestine and semi-clandestine Soviet activities the KGB wages against the free world. I never intended to use my past as my profession. I don't care to be in the spotlight or to be a celebrity. But I'm not unaware of world affairs or blind to the fact that my expertise and my life's experiences have become weapons against Soviet oppression. I've also become a researcher and an analyst specializing in certain aspects of the Soviet Union's relations with Far Eastern countries. I'm still a workaholic, and this particular job gives me much satisfaction.

It would be a lie if I said that I completely ignore the possibility that I might one day be killed by KGB assassins. They are expert at their work; they rarely leave any traces of their murders. So if I should die suddenly of a mysterious illness, or if my death should look like a suicide, please know that the professional killers from the KGB finally found me. According to the KGB's internal rules, defectors are actively sought for at least ten years. So far, I have survived for more than eight. Experts in the U.S. intelligence communities seem to think that I'm much safer here than in foreign countries. I think of that when my work takes me out of the United States.

One of the KGB's most important functions is to wreak revenge on those who have managed to escape abroad. Vengeance is essential to the Soviets, whose history, like that of the peoples of the Far East, demands that they never lose face. The affront to the Soviet Union when one of its citizens defects is enormous, and they pull out all the stops in trying to avenge the affront.

In fulfilling the directives of the Soviet Politburo, the KGB tries first to locate the defector and then to compromise him in some way so that his credibility is destroyed. In cases involving dissenters who ignore threats and harassments from Moscow (such as those I went through in their mistreatment of my family) or who speak out against the Soviet socialist system, they next set about trying to murder them. I'm a prime candidate, all right, if doing what the Soviets think are the wrong things makes me one.

By threatening the lives of these people who have escaped and by persecuting the relatives left behind in the Soviet Union, the KGB tries to shut their mouths, to scare them, and to force them into silent hiding. By threatening dissenters, especially those who were KGB officers themselves, with physical violence, the Soviet security police try to teach a lesson to those still with the KGB who might be tempted to defect. The successful murder of a defector says, "See? See what will happen to you if you should try to defect?"

As is easily seen from the numbers of people who have escaped from the Soviet Union and who are living in the United States, not all of those who escape to other countries are murdered. It isn't in every country that these KGB assassins can work unencumbered. And fortunately, many of the people who have defected are courageous fighters for a righteous cause who can't be stopped by threats. They have recognized and accepted the dangers before ever reaching the decision to sever all ties with a system they consider to be evil. Still, the KGB persistently seeks to take revenge. Some of the murders and attempted murders of defectors have been well publicized in the free countries of the world.

On February 18, 1954, Captain Nikolai Khokhlov, a KGB officer with many years of seniority, went to the apartment of Georgi Okolovich, the leader of an active anti-Soviet Russian emigré organization who lived in West Germany. "Mr. Okolovich?" he asked politely.

"Yes?" answered the apartment owner.

"I'm Captain Nikolai Khokhlov of the KGB," he told the shocked Okolovich. "The Politburo of the Soviet Union has ordered your liquidation, and the murder has been entrusted to my group. Three of us, myself and two others, have entered Germany illegally. May I come in?"

"My God!"

"No, no. You don't understand," Captain Khokhlov told him. "I can't commit murder, but you have to know what they're planning for you. As for myself, I'm fed up with the whole awful system. I resent the hell out of it. I'm going to give myself up to the West German authorities."

The two men became good friends, and Khokhlov began taking an active part in Russian emigré organizations that were working against the Soviet Union and the socialist system. A determined and courageous man, this former KGB captain made numerous public appearances, laying bare the criminal activities of the KGB against the free world. Not surprisingly, the Soviet leaders soon issued a secret directive ordering Khokhlov's liquidation.

On September 15, 1957, Khokhlov participated in an emigré organization's convention in Frankfurt. After drinking a cup of coffee during a break, he became so ill that he collapsed. He was rushed to the hospital; his condition was so grave that the doctors thought there was no chance for his survival. His face swelled, and his skin was covered with black and blue spots. His hair fell out. Finally, a group of American doctors who were treating him concluded that Khokhlov had been poisoned with thallium, a rare toxic metal, which had been subjected to intense atomic radiation.

Due to the skill of his doctors and to his will to live, Captain Khokhlov survived. After months of recuperation, he was able to resume his fight against the Soviet system. Despite barely living through the ordeal of being poisoned, Khokhlov wasn't intimidated by the KGB's assassination attempt. He has since moved to the United States and is now a professor of psychology at a major university. He's still very active, and he never hesitates to appear in public. I've always admired Khokhlov very much. Indeed, I'd like to follow in his footsteps and become a teacher in a college or university somewhere. In a time when the word "hero" is often misused, I regard Khokhlov as a real hero. Certainly he is a man I'd be proud to emulate.

Another famous incident took place in London in September 1978. A prominent Bulgarian writer, Georgi Markov, defected to Great Britain in 1969 and by 1978 was an accepted writer employed by the British Broadcasting Company (BBC). Markov, who also worked for Radio Free Europe, usually parked his car near Waterloo Bridge so he could be close to the BBC. On September 7, 1978, he parked as usual and walked toward his BBC office. As he crossed a busy intersection, he walked past a corner bus stop where a passerby bumped into him and jabbed the sharp end of his folded umbrella into Markov's thigh, leaving a slight scratch on the skin. The man murmured a few words of apology and disappeared into the crowd.

Two hours later, Markov complained of chills and a fever, as though he were coming down with the flu. Each hour he felt worse. The next day he was admitted to the hospital. He died two days later.

Scotland Yard, headquarters for the London Criminal Investigations Department, conducted a thorough investigation into the circumstances of Markov's death. They recognized at once that the Bulgarian writer had been murdered, and they suspected that it had been done by a Soviet bloc agent. The cause of death, however, continued to elude them. Then, during the autopsy, a minuscule metal pellet, nearly spherical in shape, was extracted from the scratch on Markov's thigh. Long days and nights followed as experts and specialists analyzed the pellet. From the moment it was found, doctors had suspected that it carried some type of exotic poison, but the trouble was determining what kind. Finally, the specialists who were involved in a secret defense biological warfare laboratory pinpointed it as ricin, an extremely lethal poison derived from the castor bean plant. More deadly than cyanide, ricin is a toxic substance for which there is no known antidote.

Markov was murdered because he had become one of Europe's most outspoken emigrés. In his Bulgarian language broadcasts, he sharply criticized the Bulgarian regime, disclosing the corruption of the Bulgarian leaders to his Radio Free Europe listeners. His broadcasts infuriated Bulgarian President Todor Zhivkov, who was afraid Markov's revelations would encourage the dissident movement in Bulgaria. The directive to annihilate Markov was issued in Sofia. The poisonous pellet was shot into him from a special, silent gun concealed in the umbrella. Obviously Markov's habits had been carefully studied; he was killed just across the street from the BBC offices where he worked.

There can be little doubt that the assassination was approved, and possibly even ordered, by the KGB. The KGB's top-secret laboratories are constantly at work developing such weapons and sophisticated devices as the umbrella gun, and it has since been confirmed that the Soviets have made several such guns. To tie the Soviets to the murder of a Bulgarian writer one need only realize that the Bulgarian State Security Committee is under the total control of the Soviets. They work together, hand in glove, and Georgi Markov was killed with a weapon developed by the KGB.

Markov's execution wasn't the only instance in which the umbrella gun was used. Ten days after his assassination, another Bulgarian emigré, Vladimir Kostov, was attacked in Paris under almost identical circumstances. A deadly souvenir, a tiny pellet of platinum-irridium alloy, was extracted from his back after he'd been shot with an umbrella gun as he stood on a subway platform waiting for a train. In Kostov's case the amount of ricin in the pellet wasn't large enough to be a lethal dose. He recovered from the attempt on his life and continues to fight against the Soviets and Soviet bloc socialism.

If the KGB manages to locate me, they will try to pinpoint the places I visit regularly and then set up the special death squad to prepare for the assassination. Their methods vary. A kidnapping with the execution made to look like a suicide. A "Bulgarian umbrella," or even a traffic accident. The imaginations of the KGB's specialists on "wet affairs," their term for assassinations, are almost limitless.

In the United States they probably wouldn't use their illegals for murder; it would be too risky. They might recruit an American criminal to do the dirty work. Even more likely, they would order the

Cuban Security Service (DGI) to implement Moscow's directive, since the DGI is paid for and controlled by the KGB. I know that the DGI sent a number of its agents along with the thousands of Cubans shipped to Miami under the agreement between Fidel Castro and President Carter several years ago. How easy it was for the DGI agents to disappear into the large American Hispanic population while awaiting orders from Havana.

I don't make it easy for assassins, however. For several years I lived under an assumed name. It's not simple for anyone to locate me. I move often, and I'm still good at clearing my path and avoiding being tailed. I'm protected within reasonable limits, and I don't worry overly much about a threat to my life. I don't look over my shoulder toward the rear; I'm too busy fighting what's in front.

I know, however, that the KGB has attempted to find me several times. In the fall of 1983 they let a few of my wife's letters pass through their barriers in such a way that they would be able to trace them. For security reasons, I can't reveal how the ruse was discovered and foiled. It's enough to say that their elaborate plan didn't work.

A later attempt to locate me was even more dramatic, and I am fortunate indeed that it, too, was foiled. But the KGB will try something else, I have no doubt. They mean to kill me—I know that. Meanwhile, my life goes on, and I don't think about death very often. But the people who make up my audiences always ask me about it.

"How does it feel, Mr. Levchenko, knowing that you are under a death sentence?" That is usually the first question I am asked when I throw a session open for questions. I've heard it so often that I almost resent it sometimes. I told a friend that not long ago, and she really tore into me for saying it.

"Sometimes," I'd said, "I have the feeling that some of these people would really get a cheap thrill out of seeing a KGB agent suddenly appear and kill me before their eyes."

"Stan, that's totally wrong. People don't ask that question out of malice or because they are bloodthirsty. Don't you understand that to them you are a very brave man who has risked everything—even his life—and they are in awe of it? They aren't asking you, 'What do you *think* about being under a death sentence?' They are asking, 'How do you feel . . . ?' Interpret it, Stan. They are asking, 'Are you human? Do you have feelings like ordinary people do?' And remember this: you have heard the question a million times; that particular questioner has asked it only once."

My friend was right, of course. My audiences do seem to be eager to probe for signs that will establish the kinship between us, so I try very hard now to let them see me as a fellow human being. Am I human? My God, if I am hurt, I bleed. If I hear a good joke, I laugh. And if I remember too much, I cry.

After the Soviet Union altered its phone system so that I could no longer communicate with Natalia and Aleksandr by telephone, I found a private channel through which I communicated with them. By 1984 the KGB had come very close to uncovering that route. The last two letters I received from Natalia appealed to me to "cease making public appearances" and to stop writing about the Soviet system because "such actions only hurt me and our son." The phrasing was totally out of character for her; besides, Natalia couldn't possibly have known that I was making public appearances or that my writings had been published unless the KGB had told her. From my own past experiences with matters of this sort, I knew beyond doubt that the KGB was telling her exactly what to write. I realized that I had to stop the correspondence at once, not only in the hope that the KGB would then leave Natalia and Aleksandr alone, but also because it was clear that the KGB was trying to locate me by tracing Natalia's letters.

The Soviet security system has encircled Natalia and confiscated nearly everything we had accumulated during the years we were together. They have made her write things that are completely out of character for her, and they have doctored other letters she has written. I am resigned to the fact that I will never see Natalia again in this life. The Soviet authorities will never let her out. The last few times I have tried to reach her, I have been told that she has decided that she doesn't want to leave.

I hate to give up the hope of getting my son out of the Soviet Union. Three years ago my Aleksandr tried to enter college, but the KGB ordered the superintendent of the college to reject his application. He is in the Soviet army now, and his unit is stationed somewhere in Siberia. Reason tells me that I have practically no chance of getting him out, but it is hard to accept this.

Oh yes, I'm human—human enough to know that the pain being suffered by two people about whom I care deeply is the result of actions I took for ideological reasons. But I want the bastards who are punishing them for what I did to know that no matter what, regardless of any threats from the KGB, I will never stop telling people around the world the truth about the Soviet system. This is the mission in life that fate has assigned to me. I can make no separate peace.

10

My Life in My Own Hands

OUTER BANKS, NORTH CAROLINA

It was dark by the time I'd climbed up to the sidewalk. I turned toward the hotel, relieved to see that most of the walkway was well lighted. One little stretch was dark, a single-lane sidewalk with sea oats and sand on one side and overgrown grass on the other. Just as I entered the darkness, a man suddenly loomed ahead of me. As we drew nearer to one another, I saw that he was in a police uniform.

"Evening, sir," he said cheerfully. "You want to watch your step along this bit of walkway. It's dangerous right here. The last storm washed away chunks of the pavement, and if you don't watch out . . . why, a person could fall and get hurt. You take your life in your own hands along here."

WASHINGTON, D.C., THE 1980s

Although this is the part of the book that should end "and they all lived happily ever after," the future for me is unknown—even more than it is for others. I am still under a sentence of death, and there have been moments of sadness and disillusionment in the last few years that make it impossible for me to finish my story with a fairy-tale ending. I cannot tell all the details of my private life; there are people whom I love who must be protected. Sadly, they must be protected most of all simply because they love me, and their security depends upon my not revealing anything about them. I can, and will, share what I have learned about my new country and my new countrymen, and I will share thoroughly the details of my public life.

Americans are remarkably casual in their manners and in their dress. It's a famous joke that it's impossible to figure out in a crowd who is a millionaire and who lives on Social Security because they both dress in the same manner. Americans take pride in being part of the "melting pot" with ties to countless mother countries from which their families came. They are open, fun-loving, straightforward, and hospitable. America to me is, as the poet Philip Bailey said, the real "half-brother of the world with something good and bad of every land." From the very first moment that I set foot on American soil, I was told that I could travel freely within the country, take any job I wished, have all the rights of any American citizen. I was overjoyed to know that I was accepted as an American.

After my debriefing was completed, I spent much of my first two years in the United States working for the Reader's Digest Press. Eventually, of course, I began to think that the time had come for me to become a part of the mainstream of American life. I began to look for another job and a place to settle down. It was a new and rather frightening experience for me. For the first time in my life I could look for a job that pleased me, and I suddenly felt helpless. For all of my adult life I had been told what to do, where to work, where not to work. I didn't even know how to begin to find a job. It was scary. Imagine my excitement, then, when I received an invitation to dinner from a business executive whom I shall call Mrs. Felicia Doe.

"Mr. Levchenko," she said in her phone call to me, "I've been

213

talking to——," and she named a prominent journalist with whom I had been associated during the last few months. "He thinks that you might be the person I'm looking for. I would like to meet you and get to know you because I'm hopeful that we can work out an arrangement that will be beneficial to both of us. Can you join me for dinner this evening?" She named a plush club in downtown Washington as a meeting place. I was intrigued and interested. I said yes.

"Good," she said abruptly before hanging up.

The evening I met her was one of those steam bath summer nights for which Washington is famous, but the club was delightfully air conditioned, the food superb, and Mrs. Doe a charming hostess— smooth, urbane, and cool. When we reached the coffee and liqueur stage, Mrs. Doe got down to business.

"I am the president of——," and she named a company that I shall call the Study East Group, "and I have asked you here because I want you to work for my organization as a research consultant."

"I'm flattered, of course," I told her, "but I feel compelled to ask why you think I'm the one for the job? What exactly would my job be?"

"Mr. Levchenko, I have made it my business to learn as much as I could about you. You have firsthand knowledge that would be invaluable to us. I would need you to tap the reservoirs of your own knowledge and expertise on the Soviet Union, on Soviet decision-making mechanisms, on Soviet domestic policies, and on Soviet foreign policies. Your primary job would be to research and analyze specific topics as they are assigned to you or are required of you."

"For what purpose would these monographs be prepared?" I asked.

"My company is a research and study group, and we contract with various corporations and businesses to research what they need to know. We serve a diverse clientele—banks, private foundations, and certain think tanks—and these people urgently need the information that you can provide. They require dependable data, Mr. Levchenko."

"I'm interested," I said, "but I believe that I probably should ask what the job pays, shouldn't I? That's what my American friends say is the proper procedure. It is, isn't it?"

She laughed a little, then said, "The starting salary is $25,000 a year with the opportunity to advance as you become familiar with the work."

It was a sum that seemed generous to me at the time, but then I was still a relative newcomer to the United States and hadn't learned to consider the cost of living as well as the gross pay. In any case, she sounded straightforward and sincere, so I accepted at once. A few months later, with all of the loose ends in Washington tied up, I gathered together my few belongings and moved to another city where Mrs. Doe's company was headquartered. I rented a small one-bedroom apartment and began life on my own.

The first two or three weeks were great. I was warmly received by everyone in the office. They were friendly and accommodating, helpful, considerate, and thoughtful; they understood that I was still adjusting to a new way of life and new surroundings.

Disappointment followed very soon, however. In a matter of months after beginning full-time work, I realized that the researched reports that I produced were not being used, that these monographs simply disappeared into a great void somewhere, and I wasn't being told why. I felt terrible. My self-esteem plummeted, and I felt more and more inadequate.

I made some inquiries, and some interesting facts emerged. For one thing, I learned that Mrs. Doe herself had no knowledge of or interest in those fields with which I was most familiar; therefore, she had difficulty assessing the value of my work. More important, I discovered that the main purpose of her organization was to investigate radical terrorist groups and leftist, ultra-leftist, and ultra-liberal groups in the United States. As soon as I made that discovery, I began to question just how much I really had to offer her company. I am not, nor have I ever claimed to be, an expert in those fields.

I did feel, however, that I could still make a valuable contribution to the company. If Mrs. Doe had been willing to expand her company's consultation services to include those organizations that needed factual information about the Soviet Union and the Eastern bloc countries, she could have realized a substantial profit, and I had enough contacts from my months in Washington to have made such an expansion feasible. In answer to all of my proposals, Mrs. Doe gave an emphatic "no." Finally she called me into her office and delivered a specific order.

"Stan," she said, "you are really becoming an embarrassment to me. You must stop sending me these useless contacts. They are all organizations that want information on the USSR and Eastern bloc countries. Now this is an order. Don't you ever make any contacts again unless you consult me first to get permission."

"But I thought that the purpose of a private company in a capitalist country was to show a profit. We can supply what those organizations want, so I don't understand why you won't let me do it."

"That's right," she snapped, "you don't understand the first thing about this company."

As I was leaving her office, she called after me, "You heard me, Stan. No more contacts without my permission."

That woman made me feel as fenced in as I'd ever felt in a totalitarian state. It also didn't take me long to discover that Mrs. Doe was the kind of employer who functions by building a loyalty cult among her employees, sometimes pitting one group or one individual against another, in order to know what people were thinking. As time went on she became more obsessive about her company and her work. It got to the point where she literally lived at the office. She kept extra clothes there, ate there, even slept there. That was no real hardship: the office was equipped with a bath and shower, comfortable couches, even a small kitchen with a stove, a microwave, and a refrigerator. She could easily live in the office for days at a time, and she did.

I reached the conclusion that Mrs. Doe came perilously close to suffering from a martyr complex. She really believed that she and only she could protect America from the radical elements she pursued with such single-minded devotion.

As the months went by, I became increasingly frustrated and unhappy. I had left the Soviet Union to find personal freedom, and here I was, caught up in the same pattern I had fled my own country to escape. Mrs. Doe tolerated no suggestions, no matter how minor. Anyone who disagreed with her quickly became *persona non grata*. The situation was aggravated by the company's financial status. Employees were not paid on time; indeed, there were instances when several months would pass without a paycheck.

I finally had to demand some explanations. In a very painful but brutally frank interview I at last told her the observations I've recounted here. "I cannot thank you for your frankness," she said when I'd finished, "because I think it's time you learned firsthand exactly why I hired you. The truth is that I felt sorry for you. You were and are so damned unemployable. There isn't one thing that you can do for a real organization. Actually, Stan, I considered you to be nothing more than a charity case, pure and simple."

"There are many people in your own organization who think differently," I retorted. "In fact, some of them are convinced that they wouldn't have missed several paychecks if you'd had the foresight to expand your clientele."

"This is my company, and don't you forget it! Nobody tells me what to do with my own company." She was so angry that she could hardly talk.

"Not bloody likely," I said. "The way you refuse to let people help, you will ruin the company without any help from us at all."

"Do you know what angers me the most?" She was almost spitting the words out. "I'll tell you, Mr. Stanislav Levchenko. You never understood your function in this company from the very beginning. You were hired as 'bait,' nothing more. If you'd had any sense, you'd have stayed in the background, out of sight until you were needed. I could have used you a million times to get new clients for the company, but no! You could never be depended on to play along, keep your mouth shut, and be useful to me, Stanislav, to *me!*"

I felt absolutely shattered when I left that meeting. It's a ruinous experience to be told that one is being exploited. I'm not sure there are any words to describe the impact this makes on one's sense of personal worth, but it seems to be an occupational hazard for people who seek political asylum in the United States, particularly if they have intelligence value. An article published on July 6, 1986, over the by-line of Peyman Pejman in the *Washington Post* makes the same point. I don't know exactly how such exploitation can be avoided, but emigrés, particularly those from the Soviet Union, must be alert to the danger of exploitation by unscrupulous employers.

In any case, I was frustrated and increasingly angry with the situation. I had come to America for serious political reasons, and I had to have the freedom to meet people and to make contacts. I could easily see the parallel between the way Mrs. Doe treated her employees and the mindset of the KGB. In speaking as candidly as I had, I had made an implacable enemy, and I was faced with having to rethink my position in terms of both my employment and my future.

It wasn't easy to sever connections with the relative security of a job and start searching again. But I hadn't gone through the hell I'd experienced to get out of the repressiveness of the Soviet Union only to be bound by an equally repressive job and an unreasonable employer. I began looking elsewhere for employment and left Mrs. Doe's company after nearly two years.

I've had to adjust to many things, but one of the most difficult to overcome is what I've come to call my built-in slave complex. In the

Soviet Union, you see, there is no need for the average citizen to make decisions because everything is regulated: where one works, where one lives, and what one does. There is no unemployment, and everyone has a job, even if the pay might be next to nothing. In a democratic society, however, there is a natural and dynamic competitiveness. In a free-market system each person has to take care of himself, plan his own future, and find his own job. That's independence. In America there are no common proscriptions or directives about how to behave or where to work or how to live.

Even the relationships between people are different here from those in the Soviet Union. In America most people appear to be outspoken and self-confident whether they are at work or at play. It is relatively rare to meet an American who suffers from an inferiority complex or who keeps all emotions inside. Yet I discovered that I had exactly those complexes, undoubtedly as a result of growing up in the Soviet Union. I'll even go so far as to suggest that most of the Soviet people have those same complexes. Early on during my life in the United States I recognized that I would have to make a breakthrough and rid myself of this crippling tendency to wait to be told what to do. I knew that only I could overcome it and become an independent, self-confident, self-reliant individual. It has been a long and difficult uphill battle for me.

Predictably, a few years after I left Mrs. Doe's employment, the Study East Group went bankrupt. Financial difficulties, lack of long-range planning, and a heavy burden of debts took their toll. After the collapse of the company to which she had been so obsessively devoted, Mrs. Doe became a very bitter woman, holding everyone but herself responsible for the failure of her dream.

There is no doubt that the fight against terrorism is an essential undertaking and that it is a just cause. Terrorist groups are not only threats to life and property, but they also endanger the strength and stability of entire nations. What Mrs. Doe obviously never understood, however, is that such just struggles must be undertaken by governments, not by individuals—certainly not by individuals who are motivated by personal or egocentric reasons.

After leaving Mrs. Doe's employ, I went through a period of real agony during which I searched frantically not only for a job, but for my place in American society. I wanted a position in which I would be able to use my knowledge by becoming a part of the struggle against the socialist system.

Fortunately, it wasn't long before my many friends at Reader's Digest, in the government, and in the private sector had located positions in various think tanks. I began making speeches and giving lectures to both government and private audiences, and I started writing this book. It took time to recuperate from the shock of my experience with Mrs. Doe. Indeed, I still experience flashbacks of that terrible period from time to time, but less often, now that I'm keeping busy in a most gratifying and productive way. At last I've found my own niche in American life. I'm able to meet and to make friends with people in all kinds of careers and in all types of professions. At last I live as an American with Americans.

Ever since I arrived in the United States, I've had the option to go into hiding, to disappear into a new identity, and to forget the past. In fact, many people have advised me to do so, and there certainly would be nothing wrong with that. Everyone who knows the circumstances of my case knows that the Soviet Union is completely serious about my death sentence. Others in this country—some, perhaps, with fewer reasons than I have for doing so—have opted to go into total hiding. But I have decided that I must be as public as I reasonably can. I like people and feel I owe it to them to share with them, as often as possible, what I know.

I want to go much further than that, however. It would be wrong for me to get stuck in the past, doing nothing more than repeating like a parrot what *was*. Morally and professionally, I can only be comfortable if I stay current on Soviet active measures and deliberately stay as informed as possible. I have decided to *use* the past as the means to project and predict future Soviet moves.

It isn't easy to be a defector, and I find it difficult to even use the word *defector*. My teacher friend has given me several lectures on my "ridiculous" attitude. "The word 'defector' has absolutely no demeaning connotations," she declares. "It simply means 'one who has turned away from' something."

"No, it doesn't," I answer. "Look it up in your dictionary. It's defined as 'deserter.'"

"I don't care what the dictionary says," she insists. "The word is a Latin derivative, and it translates as 'one who has turned away.'"

I still hate the word, but I am a defector, and the experiences I have had are representative of the experiences of many others like me. I have recounted the Felicia Doe incident to illustrate the vulnerability of newcomers in this country to exploitation. There are other dangers as well.

One of the problems emigrés have to face is that some Americans reject the idea that these newcomers, particularly Soviet defectors, can adjust successfully to American society. Some of these same Americans also believe that such newcomers will have to be supported, or at least assisted, by the government for the rest of their lives. I know of one case where the estranged wife of a Soviet defector attempted to extract an enormous amount of money from the U.S. government. "It's only right for the government to be the one to pay me alimony," she reasoned, "because the United States government owes a lot to that man, and, after all, they will be paying him for the rest of his life." Fortunately, cases of outright blackmail are relatively rare.

Many misunderstandings do arise, however, even under the most normal of circumstances, because Americans have difficulty in deciding how to react to defectors. That uncertainty is compounded because during the first few years in this country we don't know how to react to ourselves either. At one time or another all defectors feel what I call the "zoo complex"—as if we were exotic animals removed from our natural habitats. Americans view us with curiosity, wondering, "How will they behave? Will they adjust to their new environment or remain wild?" In human terms these questions can be translated: "Are they merely foreigners? Are they Americans? Are they really part of our world, or are they as mysterious as aliens from outer space?" I have experienced situations in which acquaintances have dropped me instantly when they learned about my background. In other cases friendships have flowered because of my past. At another extreme were relationships that were triggered by the exotic appeal of my past. I think it's fortunate that the latter never last very long.

One of the most helpful organizations in America today, one to which defectors can turn in confidence, is the Jamestown Foundation. It is a private organization that protects the interests of escapees from the Soviet system, helps them find their place in American society, and does so with a dogged, tireless determination. The people who are part of the Jamestown Foundation are selfless and trustworthy, and I am proud to be a part of their work. Thankfully, I have reached a stage in my life when I do not have to rely on their help, but I remember well the ups and downs of my struggle for identity in this country, and I want to do everything I can to help the others who come after me. I have become a senior adviser to the foundation on a volunteer basis. If all the groups that claim to help defectors were like the people who work with Jamestown, there would be few complaints about exploitations or misunderstandings.

When I left Mrs. Doe's employ, however, the Jamestown Foundation did not exist, and I went through a period of soul-searching and insecurity. Unfair as her statement was that I was unemployable and that my past could only be used as bait, the effect on my self-esteem was still crushing. It took time to get over the trauma. But I have finally come to realize that Mrs. Doe was not Mrs. United States and that there is fairness and justice in this country.

After I'd rejected the notion of getting lost somewhere in America and once I was finally settled into the mainstream of American life, I began to publish a monthly newsletter called *Counterpoint,* which analyzes the current activities of the Soviet Union. Designed for a European audience, *Counterpoint* is a joint effort with co-editor Peter Deryabin, a former KGB officer who came out some thirty years ago. Its purpose is to analyze the latest Soviet activities in deception around the world, to examine the newest disinformation attempts (forgeries, for example) by which the Soviets try to shape public opinion or the policies of other countries. We aimed toward a Western European readership because we both felt that the people needed to be made more aware of the extent of the KGB's active measures, which are both sophisticated and effective.

I have also become a consultant to the Washington office of a private organization, the National Strategy Information Center, a group that studies many subjects in the intelligence and security fields. I'm currently on the advisory board for a newsletter called *Disinformation,* a quarterly American publication published by Dr. Roy Godson, an associate professor at Georgetown University. The purpose of *Disinformation* is to analyze Soviet deceptions, the goals they hope to achieve, their strategies, and the methods they employ. Aimed at both American and foreign readers, the newsletter projects future Soviet actions through these analyses.

Both of these newsletters have been well received, and I take pride in my contributions to them. I've also supplied material that was used in a book entitled *Dezinformatsia: Active Measures in Soviet Strategy.* Co-authored by Dr. Roy Godson and Professor Richard Shultz, it analyzes Soviet deception around the world.

My work is centered in Washington but takes me to many different cities and often plunges me into some exciting and newsworthy situations. Sometimes it still seems as though the most important moments of my life are heralded by telephone calls. In early 1985, I got a call from John Martin of the Justice Department.

"Stan, I think you can help us with a few little problems that we have over here," he told me after the usual amenities were out of the way. "I am chief of the Internal Security Section: all of the espionage cases that the Justice Department handles are under my supervision." I now know this soft-spoken man to be one of the real VIPs at Justice.

"What can I do for you?" I asked when I recovered my wits and my voice.

"Well," he said carefully, "we have a few cases over here that we're not sure about. We need a little help to see if we're right in our translations and interpretations. Wonder if you'd mind lending us a hand?" I was pleased and flattered to be asked to assist in whatever cases he was referring to, and we set the time to meet later that same day.

John Martin is as pleasant in person as he is over the phone. He's a lawyer, of course, and an unpretentious and gentle person. But I've also had the opportunity to watch him doing business, and then he is as tough-minded and unyielding as is necessary to do the job correctly. He is quite a man, and I'm proud that I can number him among my friends. I went to his office on Tuesday, March 5th, and when we got down to the matters at hand, it turned out that his "little problems" were very intriguing indeed.

"I want you to meet an interesting couple," he said. "Not in person, you understand. A photograph." He settled me down and offered coffee as though I were a guest instead of a business appointment. A picture flashed up on the screen, a shot of a woman who, though not beautiful, was attractive.

"Svetlana Ogorodnikov," John said.

Another picture took the place of the first. This time it was of a short man, nude from the waist up, out of shape and overweight. He had a tattoo on his chest, a huge eagle that covered almost his whole front.

"Mr. Ogorodnikov, the husband. Ever heard of them?"

"No," I answered. "Should I have?"

"Might be a good idea," John said, smiling a little. "They've certainly shown a lot of interest in you. Let me tell you a little story."

The story he told me was fascinating. The Ogorodnikovs had been in the United States for some ten years, living in California where Mrs. Ogorodnikov worked as a distributor of Russian-language films.

The couple finally attracted the attention of American counterintelligence officers because of their suspicious behavior. Mrs. Ogorodnikov traveled frequently to the Soviet Union and was also quite obviously collecting counterintelligence information on the Russian emigré community in Los Angeles. Finally, the FBI discovered to its dismay that one of its own agents in the Los Angeles field office, a man named Richard Miller, had been seduced by Mrs. Ogorodnikov and subsequently recruited by her to work for the KGB. After months of surveillance, both she and Miller were arrested when she gave Miller a ticket to fly to Vienna to meet his Soviet handler.

In the course of the American investigations of the Ogorodnikovs and Miller, many previously unknown details came out, and that's where I entered the picture. In 1984 the Ogorodnikovs had hired an American attorney to fulfill a bizarre request.

"We can offer you up to $10,000 if you can locate a man who is in hiding in this country," Mrs. Ogorodnikov had told the attorney. "Much will depend upon the outcome of your search." The attorney was understandably confused by the request, phrased as it was.

"I'm not sure I understand what you're asking," he answered.

"I have a friend," Mrs. Ogorodnikov told him, "and she is desperate to find a man named Stanislav Levchenko. She is the one who will pay up to $10,000 to find him. Of course, she will pay a generous fee for your efforts in any case, but she really wants to locate this man because she is going to file a paternity suit against him." A rather typical KGB cover story, I thought.

The Ogorodnikovs did not limit their efforts to that one attorney. After Mrs. Ogorodnikov had recruited Richard Miller, she asked him to find me through the facilities of the FBI field office in Los Angeles. Fortunately for me, both the Ogorodnikovs and Richard Miller were arrested before any progress was made in their search. By the time John Martin and I listened to the tape, the case had been under investigation for some time, and the government was preparing its evidence for the courts.

John Martin also let me listen to a tape of Svetlana Ogorodnikov and her Soviet handler, a KGB officer named Grishin who was attached to the Soviet consulate in San Francisco. The FBI had recorded this conversation while Mrs. Ogorodnikov was under surveillance. The dialogue was clear and easy to hear, but was conducted in a kind of colloquial Russian that caused the translators a bit of trouble.

The Ogorodnikovs and Richard Miller were tried for many

things they were reputed to have done against the United States, and the government's case against them was strong enough to convict them. I was but a small part of the picture, but for me the case was a grim reminder that the KGB does not cease its efforts to find me. They had failed this time, but they will undoubtedly try again.

John Martin was painstaking in briefing me about the Ogorodnikov couple and about the connection between Svetlana Ogorodnikov and Richard Miller. Then he carefully went over what the Justice Department had concluded from the tape he had shown me and about the portions of it that were puzzling to their analysts. Happily, I was able to correct a few misinterpretations and translate the more puzzling aspects of the tape for John, a job I've been called upon to do in other situations since then.

John and I remain friends and have even gone fishing together on the Chesapeake Bay on several occasions. Sometimes, when we are both pressed for time, we share a cup of coffee or a drink on the run. But I can honestly say that from the very first moment I met him until now, he has never changed one iota from the soft-spoken, kind gentleman he was in the beginning.

The summer of 1986 was chock-full of spy news, one sensational story after another: the Walker spy ring; the trial of John Walker's accomplice, Jerry Whitworth; the sentencing of Richard Miller; the Nick Daniloff case; on and on. Shortly after the arrest of Jerry Whitworth, John Martin called me again.

"Stan, I've got a serious case I'd like to clue you in on. It's really a kind of shock wave, a spin-off from the Walker case. Want to know more?"

"Of course," I replied at once.

"OK, when can you get over here?" I knew that "over here" was the Justice Department. We set a time, and I was there with minutes to spare.

Once again John was painstakingly careful in briefing me, this time about the indictment of Jerry Whitworth. When he got to the end, he waited a few seconds to see if I had any questions, then got to the reason for his call.

"Jerry Whitworth was a career navy man who had access to the most top-secret codes the U.S. Navy possessed. He was recruited by John Walker to sell those codes and God knows what else to the Soviet Union. He was—maybe still is—John Walker's best friend. It's an important case, all right, and it's got to be handled just right. Do you know William Farmer?"

I shook my head no.

"William Farmer, nicknamed 'Buck,' is an assistant U.S. attorney in San Francisco. He's the prosecutor in the Jerry Whitworth trial. Would you mind lending him a hand? Kind of serving as a consultant?" John was understated as always, but by then I knew him well enough to know that this was important to him.

"Of course, John. You know I'm always ready to help if I can."

The Whitworth case was indeed a spin-off of the John Walker case, one of the most shocking espionage cases in history. John Anthony Walker, Jr., was a career navy man with twenty years' service at the time of his retirement in July 1976. (There is an irony in that retirement date, the month when all the states in the union and their citizens were celebrating the bicentennial of the birth of the nation, the land of the free.) Walker's insult to his homeland lay in the fact that he had for years been a spy for the Soviet Union, that he'd built a spy ring to continue his spying activities after his retirement from the navy, and that he had no regrets about his activities when he was finally arrested. He enjoyed living in a free nation, but he betrayed it for money and thrills.

Morally shocking as the espionage charges were against Walker, there were even more shocks to come. John Walker had recruited his son, Michael Lance Walker, his brother, Arthur James Walker, and his best friend, Jerry Whitworth, to spy for the Soviet Union. John Walker's daughter said that he'd also tried to recruit her as a spy. Michael Walker was assigned to the aircraft carrier *Nimitz,* where he gathered information his father asked him to get and, it was subsequently revealed, blatantly kept the documents in a box under his bunk. John Walker was handled by Alexey Gavrilovich Tkachenko, a vice-consul at the Soviet embassy in Washington who was recalled to Moscow shortly after Walker's arrest.

The day before John Walker's arrest, the FBI tailed him to Poolesville, Maryland, where he made a drop of some 129 secret navy documents. He was arrested in a motel in Rockville, Maryland, in a dramatic pre-dawn raid. Father and son pleaded "not guilty" to the charges against them, and a trial date was set for October 28, 1985. John's trial was postponed, however, probably because a plea bargain agreement was being worked out. By August 1986 the terms of the agreement were well known. John Walker agreed that he and Michael would give a total accounting of their activities over the years, John would testify against Jerry Whitworth, and in return, Michael would receive a specific sentence of 25 years.

I was asked to work with the prosecutor in the Whitworth trial. Jerry Whitworth was a retired senior chief radioman, a petty officer. He was the first person outside of the Walker family to be charged. It was revealed during the course of his investigation that Jerry Alfred Whitworth was known by and worked under the code name of "D." He was being held without bond and faced a twelve-count indictment. This case was some spin-off!

A few days after the conversation with John Martin at the Justice Department, I got a call to come over and meet William Farmer. "I think you're going to like him," John told me. "He's a real gift to the Justice Department, and we expect him to shoot up like a meteor in the organization. I think he's probably a genius."

"High praise, John," I remarked.

"He deserves it," John answered. "Wait till you meet him."

In his mid-forties, Buck Farmer was an energetic man with piercing eyes and an easy smile. Young as he was, he was also completely bald. I learned the story about that from John Martin, and because it is so illustrative of Buck Farmer's courage and determination, I think it's worth recounting. Buck was the prosecutor in several cases involving Colombian drug figures. In the course of these cases, threats were made against his children. Anonymous notes would appear, telling him that if he didn't lay off and drop the case, his children would be kidnapped and murdered. His marriage collapsed under the pressures of the constant danger, but Buck couldn't quit and let those people go free. The penalty that he paid for his determination was that in a matter of a few short weeks, because of the stress he was under, he lost all his hair.

I had a good chance to see this brave man in action during the course of the Whitworth trial. I agree completely with a courtroom observer who commented, "You've got to admit it about Farmer—the man's got balls."

Throughout the trial I worked with Buck as a consultant. I went to San Francisco several times and read thousands of pages of transcripts. Visiting Buck in his comfortable townhouse, I got to sample some of his gourmet cooking. I'm proud that Buck Farmer can be numbered among my colleagues. I also met the co-prosecutor of the

Whitworth case—tall, lovely, and very intelligent Assistant U.S. Attorney Leida Schoggen. During the preparation of the trial and the trial itself I stayed in close touch with both of them. If I wasn't out in San Francisco, then we were conferring by telephone.

John Walker testified against Whitworth during the trial, readily admitting that he had recruited Whitworth. Buck Farmer told me about Walker's personality. "The man's a clown," he said. "When he gets to talking he's as funny as any stand-up comic I've ever seen. I go in to talk to him seriously, and the next thing I know I'm laughing my head off. He knows how really bad this is, too, but the son of a gun can't help being funny."

When Walker was asked why he'd recruited Whitworth, his answer revealed his knowledge of how to read people. "Well, I knew him, you see," he said. "He and I were friends, and we talked. I hadn't known him very long before I knew he had larceny in his heart."

Interesting! John Walker could tell almost at once that Jerry Whitworth wouldn't refuse to do something dishonest—if the price were right. I said as much to Buck Farmer, and he just shrugged. "Maybe it takes one to know one, eh?"

"Maybe so," I answered.

I thought more about it, however. There was a little item buried in the masses of evidence collected about John Walker that might be more important than it seemed. When John Walker was seventeen years old, he was convicted of four burglaries. He was put on probation because of his youth, but the record was there, and the navy was aware of it. They knew Walker had committed those burglaries, certainly indicative of the larceny in his own heart, yet they had granted him a Top Secret, and later a CRYPTO, clearance.

Whitworth was convicted in the summer of 1986 and given 365 years in prison for his part in espionage against his country. A fine of $410,000 was levied against him, but as one observer noted, "That's not such a big fine when you consider that Whitworth was so valuable to the Soviets that his pay from them was $1,000 to $4,000 a month. C'mon, folks, that's not peanuts they were paying our Jerry."

Personally, I think he missed the point. The Soviets got a real bargain in Whitworth; the value of the information he supplied was dozens of times more than he was paid. These spies put the U.S. Navy itself in peril.

My part in the Whitworth trial was to interpret the actions of the Soviet Union in terms of what they wanted from Whitworth, why they wanted those things, and what we could extrapolate from the evidence for future use. I wish I could say the case is unique, but Soviet espionage will not stop, and I know there will be other trials to keep me and many others busy.

Such activities are not limited to the United States, of course. In 1985 I testified as an expert witness at the trial of Arne Treholt in Norway. When he was arrested by Norwegian counterintelligence in 1984, Treholt was the chief of the Press Department of the Norwegian Foreign Office. In this position he had access not only to the highest-ranking government officials in Norway, but to important military information, and because Norway is a member of NATO, to NATO military secrets as well. The investigation revealed that Treholt had been a Soviet agent since the 1960s. At the time of his arrest, he was on his way to Vienna to meet his Soviet handler, and his briefcase was found to contain more than sixty documents that he intended to hand over to the Soviets.

Another important event of the summer and fall of 1986 was the Daniloff case. As a result of the painstaking care with which the FBI works, early fall brought the arrest of a Soviet spy in New York City. The agent, Gennadi Sakharov, had been the object of an FBI investigation for nearly two years before he was arrested in the act of picking up classified documents from a drop. The Soviet Union, in retaliation for Sakharov's arrest, framed Nick Daniloff, the Moscow correspondent for the prestigious news magazine *U.S. News and World Report*. Nick Daniloff, who was in the process of bidding goodbye to friends and acquaintances before his return to the United States, met a Russian friend who handed him a sealed envelope, which was supposed to contain a few interesting little clippings.

The moment the envelope was in his hand, Daniloff was surrounded by KGB men who arrested him because he was "caught red-handed with secret documents." It was perfectly obvious to thinking people the world over what Daniloff's arrest was all about. The United States had caught a Soviet spy, and in retaliation the Soviets took Daniloff as a hostage. During the weeks when Nick was being held by the Soviets in Lefortovo Prison, I was invited to be a guest on a variety of television programs: Washington, D.C.'s *Panorama,* a daily news magazine program on Channel 5; Cable News Network's *Newsmaker, Sunday* with Charles Bierbower; twice on ABC's *Nightline* with Ted Koppel; Channel 5's nightly news program; *One-on-One* with NBC's John McLaughlin; and *The Larry King Show.*

The questions I was repeatedly asked indicated to me that there are many Americans who are not fully aware of the magnitude of the Soviet threat to the free world. It seems I've always sensed this fact to some degree; that's one of the reasons I've been so determined to write this book for free people. A teacher once told me that the best way to get people to understand and remember a lesson is to "teach it, then reinforce it—over and over again." I'm certainly trying to follow her advice.

My sense that there is much naiveté about Soviet and KGB determination was recently reinforced by my experiences as a consultant to the Department of Justice at the trials of the U.S. marines after their tours at the U.S. embassy in Moscow. Even these carefully selected and disciplined military men were deceived by the KGB.

The final section of this book, a postscript, contains a number of the questions I've been asked many times, my answers to them, and the reasons why I believe these points are generally misconstrued. I no longer make the mistake of thinking that, because a question is repeated, it shouldn't be answered. I realize that the questioner has asked it only once, even though I might have heard it a hundred times. But the fact that it is asked over and over does show that too many people don't know some important truths that I hope I can help them to see. The final section of this book is thus intended as my personal primer on the Soviet threat.

I read somewhere that each cell in the human body dies and is replaced every seven years. If that is so, then I am indeed totally different from the man who came to America in 1979. All the Soviet cells have been replaced by purely American ones. I know that I feel very American—and I love it. This is my home, my corner in the sun, and I am committed to working for the safety of my new homeland and the whole free world.

As I became more and more settled in the free world, the time came when I realized that the past is past, that I had to start living in the present. I had to admit to myself that any further attempts to get Natalia and our son out were useless. Reluctantly and with infinite sadness, I divorced Natalia in the hope of freeing her from the continual KGB pressure. I pray to God that things are easier for her now, but news is sparse from the Soviet Union, and I don't know enough about her situation to feel confident that my action helped her at all.

Meanwhile, I am in America, making a new life. I have finally adjusted fairly well, I think. There are times when I get so weary that I feel depressed, but I have found much satisfaction in working for the things I believe in. I always greet the new day with enthusiasm, eager to get going again. The first thing I do each morning is read the newspapers thoroughly. Even when my enthusiasm falters a bit, a careful study of the day's news always stokes the furnace of my determination by revealing how much remains to be done.

I have my hobbies: photography, collecting classical records and tapes, going to the theater and to symphony concerts. I read a great deal—best sellers, classics, books in English or Russian or Japanese. And I love movies. I often stop by a movie rental store and check out half a dozen films. Then I go home, settle into my easy chair, put a film in the VCR, and relax.

I love the sea! Whenever I can find the time for a free weekend, I head for the ocean, check into a seaside hotel, and go for a long walk. Nothing feeds the soul like a walk along a deserted beach. Any time of the year is the perfect time to refurbish the spirit by just listening to the sounds and smelling the indescribable scents of the seashore.

The story of my odyssey from Moscow to Washington is nearly finished. In these pages I have tried to give the reasons for my decisions, the motives that impelled me to leave the land of my birth, and to show how those motives and decisions developed. I have tried to open my soul so that people will know that inside the KGB officer there existed a man with feelings and a heart and sensitivities. At times, I feel that this book is a form of spiritual surgery, a catharsis, a cleansing of old wounds.

I know that the Soviets will not stop their search for me, that they are determined to kill me if they can. I know that my declaration of a private war against the Soviet system only heightens their efforts. I accept that. But I feel American now. When I walk down a street with a spring in my step and a sense of well-being in my heart, I know it's because I'm free in every way that really counts.

Over the years from 1979 to the present, there have been so many things that I have had to do for my own safety that have grated, and I'm tired of them. I'm tired of sitting with my back to the wall in restaurants. I'm tired of using the protective coloration of disguises when I'm out in public. I'm tired of changing my residence several times a year. I'm tired of the damned cat-and-mouse games. I'm tired of being tired.

There is one thing I'm not tired of, however. I will continue to appear before audiences that will listen to what I have to say. I will continue to tell the truth about the Soviet system. I want every person in the KGB and in the Soviet Union to know that I declared this war, that I tell it like it is. Me! Stanislav Levchenko, a free man! My life is in my own hands now, and I can make of it what I wish.

Once when I was very young and still in school, I saw a Japanese film about a noncommissioned officer who was tried as a war criminal. He was the scapegoat for higher-ranking officers under whom he served, but he was found guilty and sentenced to death for their deeds. While he was in prison, waiting to be executed, he meditated on the meaning of his life. At last he reached a stage where he achieved serenity of spirit. He decided that when he died, he wanted to become a seashell and to spend eternity being endlessly rocked by the rhythms of the ocean, being washed gently onto the shore and then being pulled back into the great womb of the sea, the mother of all life.

I have empathized with that soldier all my life. Like the Russians in the works of Turgenev and Tolstoy, I have endured great pain and known great joy. Indeed, I have been an example of the Russian tragedy and a part of the Russian comedy. I have also spent much of my life learning to think, sense, and feel as the Japanese do. I have taken as my own the love of the sea, which is so much a part of the Japanese character. Even in telling my own story, I've had to come to the sea to think it through.

Like the soldier in the film, I, too, in my meditations, have chosen my own symbol for eternity. I see the beach as countless grains of sand, each grain representing a human soul, and that is all I want to be: one grain of sand among all the others, one among mankind. Perhaps then I will understand the meaning of my own life. Perhaps then I will know at last whether I have served mankind well.

Until then, I will go on fighting with all my strength and all my mind and all my heart. I can do no less for those I love. I can do no less for America, the country that made me free.

* * * *

KILL DEVIL HILLS, NORTH CAROLINA

The sea was deep purple and mysterious in the pre-dawn light as I made my way down to the beach on my last day in North

Carolina. I could barely make out the words Kill Devil Hills *on the sign at the top of the stairs.*

"Kill Devil Hills," I said to myself. "That's some name."

I had been told several versions of the origin of the name. Some said that Kill Devil was the name of an old patent medicine. The version that I like best was that the Indians used to meet on the sand hills while the medicine man killed the devils that brought troubles to the tribe.

"Yes," I mused. "I like that one best. That's why I'm here, to kill all the devils that haunt me."

I went down the flight of steps and scuffed through the loose sand to the wet beach that skirted the gentle froth of the waves. A tired-looking seagull barely moved aside as I passed by.

"I know how you feel, old-timer," I said to him. "I am as old as the sea itself and tired, bone-weary."

I picked up a handful of sand and let it trickle through my fingers.

"I feel like a grain of sand. . . ." I could almost hear Natalia saying those words, her voice muffled over the long-distance telephone lines.

A grain of sand . . . a grain of sand.

The sun blazed up suddenly out of the sea, and the wet sand at my feet seemed to sparkle, almost as though each grain were separate and distinct in the bright light.

My tiredness was suddenly replaced by serenity, and I smiled to myself.

"Not bad," I told myself. "Not bad at all. And if this is the way your life ends, that's not bad either."

A grain of sand. . . .

There's a lot that can be done with a grain of sand.

A PERSONAL PRIMER
ON
THE USSR AND THE KGB

This section should be informative because it answers the questions that I'm always asked. These questions reveal that many people in the free world harbor some dangerous misconceptions. Americans in particular often do not see the realities of Soviet thinking and objectives. I consider all of these questions and answers to be of equal value; all of them are important. My final message is that the free world must be on guard against the KGB.

* * * *

Your account of the KGB and the people who work in it puts a very human face on the organization and the personnel. Why should the free world fear them, then? After all, they're only human, aren't they?

People in the free world had better fear them.

Since its inception the Soviet socialist system has rested on two pillars—the KGB and the Soviet army. It needs these two pillars in order to survive. The Soviet military forces are essential to protect the country from what it perceives as threats from outside. But the Soviet system has to be protected also from its own people, and the KGB is responsible for that task. It protects the system and its elites from any possible dissent and from any dissident organizations that could alter totalitarianism into a form of democracy. The KGB has hundreds of thousands of informants who report to it on virtually everything. It also has tens of thousands of informants and full-time KGB officers in the ranks of the Soviet military to ensure that the military does not deviate. And, of course, the KGB's external intelligence service—First Chief Directorate—has its officers and agents in every country in the world.

The people who work for the KGB have very human faces and share some very human problems and weaknesses. They are overworked; they succumb to alcohol; they become disillusioned and weary; there is an extremely high divorce rate. At first glance they might be found in the CIA or in Britain's counterintelligence services. But these KGB professionals are exactly what they say they are: people who are devoted to achieving the goals of the Soviet Union as professionally as they can, with fanatic perseverance. Their humanity or "human faces" are to be expected, but these are compensated for by the vast size, resources, and tight control of the KGB.

What exactly is the KGB?

The KGB gets its name from the Russian words *Komitet Gos-udarstvennoy Bezopasnosty,* which translates as the Committee for State Security. It is an incredibly large organization that concerns itself with all aspects of Soviet life. Espionage is but a small part of the activities of the KGB. Still, the KGB's First Chief Directorate is the largest intelligence service in the world. The KGB is spread through-out the world with an estimated employment of over 250,000 people, including Border Guard troops. Five KGB divisions always stand ready to crush any attempted riots or revolts in the USSR. There is no organization in the world to match its size, the scope of its operations, and its freedom to act without restraint. It is the largest oppressive and punitive force in the history of civilization.

Is the KGB answerable to anyone or any group in the Soviet Union?

The KGB is answerable to only one group, the Politburo of the Communist Party of the Soviet Union (CPSU). The Politburo is akin to a collective dictatorship that decides the destiny of the Soviet Union and its citizens. It is a policymaking body of the CPSU and is com-posed of the highest-ranking members of the party. As a policymak-ing body, the Politburo is not to be confused with the Presidium of the Supreme Soviet of the USSR—a rubber-stamp parliament that has almost no influence on the political and economic life of the country.

Daily activities of the KGB are supervised by the Administrative Organs Department of the Central Committee of the CPSU, which reports directly to the Politburo. Unlike the intelligence community in the United States or other free-world countries that are subject to legislative oversight, there is no democratic legislative organ in the Soviet Union to regulate or check the KGB's activities. The KGB's operations, budget, and personnel problems are considered top secret, and nobody except the Politburo and the Administrative Organs Department has access to any information on the KGB.

At the same time it is important to realize that the KGB is not a totally independent organization. It enforces the goals of the leadership of the CPSU, and every part of its activities is approved or guided by the Politburo and personally by the secretary general of the Central Committee of the CPSU.

During the time when Nicholas Daniloff, the correspondent for the American magazine *U.S. News & World Report,* was in a Moscow prison, I was a guest on several news programs. I was asked by almost all of the moderators whether I thought that Mikhail Gorbachev "knew in advance" that the KGB was going to arrest Mr. Daniloff. The answer is yes. It was a considered and deliberately undertaken move to accuse Mr. Daniloff falsely of being a spy, a move that may have been conceived by the KGB but was at least endorsed by the Politburo. The KGB can arrest any Soviet citizen on the street without explanation, but they don't have the power to do that to a foreign correspondent. Such a move must be approved by the Politburo. Mr. Gorbachev is the most important member of the Politburo. Of course he knew in advance.

What are the overall goals of the Soviet Union and the KGB?

The leaders of the Soviet Union are implacably committed to undermining the position of the free world through military superiority, subversion, traditional espionage activities, active measures, and conventional diplomacy. They seek to destabilize the politics, the economies, and the social fabrics of the societies of free world countries and eventually to dominate world politics. Democracy and the free-market system are defined as hostile to socialism by Marxist-Leninist theory. Since the 1950s the Soviet leaders have considered the United States their No. 1 enemy, and the main thrust of the KGB's activity on a global basis is directed against the United States. I know this is true because that goal was exactly what I was committed to serving for so long, especially during the turbulent four years and eight months I served as a political intelligence and active measures officer in Japan.

I often hear people say that Mr. Gorbachev is a "new Russian," that his new image indicates a new approach in Soviet politics. Mr. Gorbachev, regardless of the reforms he promises in industry and agriculture, does not intend to change the main goal of socialism, clearly defined by Marx, Engels, Lenin, and Stalin. According to their theory, which all Soviet leaders, including Mr. Gorbachev, have been and are implementing in practice, the socialist system should prevail over capitalism—everywhere.

Socialist theory and practice are quite flexible when it comes to morality and fairness in international politics. Any means to achieve advantage over the free world (including subversion, sabotage, lies, violations of bilateral and international agreements) are considered moral if they advance the cause of socialism in the world and therefore are readily approved by the Politburo.

The Soviet army is the largest offensive peacetime force in the history of mankind. Military expenditures in the USSR as a percentage of gross national product are the highest in the world, despite the problems of Soviet industry and agriculture, the low standard of living of Soviet citizens, the poor quality of national health care, and other handicaps.

To ensure military superiority, the Soviet military-industrial complex badly needs Western technology. Whenever it is impossible for the Kremlin to buy high-technology products and processes from the West, the KGB steals them through its global espionage network.

What exactly are active measures?

The term *active measures* came into use in the Soviet Union in the 1950s, the years Americans called the Cold War. However, the Soviet leadership had been implementing this type of activity since the inception of the Soviet state seven decades ago. It is a catch-all phrase that describes both overt and covert techniques for influencing the actions, events, and—sometimes—the behavior of foreign countries. Active measures may be used to undermine the confidence a citizenry has in its leaders, to destroy a leader's or a nation's credibility, or to disrupt relations between nations. Frequently, active measures will attempt to skew public perceptions of events or of the meanings of those events.

Active measures can be overt and covert. For example, officially sponsored exchange programs for students and for cultural groups are popular propaganda devices (overt active measures). Covert active measures may involve the dissemination of disinformation, the use of agents of influence, planting forgeries, penetration of political and public organizations and the mass media, subversion, penetration of business communities, and so on.

I worked most of the time in the interests of the Active Measures Service of the KGB, which is usually identified as "Service A" and is one of the most important components of the First Chief Directorate of the KGB. It functions in close cooperation with the International Department of the Central Committee, CPSU. By the time I worked in active measures, the term was used to distinguish influence operations from espionage and counterintelligence, but the term isn't limited to intelligence alone. Rather, Soviet active measures involve activities by virtually every element of the Soviet Communist party and by the state structure. Active measures are regarded as a valuable supplement to traditional diplomacy and are relied on to function in this manner.

In 1979 the Active Measures Group in the Tokyo residency consisted of five officers. However, many more officers and their agents were involved in active measures operations on a regular basis.

The KGB penetrated most of the major newspapers in Japan. Among agents of influence were a former cabinet minister, a prominent Liberal Democrat, several high-ranking politicians from the Japanese Socialist Party, and important members of the academic, journalistic, and business communities.

What were the major objectives of your operations with active measures in Japan?

We were instructed to carry out programs of very specific dimensions, and though we were working in Japan, the overall purposes are much the same wherever the KGB uses Service A—and that is pretty much all over the world. In Japan we were told to:

- prevent a further deepening of political and military cooperation between the United States and Japan;

- provoke distrust between the United States and Japan in political, military, and economic arenas;

- prevent further development of good relations between Japan and the People's Republic of China, especially in political and economic relationships;

- eliminate by any means the possibility of the creation of an anti-Soviet triangle (Washington/Beijing/Tokyo);

- create a new pro-Soviet lobby among prominent Japanese politicians—first, in the Liberal Democratic Party, then in the Japanese Socialist Party—in order to develop close economic ties with the Soviet Union;

- convince the leaders of the Japanese government, through high-ranking agents of influence, prominent business leaders, and the mass media, that significantly broadening economic ties with the USSR was essential;

- organize a movement in Japanese political circles favoring the Friendship and Neighborly Relations Treaty between Japan and the USSR;

- deeply penetrate the main opposition parties, beginning with the Japanese Socialist Party, in order to influence their political platforms and to prevent the Liberal Democratic Party from creating a political monopoly in the Japanese Diet;

- discourage the leaders of the opposition parties from creating a coalition government because the Soviets need a politically stable Japan in order to make the best use of the existing network of agents in which they have invested so heavily.

Of course, the Soviet Union hasn't achieved all of these goals, but trying to attain them has been declared the official policy, and the Active Measures people continue to work to achieve them. As is said in America, they "win a few, lose a few," and the thing to be careful about is that they do have many successful operations, due primarily to their agents of influence.

How do you define "agent of influence"?

Agents of influence are citizens of foreign countries who use their influence, reputations, positions, power, or credibility to promote the objectives of the Soviet Union in ways that cannot be linked to Moscow. In general, there are three types of agents of influence.

There are the controlled agents who have been recruited by the KGB to advance the interests of the Soviet Union as they are ordered to do so. Trusted contacts are those who consciously collaborate in furthering the USSR's objectives but who have not been formally recruited. Finally, unwitting individuals are those who are manipulated into aiding the Soviet Union without recognizing that they have been exploited.

If the KGB is such an enormous organization, doesn't the possibility exist that the entire machine might be too unwieldy to run effectively?

I cannot answer that question without first explaining what the structure of the "machine" actually is. Structurally, the KGB consists of a number of chief directorates and directorates, which are further divided into various services and departments. A cursory glance at the structure, size, scope of functions, and missions undertaken can give a false impression that the "machine" is unwieldy.

The reason that this impression is false is that each directorate has its clearly defined functions, and its operations are highly compartmentalized. The directorates cooperate with each other only when it is strictly necessary. Their officers even have different professional educations: there are separate schools for intelligence, counterintelligence, surveillance, and Border Guards. The KGB must be taken seriously by the free world. Its personnel are professionals who have been thoroughly trained to do their jobs, have virtually unlimited funds with which to work, and have no constraints to guarantee that they follow moral or ethical rules in achieving their goals. Unlike the CIA, which is policed by several watchdog groups, the KGB has nothing to stop it from doing whatever it deems necessary. No Soviet citizens write books or articles about the KGB, and demonstrations against this organization are unheard of or last about ten minutes.

The case of Nicholas Daniloff, who was arrested in retaliation for this country's arrest of a Soviet spy, brings up a question that many would like answered: why does the Soviet Union treat all journalists as though they were spies?

The Soviet leaders and the KGB realize that due to the laws passed by the U.S. Congress in the 1970s, the CIA is forbidden to use journalistic cover for intelligence operations. Nonetheless, they arrested Mr. Daniloff and, during several years prior to this incident, expelled several American journalists from Moscow for the following reasons:

- The Kremlin wants to isolate foreign journalists from the Soviet public. The Soviet leaders are angered every time the truth about human rights violations in the USSR, about hypocrisy and corruption of the Soviet elite, are leaked out to the free world media.

- Many foreign journalists in their contact with Soviet citizens tell them about the true reaction of foreign governments and world public opinion to Soviet foreign and domestic policies—subjects that are routinely distorted by the heavily censored Soviet media. This flow of news from the West undermines the credibility of the Soviet propaganda machine.

- In the KGB's opinion, the best way to prevent contacts between foreign journalists and ordinary Soviets is to create a widespread suspicion that journalists are spies. The KGB wants people to be afraid of being accused of contacts with Western intelligence services. It is one of their usual scare tactics.

In the future there may be more cases of intimidation and harassment of foreign journalists. The KGB has to do it periodically to remind the Soviet people of the dangers of contact with foreigners. The fact is that the Soviets do use their journalists as spies. My own past proves the point. I was stationed in Tokyo as a correspondent for a magazine, and I have just told the readers the full story of what my activities actually were. About fifty percent of the Soviet journalists stationed abroad are full-time KGB or GRU intelligence officers.

Several times you mention the Soviets' military organizations, and then (seemingly as an afterthought) you say, "and, of course, the Border Guards." What is unusual about the Border Guards, and how do they fit into the military structure of the USSR?

The Border Guards are actually a chief directorate in the KGB. They are a separate military force, very well trained, very well equipped. They have their own tank units, artillery, naval vessels, and air force units. Ostensibly, their main mission is to guard Soviet borders, and military units of Border Guards are deployed along Soviet frontiers.

The Border Guards Directorate has its own intelligence, which collects information on military and political developments in the areas bordering on the Soviet Union. For instance, officers in the Border Guards intelligence recruit Japanese fishermen whose boats are based in Hokkaido. Their approach is to detain the boat crews when they are caught in Soviet waters. Once these vessels are in the hands of the Border Guards, it becomes relatively easy to strike deals with them, and they get numbers of Japanese in this way. For example, twenty-seven fishermen were detained in 1982 alone. The deals that the Border Guards make begin in this way: First they promise to grant permission to the fishermen to trawl in the Soviet-controlled waters in exchange for consumer goods. These "report ships," called *reposen,* then start bringing such items as cigarette lighters, ball-point pens, and digital watches to Border Guards. In time, a top-category ship owner, called a *motojime*—a derogatory term, actually a pejorative word for a croupier—is asked to supply more valuable goods: high-grade integrated circuits, militarily useful computers, expensive office equipment, and cars. Some are even asked to bring Japanese bar girls. Finally, some of the captains are recruited to collect intelligence. Valuable information on Hokkaido's Self-Defense Force and its installations are known to have been transmitted to the Soviets in this way.

As is known, the Soviet leaders deprive their citizens of the right of free travel or emigration abroad. They also do not want to let their subjects escape from the country. That is one of the reasons why the KGB's Border Guards literally seal the Soviet border. Many thousands of miles long, it is covered with electronic detectors, minefields, and in some places, a wooden or barbed-wire fence. In view of the scope of their work, it's hardly surprising that the Border Guards are so well trained and so well equipped, nor is it surprising that the Border Guards are a separate military force answerable only to the KGB.

You have used the acronym MICE (for money, ideology, compromise, and ego) as the reasons why people become spies or, sometimes, traitors. In the wake of America's spy trials, it seems clear that Americans who become Soviet spies do so for money, yet we have one of the highest standards of living in the world. What do you think makes people like the Walkers and Jerry Whitworth willing to betray their country for money?

I don't pretend to be a psychologist, so my answer is just my personal opinion. But for what it's worth, I will advance a few views for you to consider. First, the United States is the prime consumer country in the world. People in this country are brought up on television, and one of the things that television does well is saturate generation after generation with attractive pictures of the good life and the promise that this good life will be better if such-and-such product is added to it. Children seem to grow up expecting that they will be able to buy what they want when they want it. Unfortunately, there are many people who will not reach such heights in income and purchasing power. When that is compounded by the easy availability of credit cards and the promise of "buy now, pay later," the risk of finding oneself in debt certainly exists. It is possible that some who sell out to the enemy are people who have entrapped themselves by assuming that they have a right to more and more consumer goods and unwisely have gone too deeply into debt in order to get them.

Soviet intelligence is continuously gathering information on those who have access to secret information and who get themselves into financial trouble. This information is obtained through existing agents, conversations with overt contacts (some of whom may be called "willful idiots" because of their loose mouths), and easy access to public records.

The second factor that I want to address is ego and excitement. In the case of the Walker family, for example, these factors were very much at work. John Walker was smart, he knew he was smart, and there was an enormous satisfaction to him in knowing that he was outwitting his superiors and that he had been doing so successfully for many years. He enjoyed the challenge. Of course, he could and did use the money, but the boost to his ego was satisfying to him.

If I had to declare what I think are the real reasons for these and other Americans to sell out, I'd say that the desire to prove they can get away with it is high on the list of motives. Another motivation for such people is to establish that they are intelligent enough to play a dangerous game and win. Some people—like John Walker—find a certain enjoyment in the cloak-and-dagger game simply because it is exciting. Americans should not blame their way of life or feel responsible for the actions these people endorse. The fault lies in the spies; they are the ones with the tragic flaw that flies in the face of loyalty. Blame them, not their countries.

It is important to realize also that the KGB and the military intelligence GRU target Americans on a global basis. Tens of thousands of American military personnel, diplomats, businessmen, and students spend several months or years abroad. The highest priority target of the Soviet intelligence services abroad are Americans. For recruitment of an American agent, the KGB officer automatically gets one of the highest awards in the Soviet Union.

If you could give one piece of advice to every young person in the United States (particularly to those still in school) regarding the future, what would it be?

I would say, "Train yourself to read the front pages of your newspapers, and read them every day. Read news magazines; read important books."

I was amazed to discover that Americans do not read very much. The majority of the people in this country subscribe to newspapers, but as a rule they don't read international news. They might look at the headlines, but they usually listen to the accounts on the television news programs rather than read about the events for themselves. Too often their reading is limited to local news, sports, and the comics.

I would advise young people to read for themselves every day because that is the way to know for themselves. The more they read, the better prepared they are to make valid judgments, and the less likely they will be to rely on newscasters to interpret the world situation for them.

Many Americans say that they are dissatisfied with the various media. They say they don't trust the newspapers. "Newspapers are too liberal," some say, while others say that "the reporters manage the news." Whether these charges are true is irrelevant. The press in democratic countries is there to serve the readership. That is why my best advice for the future of the free world is read, inform yourselves, make your own interpretations, and draw your own conclusions. Informed readerships will guarantee real freedom of the press. In the long run, informed citizens will demand and get the most dependable kind of reporting from the media.

I would tell young people to realize that they will have tremendous responsibilities for the protection of freedom and the free-market system against the expansionism of the totalitarian Soviet Union and its allies.

To know how to protect the free world effectively, it is essential to learn as much as possible about that world's adversary. Do not be naive about the Soviet Union. Learn how to distinguish overt or covert Soviet propaganda and disinformation from information on the real goals of Soviet external and internal policies. Only in that way can you ensure that all of us won't end up "on the wrong side."